The Incestuous Workplace

The Incestuous Workplace

Stress and Distress in the Organizational Family

WILLIAM L. WHITE

⬛ HAZELDEN®

Hazelden
Center City, Minnesota 55012-0176
1-800-328-0094
1-612-257-1331 (FAX)
http://www.hazelden.org

Library of Congress Cataloging-in-Publication Data
White, William L., 1947–
    The incestuous workplace : stress and distress in the
organizational family / William L. White.
        p.   cm.
    Includes bibliographical references and index.
    ISBN 1-56838-154-9
    1. Job stress.   2. Burn out (Psychology)   3. Organizational
behavior.   I. Title.
HF5548.85.W463   1997
158.7—dc21   97-26530
                                                          CIP

02 01 99 98 97   9 8 7 6 5 4 3 2 1

Book design by Will H. Powers
Typesetting by Stanton Publication Services, Inc.
Cover design by David Spohn

Editor's note
Hazelden offers a variety of information on chemical dependency
and related areas. Our publications do not necessarily represent
Hazelden's programs, nor do they officially speak for any Twelve
Step organization.

Contents

Figures

Acknowledgments

There are several people who helped birth this book and nurture it to its current state of development. Alan Walker of Goddard College first encouraged me to write down my observations of what I had come to call "incestuous organizational families." Bruce Fisher and Roger Krohe provided early assistance in applying family systems concepts to my understanding of how individuals become casualties in distressed organizations. Jerry F. X. Caroll first introduced me to an ecological model of problem analysis pioneered by Urie Bronfenbrenner that became the conceptual skeleton of this book. Early presentations of the material in this book were published first by Health Control Systems and later by Chestnut Health Systems. The feedback from all over the country on these early publications greatly enriched the current version.

This book has also been blessed by a series of editors, first Keith Corley and more recently Steve Lehman, who brought great passion and skill to their work on this project. Steve and the editorial staff at Hazelden were particularly helpful in refining my original work for a much broader audience.

Finally and always, there are my wife, Rita Chaney, and my daughter, Alisha, who have brought immeasurable joy to my life.

Introduction

This book is about the complex relationships between organizations and the people who work in them. It's about how individual workers, an organization's leaders, and entire organizations can self-destruct in the face of excessive demands for adaptation, and how distressed individuals and organizations can regain their health.

I have struggled for three decades to define the laws and principles that govern the rise and fall of organizations and their leaders, and the laws and principles that govern the relationships between people and the environments in which they work. Many of these concepts have revealed themselves slowly, and it seems that they operate predictably in organizations of all sizes, settings, and purposes.

We will explore in the coming pages how organizations are born and how they grow, create new organizations, decay, renew themselves, die, and occasionally rise from the dead to thrive again. We will look at how organizations in these cycles of decay and renewal have the power to do harm—to themselves, to their leaders, to those who work in them, and to the public. And we will become familiar with a story of hope—a story of organizational and personal resilience, a story of how severely distressed organizations have recaptured their health, and how workers have survived in, escaped from, or helped to transform toxic organizational systems.

A central tenet of this book is that the workplace can be seen as an organizational family system and that problems of distress in organizations can be understood by applying a knowledge of family systems to the workplace. We will look at a type of workplace I describe as a "closed organizational family." We will see the propensity of these "families" to develop an incestuous dynamic in which organizational members, isolated from the outside world, increasingly meet their personal, professional, social, and sexual needs inside the boundaries of the organization. We will see how this dynamic can wound organization members, as it can family members, and lead to the disruption and potential demise of the entire system. Considerable time will be spent in exploring how to prevent such damage, as well as in describing how to open up systems that have become progressively closed.

The following pages are an operations manual for sustaining the health of organizations in which the environment has become increasingly turbulent and threatening. They are also a survival manual for people who work in toxic environments. I hope the ideas here will serve as catalysts to enhance the health of organizations and individual workers. The book is designed to be an ongoing resource. A detailed table of contents, an index, and extensive subtitling are provided to help you return to particular topics easily. The glossary will assist you with many unfamiliar terms, and the bibliography provides additional resource material on various topics discussed in the book.

I welcome your comments, criticisms, and ideas. Correspondence can be sent to

BILL WHITE
Senior Research Consultant
Chestnut Health Systems
720 West Chestnut
Bloomington, Illinois 61701

《 1

Professional and Organizational Distress: Definitions, Assumptions, and Indicators

This chapter will cover key terms and concepts we will use to explore what happens when the relationships between organizations and the people who work in them are strained to the breaking point. We will begin by defining such terms as "stress," "stressor," "stress response," "professional distress," and "organizational distress," and then look at signs and symptoms and assumptions about professional and organizational distress.

1.1 Terms and Concepts

Theorists from fields as diverse as internal medicine and cultural anthropology have tried to describe the nature of stress and its impact on individuals and groups. The literature of stress is filled with disagreement over terms, definitions, and theories. I offer the following definitions not as a contribution to these intellectual debates, but merely to convey the meaning of the terms as they will be used in future chapters. The definitions are based, in part, on the pioneering stress research done by Hans Selye (Selye 1974, 1956).

STRESS *is a demand upon the body and mind for adaptation.*

Demands for adaptation occur constantly and are of concern mainly when the level of stress exceeds our capacity to effectively respond. Stress and the body's continual response to it represent the intricate mechanism by which we maintain balance with our social and physical environments. To be free of stress is to cease living. Most of us have an optimum level of stress, a level at which we function best. Some thrive on a very high level of demand for adaptation while others function best at a much lower level of demand. And, of course, these optimum levels

1

are subject to change as our personal circumstances alter. Some change in our capacity to respond to stress occurs simply as a function of age.

When we say someone is under a lot of stress, we usually mean excessive and unpleasant stress, or "distress." The focus here will not be on stress, which, according to our definition, might represent some of the most positive and meaningful challenges we face in life. The focus instead will be on distress, and in particular, professional distress.

> DISTRESS *is a state of physical and emotional suffering produced by excessive demands for adaptation.*

This book is not about normal day-to-day work demands. Rather, it is about demands for adaptation in the workplace that reach levels of great intensity and that must be endured for prolonged periods of time. It is also about the kinds of stressors that can create such distress.

> STRESSORS *are factors or conditions that create excessive demands for adaptation.*

The coming discussions will focus on psychosocial stressors—stressors that emerge in professional relationships with one's superiors, co-workers, and clients.

> STRESS RESPONSE, *as used here, refers to the generalized and specialized reactions of an individual to excessive demands for adaptation.*

The generalized nature of how humans respond to stress was defined by Selye, who pioneered the concept of the general adaptation syndrome (GAS), which represents a stereotyped response of the body to a stressor. This generalized stress response occurs in three phases: (1) alarm reaction, (2) resistance, and (3) exhaustion. Each phase is marked by different physiological and psychological changes. Selye's research was remarkable in that it documented similar responses to excessive demands for adaptation regardless of whether the demand was experienced positively or negatively (Selye 1974, 1956). Americans spend billions of dollars every day in gambling lotteries, and the befuddled winners usually mumbling something about how their lives aren't really going to change. The fact is such windfalls are usually extremely stressful and life-disrupting.

In addition to the generalized nature of the GAS, an individual responds in his or her unique manner to prolonged and excessive stress. This specialized adaptation to stress represents a person's style of stress management. Chapter 11 will cover stress management and those factors that serve to increase or decrease our vulnerability to professional distress.

> PROFESSIONAL DISTRESS *is a deterioration in personal and interpersonal performance and health directly attributable to continued contact with high-stress work environments.*

Professional distress centers on demands that threaten our self-esteem and prevent the effective performance of our role in an organization. The subject of worker distress has received considerable attention, but often in a superficial or faddish manner. Following Herbert Freudenberger's early monographs and book on what he called "staff burnout," the term "professional burnout" came into common usage in many occupational circles. The term served to describe the anguish of the distressed workplace, but provided little as an organizing metaphor for positive change. In fact, the word had a rather terminal sound to it, implying that once burned out, there was little opportunity for reignition. "Distress," in contrast, has a more enduring usage and meaning within the culture, and suggests that professional distress, like life's other distresses, may be transitory, that it may be alleviated through the use of resources within and beyond ourselves. The term will also be applied to organizations.

> ORGANIZATIONAL DISTRESS *is a stage of deteriorating organizational health that occurs when tasks essential to the survival of an organization are not adequately completed due to the stress-related decline in performance of key organizational members.*

Much of this book will look at the reciprocal relationship between individual and organizational distress.

1.2 Individual Indicators of Professional Distress

Individuals who experience acute or prolonged distress in the workplace show predictable signs and symptoms of that distress. They can be generally classified as health indicators, excessive behavior indicators, emotional adjustment indicators, relationship indicators, attitude indicators, and value indicators.

Health Indicators. Evolution has provided humans with remarkable physiological mechanisms to respond to real or perceived threats. These mechanisms are automatic and consistent regardless of the nature of the stressor that triggers them. When we experience a high-intensity stressor, the following physiological changes occur instantaneously:

- The heartbeat quickens; blood vessels constrict, raising blood pressure; blood is diverted from the extremities into the muscles; and blood-clotting factors increase.
- The hypothalamus triggers the pituitary gland to produce and release adrenaline and related hormones, creating a state of high physiological arousal.
- The nervous system signals the lungs, heart, and muscles to be ready for action.
- The liver converts glycogen to glucose for energy.
- Breathing becomes more rapid, increasing the supply of oxygen to the brain and muscles.
- The body is flooded with endorphins—morphinelike substances produced in the brain that self-medicate physical and emotional pain.
- The body's senses—particularly sight and hearing—become more acute.

These changes are designed to prepare us for action, either fighting a life-or-death struggle or fleeing. While such reactions were very practical in confrontations between early humans and saber-toothed tigers, they are extreme for an encounter in a staff meeting or boardroom. And therein lies the problem.

The constant triggering of these physiological mechanisms—particularly when they are not accompanied by a release, a discharge of physiological arousal—can be extremely detrimental to our health. Over time, these frustrated automatic responses can damage many of the body's major systems and produce a number of distress-related symptoms that can be at best uncomfortable and at worst life-threatening. This section will not review in detail the mechanics of how this damage occurs; those interested in an in-depth treatment should refer to two classic works on the subject: Selye's *The Stress of Life* and Pelletier's *Mind as Healer, Mind as Slayer*.

The range of health indicators of professional distress identified in my early studies of workplace distress includes fatigue and chronic exhaustion, headaches, frequent and prolonged colds, ulcers, sleep disturbances (insomnia, nightmares, excessive sleeping), sudden weight gain or loss, injuries from high-risk behavior, flare-up of preexisting disorders (diabetes, high blood pressure, asthma), muscular pain (particularly in lower back and neck), increased premenstrual tension or missed menstrual cycles, bruxism (grinding of teeth), skin disorders, excessive sweating and urination, cardiovascular crises, colitis, diarrhea or constipation, and other gastrointestinal disorders.

Excessive Behavior Indicators. Most human beings are predictable. The variation in our day-to-day activities, values, lifestyle, and personal temperament is minimal. Such predictability constitutes our identity and helps provide security and consistency both for ourselves and for those who live and work with us. Under conditions of high stress, we begin to lose that predictability as behavior moves out of the familiar range and becomes excessive. Many distressed workers, for example, develop sleep disorders. For some, sleep is unattainable. They have trouble getting to sleep, and when they do sleep, they wake up repeatedly and rise unrested. For others, sleep becomes life's most seductive experience. The alarm goes off and they lie under the covers assessing whether some body part is uncomfortable enough to allow them a guilt-free call to report in sick and then escape back into the warmth and safety of their beds. What both groups have in common is the movement of their behavior from a medium predictable range to an extreme. Examples of excessive behavior described by distressed workers interviewed in my studies are noted below.

Flight Response	Fight Response
Rigid, compulsive behavior	Risk-taking behavior
Lethargy and detachment	Hyperactivity
Sexual dysfunction	Hypersexuality/undereating
Overeating/passivity	Violent/aggressive behavior

Excessive behaviors on the flight-response end of the continuum are meant to reduce distress through withdrawal from interaction with the environment. Excessive behaviors on the fight-response end are meant aggressively to remove stressors or to compensate for the feelings stressors generate. People feeling powerless in the work setting may attempt to demonstrate their potency and increase their supports through frantic sexual activity. People who feel emotionally numb from prolonged distress, and who interpret such numbness as craziness, may discover that they can only experience "normal" emotions in high-risk situations.

Many of the accidents that occur to distressed workers are due not only to risk-taking behavior but also to the constant preoccupation with work stressors. One man I interviewed was playing out a number of distressing work situations in his head so intensely while painting his house that he stepped off a scaffolding, oblivious to the fact that he was painting on the upper story and not on the ground level. Sound improbable, even impossible? Have you ever been so involved in or upset about a situation as you left work and continued to think about it, that you were startled by the realization that you had been driving your car for some time with no awareness of what you were doing or where you were?

Violent and aggressive behavior in response to professional distress is most often discharged on those with whom we feel safest—our intimate partners, children, and friends. It is frightening to think of the following sequence: Under extreme distress, a worker is physiologically prepared for violent activity. No safe outlet for that physical and emotional energy is available. The worker then leaves the work setting to go home to his or her family. The worker, feeling defeated and powerless at work, may use aggression at home in an attempt to demonstrate that in at least one area of life he or she has power and control.

The most common excessive behavior used to counter professional distress is self-medication with psychoactive drugs. In some organizations, one could monitor the aggregate level of distress simply by observing the changing levels of consumption of caffeine (coffee, tea, colas), nicotine, and over-the-counter medications, as well as the broader use of alcohol, psychoactive prescription medications, and illegal drugs. And, of course, this discussion would be incomplete if we failed to mention one of the most powerful sources of self-medication known—chocolate.

The problem with these substances is that they work—too quickly and too easily. When we look at such substances as rewards ("I owe it to myself," "It's been one of those days") self-medication can become very seductive—so seductive, in fact, that workers may develop drug problems.

Emotional Adjustment Indicators. Each of us has what John Wallace has called a "preferred defense structure," which he defined as the unique style each of us develops to manage our emotional life in a manner that ensures our safety and helps maintain our self-esteem. As this defense structure is worn down over time by professional distress, it can become fragile and periodically break down, producing symptomatic behavior that can include paranoia, decreased emotional control, feelings of hopelessness, feelings of being trapped, undefined fears and anxiety, increased time daydreaming, exaggerated blaming of others, undefined anger, intellectualization, grandiosity, and preoccupations with power and control.

The common thread here is loss of control over when and how emotions are expressed. From unwanted tears to impulsive angry outbursts to fearful retreats into isolation, prolonged professional distress can eat away at our capacity for emotional control or create an ironlike rigidity that eliminates any chance for spontaneity.

Relationship Indicators. While under intense prolonged stress, our response to relationships, like the excessive behavior indicators, tends to go to one extreme or the other. 'At one extreme, we may begin to emotionally distance ourselves from others, moving out of relationships toward isolation. In service agencies, such a stance can result in a worker turning a human being into "the coronary in 410" or an account number or some other label, spending less time with clients, responding to customers in a mechanical manner (shifting from a focus on people-serving to a focus on paper-processing), or isolating himself or herself professionally and socially at and outside of work.

At the other extreme, one may become overinvolved with clients and co-workers during periods of professional distress. This may be reflected in a worker developing intimate relationships with one or more co-workers, developing excessively dependent relationships with co-workers and supervisors, using clients to meet his or her own needs, becoming angry with clients, having increased interaction and conflict with co-workers, or having increased problems in intimate and interpersonal relationships away from work.

Later, we will look at the ways professional distress can spill out of the work site and affect our ability to sustain healthy, intimate relationships. It is alarming to see the high number of marital and other relationship casualties that occur among people going through periods of professional distress. Many of these relationships are shattered, then explained away in the rhetoric of "irreconcilable differences," with none of those involved having any awareness of the disruption caused by professional distress.

Attitude Indicators. Something happens to the attitudes of people exposed to prolonged professional distress. Feeling progressively worse about themselves and their situations, they can take on an air of righteous grandiosity, passing judgment on the shortcomings of their bosses and co-workers. Distressed workers express attitudes that can vacillate from hypercritical to bored to hopeless.

When an entire organization or organizational unit is going through a period of acute or sustained distress, these attitude changes can take on a contagious quality. Communication in the organization can deteriorate into repetitive games of "Ain't It Awful" and "Waiting for Santa Claus": First everyone takes turns sharing the latest details of how screwed up things are, then they talk about how great everything would be if they could retire or quit or if they could get beyond the current crisis.

Value Indicators. Barring the hormone-induced brain trauma of adolescence and, for some, midlife, most people maintain a fairly consistent set of personal values throughout their lives. When sudden, radical value changes occur, they are usually under conditions of distress.

Many of the individuals in my early studies of professional distress underwent radical changes in their value systems. The changes included conversion to extreme religious or political beliefs and violation of values and beliefs that workers had held to be important throughout their careers. Examples of such transformations are not hard to find: the cop who goes on the take after years of refusing to fix even a parking ticket; the teacher who assaults a student out of anger and frustration; the business executive who abandons a career to become a social worker or missionary; the historically ethical therapist who gets sexually involved with a client; or the priest who leaves the priesthood because of a loss of faith.

A value change can happen to individuals, and it can happen to entire organizations during periods of acute distress. Chapter 5 will cover how an organization can experience such a conversion of values and beliefs.

The individual indicators of professional distress we have reviewed are summarized in figure 1-A.

Figure 1-A
Individual Indicators of Professional Distress

HEALTH INDICATORS	EXCESSIVE BEHAVIOR INDICATORS	EMOTIONAL ADJUSTMENT INDICATORS	RELATIONSHIP INDICATORS	ATTITUDE INDICATORS
Fatigue and chronic exhaustion	Increased consumption of caffeine, tobacco, alcohol, over-the-counter medications, psychoactive prescription drugs, illegal drugs	Emotional distancing	Isolation from or overbonding with others	Grandiosity
Frequent and prolonged colds		Paranoia	Increased interpersonal conflicts with co-workers	Boredom
Headaches		Depression (loss of meaning, loss of hope)		Cynicism
Sleep disturbances (insomnia, nightmares, excessive sleeping)		Decreased emotional control	Increase problems in marital and other interpersonal relationships, including relationships with one's children	Sick humor
Ulcers	Risk-taking behavior (auto/cycle crashes, falls, "high-risk" hobbies, general proness to accidents and injuries, gambling, excessive spending/use of credit)	Martyrdom		Self-righteousness
Gastro-intestinal disorders		Fear of "going crazy"	Abuses of power (sexual harassment scapegoating)	Hypercritical of organization peers, or both
Sudden weight loss or gain		Increased amount of time daydreaming/ fantasizing		Expressions of hopelessness and frustration
Flare-ups of preexisting medical disorders (diabetes, high blood pressure, asthma)	Extreme mood and behavioral changes	Constant feelings of being "trapped"		―――――
				VALUE INDICATORS
		Undefined fears		Loss of faith
Injuries from risk-taking	Increased propensity for violent and aggressive behavior	Inability to concentrate		Spiritual crisis
Muscular pain, particularly in lower back and neck	Hyperactivity	Intellectualization		Sudden and extreme changes in one's values and beliefs
	Change in sexual behavior (sexual dysfunction or hyper-sexuality)	Regression		
Increased premenstrual tension				
Missed menstrual cycles	Over- and undereating			
Excessive sweating and urination				
Bruxism (grinding of the teeth)				

1.3 Organizational Indicators of Professional Distress

The consequences of professional distress can be measured in both collective and individual terms. Wounded by the organization, distressed workers in turn wound the organization. The cost to companies of professional distress can be measured in increased health care costs, deteriorating productivity, heightened intra- and interunit conflict, increased employee turnover, and declining quality of services and products. Distressed workers in key positions and key units can threaten the very survival of an organization. Figure 1-B provides a brief listing of some of the organizational indicators of professional distress that will be discussed in later chapters.

Figure 1-B
Organizational Indicators of Professional Stress

HEALTH CARE COSTS	PRODUCTIVITY COSTS	ISSUES IN SUPERVISION

Increased sick days
Increased worker
  compensation claims
Increased on-the-job
  accidents and injuries
Increased stress-related
  health disorders
	Decreased productivity
	Damage to equipment
	  from employee sabotage
	  and vandalism
	Increase in employee
	  theft
	Increased tardiness
	Increased frequency
	  of work slowdowns and
	  strikes
		Increased grievances
		Extreme employee
		  competitiveness over
		  status and turf
		Distrust, leading to
		  demands that rights,
		  responsibilities, and
		  relationships be
		  formally codified
		Scapegoating of
		  organizational leaders
		Conflicts over
		  authority

EMPLOYEE TURNOVER	PROFESSIONAL RELATIONSHIPS	QUALITY INDICATORS

Extremely low or high
  turnover
High level of
  employee exit without
  notice
Increased requests for
  employee transfers
Disgruntled employees
  making public
  accusations about the
  organization
	Increased inter-
	  personal conflict
	Increased inter-
	  departmental turf battles
	Emotional detachment
	Low morale
	"We-they"
	  polarizations (union
	  versus management)
		Increased consumer
		  complaints about
		  products or services
		Increased liability
		  from malpractice suits
		Loss of professional
		  and organizational pride

1.4 Assumptions about Professional Distress

This section will introduce some assumptions about the progressiveness, inevitability, importance, uniqueness, and complexity of professional distress.

Progressiveness of Distress. Professional distress can best be examined as a process rather than an event. While we can experience distress during a relatively short but turbulent period in an organization's life, most professional distress is progressive and cumulative. It is the ever-accelerating and unrelenting demand for adaptational energy that takes its toll on workers. Professional distress over a prolonged period can produce a loss of adaptational energy and a feeling of increased vulnerability. As our personal health and emotional defense structures weaken from prolonged stress, even a relatively minor work-related problem can trigger a dramatic deterioration in our performance. While our reaction to such an irritant may be judged as extreme, it was the cumulative effect of distress and not the last stressor that produced our response.

Hans Selye called stress "the rate of wear and tear in the body." He believed that each of us has a set quantity of adaptational energy that when depleted, means the end of life. He viewed stress as an aging process—the progressive consumption of our adaptational energy. When demands become too intense and too prolonged, the performance of the human organism begins to deteriorate and develop what Selye called "diseases of adaptation." To live long and live well, we must find ways to cultivate positive stress in our lives while avoiding the cumulative toxins of distress.

The Inevitability of Professional Distress. It is nearly impossible to eliminate professional distress. While such experiences cannot be prevented, it is possible to develop both personal and organizational strategies that prevent the extreme casualty process caused by prolonged professional distress. We can develop strategies that can decrease the frequency and duration of these episodes in our professional lives. The early stages of distress may be inevitable, but we can take responsibility for and control of our organizational structures and group processes to reduce the growing number of distress-related personal casualties in our work environments.

Recognizing Distress. Although we tend to think of professional distress in negative terms, its early stages may be extremely important in indicating areas of needed change and development. Distress is an early-warning system, if we can recognize it as such. Professional distress may indicate areas of needed skill development, a need for a time-out period (a long weekend or vacation), a need to take the next step in our professional development (seeking a job change, returning to school), personal needs outside the work setting that are being neglected, or a need to reestablish a better balance between our professional and personal lives.

The symptoms we associate with professional distress can be viewed as an important internal feedback system. This will become particularly important when we discuss personal strategies for managing professional distress in chapter 11.

The Uniqueness of Distress. There are aspects of professional distress that are unique to professions and organizational settings, meaning that strategies to lesson distress must be based on those unique stressors that characterize particular professions. The stressors triggering distress are likely to be different for the receptionist, the police officer, the nurse, the pilot, the lawyer, the homemaker, the social worker, and the factory worker.

It is important that we avoid simplistic answers to worker distress— those that fail to address the unique circumstances of professions, organizations, organizational units, worker roles, and the individuals who fill those roles. We must resist one-size-fits-all approaches to resolving professional and organizational problems. Rather, we must seek personal and organizational principles that are tempered by an understanding of idiosyncrasy, complexity, and subtlety.

1.5 Assumptions about Organizational Distress

To further introduce some of what lies ahead, we will briefly explore some propositions about the nature of organizations and their responses to individual and collective distress.

Personal and Organizational Synergism

There is a relationship between system distress and personal distress. Each can be a symptom of the other.

There is, in fact, a synergism between organizational distress and the professional distress of an organization's members. Each type of distress feeds into and increases the other in ways that can accelerate uncontrollably. This synergism requires intervention strategies that focus on multiple levels of what I call the "organizational ecosystem."

Distress and Developmental Maturation

Professional distress and system distress often are symptoms of developmental maturation.

There are developmental stages in the life of every worker and every organization. Professional adaptation styles that worked well early in one's career may not work well in the middle or latter phases. Distress may spring not from changes in the environment but from our developmental maturation. Likewise, structures and processes that worked well in one developmental stage of an organization often do not succeed in future stages. Personal and organizational distress often accompany the shift from one developmental stage to another. Such stages can be anticipated, recognized, and actively managed.

Distress and Organizational Character

Professional distress, though most often emerging from temporary aberrations of organizational processes, can sometimes reflect more enduring and toxic dimensions of organizational character.

There are organizations in which conditions become injurious to those who work in them and to those who interact with them. We will explore the difference between an otherwise healthy organization going through a distressing period and an organization whose character has become essentially predatory.

Resistance to Change

The first instinct of most organizations is to deny that distress exists, reframe the stressor as something familiar, and resist the very changes that would seem to be indicated.

Organizational systems are inherently conservative and self-perpetuating. They respond to crises mechanically and superficially, in ways that prevent or contain change. A committee is formed. A study is conducted. A person is hired to address the special problem. A policy is written. This is not how organizational systems change; this is how organizational systems avoid change. In the chapters on organizational intervention, we will look at the importance of getting inside the soul of an organization to change or refine its character, structure, processes, and culture.

The Cost of Cosmetic Change

When a distressed organization responds with cosmetic change rather than substantive change, the system's feedback mechanisms shut down, allowing once-resolvable problems to attain life-threatening proportions.

The strategies that work in the short run to relieve professional and organizational distress can result in a later intensification of distress. Like progressive physical ailments that are misdiagnosed and whose visible symptoms are suppressed by medication, organizational distress can reach terminal proportions before anyone notices. In such a case, an organization could die not from its "disease," but from the palliative measures that created the illusion that everything was fine.

The Dynamics of Change

Change in one part of an organization can trigger accommodating changes in all other parts of the organization, raising the potential for unforeseen consequences whenever problem resolution is attempted.

Actions that alleviate distress in one unit or on one worker may inadvertently increase distress in another unit or on another worker. The principle recognizes the dynamics and infinite complexity of organizational systems. Everything is connected; no organizational issue or problem can be addressed in isolation.

Potential Iatrogenic Effects of Ill-Planned Interventions

Poorly designed and implemented interventions aimed at lowering system distress or individual distress can have the opposite effect.

The medical term "iatrogenic illness" means inadvertent physician-caused harm or treatment-caused injury. It means that a patient suffers or, perhaps, dies not from his or her original ailment but from the unintended effects of treatment. The principle can apply to organizational interventions. Because historically successful organizations have proved so resilient in the face of internal and external threats, we tend to see organizations as nearly immortal. But for those readers who are CEOs, managers, and supervisors, my message is a simple one: Be aware that unforeseen side effects can occur from poorly planned interventions to alleviate worker distress. Later, we will cover organizational intervention strategies and the importance of implementing those strategies only after careful assessment of an organization and its workforce's characteristics. The ethical guideline for organizational intervention should be the same as that which applies to physicians: "First, do no harm!"

⫷ 2

Organizational Responses to Distressed Workers

When Hans Selye introduced the term "stress" into the field of medicine in 1936 through his description of the general adaptation syndrome, it generated heated debates that lasted for decades. Many of the early debates included disagreement over the existence of biological stress and criticisms of Selye's definition of stress. I have no intention of entering this semantic debate, but there is a way in which the definition of stress and distress interest me greatly. This is how the definitions are revealed by, not scholars, but organizational managers and supervisors through their responses to those phenomena in the workplace.

Organizational managers reveal their theoretical approaches to professional distress through their organization of the work environment and their responses to distress-related performance problems. These approaches, which are revealed through managerial behavior but are rarely articulated explicitly, are based on powerfully held beliefs and values about human nature and the relationship between people and work. A systematic study of professional distress must begin with an examination of these beliefs and values that define responses to distress in the workplace.

During the past three decades, I have had the opportunity through varied research, training, and consulting activities to work with a large number of organizations. These opportunities provided a unique vantage point from which to observe organizational approaches to professional distress and to develop a typology for analyzing these approaches. The following pages will classify, describe, and critique these six organizational approaches to professional distress:

- The authoritarian-moral approach
- The clinical approach

- The cognitive approach
- The training approach
- The environmental approach
- The systems approach

Note that each approach described has profound repercussions on those experiencing professional distress and on the future incidence of professional distress in the organization.

Ideally, this schema will provide managers an opportunity to review their own assumptions about worker distress and to assess their own supervisory responses to those experiencing professional distress. Undertake this self-examination in a spirit of openness, and check the natural tendency for defensiveness. The criticism of various approaches is based on the knowledge that many of us have exemplified some of these styles at different stages of our managerial careers.

2.1 The Authoritarian-Moral Approach: Professional Distress as Bad Character

The authoritarian-moral approach to professional distress reflects what Douglas McGregor called the "theory X" philosophy of management. Theory X is based on the assumption that most people dislike work, lack ambition, are essentially passive, avoid responsibility, resist change, and are self-centered and unconcerned with the needs of the organization. The role of the manager is thus to direct, motivate, manipulate, persuade, control, reward, and punish the worker to effectively respond to the needs of the organization (McGregor 1967, 1973).

Within the organization managed by the propositions of theory X, even the existence of professional distress is adamantly denied through such flippant phrases as, "There's no such thing as stress, only staff who don't want to work." Behavior indicative of professional distress is viewed as emerging from character flaws in the worker. While the authoritarian-moral approach is usually applied to workers on an individual basis, it may be broadened to encompass stereotyped responses to particular subgroups of workers. In the latter case, distress-related behavior of the individual worker is seen as justifying the manager's view of the unreliable and irresponsible character of a group of workers, most often women, people of color, or older workers.

Organizational managers who typify the authoritarian-moral approach are intensely invested in their work and have great difficulty accepting workers whose time and emotional commitments to the organization do not match their own. In spite of these leaders' extensive investment of time and emotional energy in the work setting, they may work for years before they experience the extreme effects of their own distress. They are what some have called "stress carriers." These managers externalize their distress to others through verbal reprimands, excessive and unrealistic role expectations, and impulsive and frequently contradictory task assignments. The stress carriers often bolster their own self-esteem at the expense of their employees through repeated variations of the following scenario:

The stress carrier storms into an office where three workers are engaged in various work assignments, turns to one of the workers and says, "Jane, I need a summary report on _____ (stated quickly, vaguely, and without reference to where the information can be obtained) for a 2:00 meeting tomorrow afternoon." The stress carrier rapidly leaves the office not allowing time for clarification. Jane, finding no help from her colleagues clarifying what precisely the boss wants, and unable to get access to him for further instructions, does the best job she can, summarizing what she guesses he wants. At 1:30 the following afternoon, the stress carrier rushes into Jane's office and responds with outrage that what Jane prepared was not what he wanted at all, and that he can't understand why the project didn't get done as he'd requested.

Such scenarios serve to build up the self-esteem of the stress carrier, emotionally devastate the workers playing the scapegoat in the drama, and reinforce the motto of the authoritarian-moral approach: "If you want anything done right, you have to do it yourself."

The stress carrier is typified by the manager who flippantly boasts, "I don't get ulcers; I give ulcers." The authoritarian-moral approach places impossible burdens on workers and then penalizes them for not being able to stand up under the weight. Organizations characterized by the authoritarian-moral approach respond to distressed workers in a punitive fashion either through disciplinary action or by forcing the victims out of the organization. As might be expected, this organizational approach produces an extremely high rate of staff turnover. When such organizations eventually self-destruct, as most do, and the stress carriers are later asked why they got out of the business, they most frequently lament that they just couldn't find good help.

There are severe disadvantages to the authoritarian-moral approach to professional distress. The focus on the character of the distressed worker camouflages the need to modify the high-stress environment in general and the leadership style in particular. This approach does nothing to eliminate those organizational conditions that will continue to produce a high rate of professional distress. The approach also creates a deterioration in the relationships and communication processes that would be necessary to reduce stressors and increase supports in the work environment.

The authoritarian-moral approach is also immune to corrective feedback. Its moral arrogance and punitiveness almost guarantee a self-prophetic outcome. As staff become increasingly distressed from the working conditions, they do indeed avoid responsibility, develop malicious attitudes toward the organization, and commit acts of sabotage against the organizational leadership. As new staffers enter the organization, they are lauded by the leader for their expertise and all that they will accomplish for the agency. As the new staff's performance then deteriorates under the high-stress conditions, they are sequentially scapegoated and forced out like the workers who preceded them, with the stress carrier lamenting, "They were just like all the others."

2.2 The Cognitive Approach:
Professional Distress as Faulty Expectations

The cognitive approach to professional distress views the phenomenon as emerging from unrealistic ideas, beliefs, and expectations held by workers about themselves and their profession. The contradiction between one's notions of how things ought to be and the realities confronted in the work environment are viewed as leading to a loss of professional idealism, a loss of personal enthusiasm, and the onset of pessimism and hostility. The cognitive approach to professional distress is most often utilized to explain the personal changes that occur early in one's professional career.

In the cognitive approach, professional distress is often seen as a product of faulty professional socialization. Marlene Kramer and Claudia Schmalenberg eloquently described the "reality shock" they experienced in the transition from nursing school to the new and unfamiliar world of nursing practice. Each of these subcultures has a set of distinct values and specific role behaviors that the participants must perform. The vast discrepancy between the two subcultures is a source of intense distress and contributes to the large number of nurses who leave the

profession (Kramer 1974; Schmalenberg and Kramer 1976). Similar reality shock tramples the idealism of many physicians, teachers, lawyers,
police officers, engineers, and public servants.

Organizations that respond to professional distress using the cognitive model attempt to resocialize the worker to bring greater harmony
between professional expectations and professional realities. Since professional distress is viewed as a problem of intellect, the manager's task
is viewed as indoctrinating workers with beliefs and expectations that,
while reducing idealism, produce a greater level of professional satisfac-
tion and contentment. The manager using this approach has relationships that can be characterized as tutorial rather than punitive.

There are a number of strengths to the cognitive approach to
alleviating psychological distress. The approach clearly raises the importance of professional education in instilling values, beliefs, and expectations that fit the real world. Managerial practices emerging from
this approach do impact the incidence of worker distress by establishing clear role expectations and realistic belief systems for workers. In
its response to distressed workers, the approach also avoids the demor-
alizing and stigmatizing effects of more punitive approaches.

The disadvantages of the cognitive approach are threefold. By defining the source of worker distress as irrational and unrealistic ideas and
beliefs, the approach tends to ignore both the emotional vulnerabilities
and the skill deficiencies that a worker may bring to the work setting. A
broader criticism of the approach is that it often serves to support the status quo by adapting the worker to the imperfections of the work world
rather than pushing the work environment toward, if not perfection, at
least progressive improvement. A final criticism is that the approach ignores other factors, particularly factors in the work environment, that
will continue to produce professional distress even after the workers are
"appropriately" socialized.

2.3 The Clinical Approach:
Professional Distress as Psychopathology

The clinical approach to workers affected by professional distress defines such distress as emerging from the poor emotional health of the
worker. This approach is particularly prevalent among human service
agencies whose members have a propensity to see the world through
such diagnostic labels. The models used by these workers to understand
the emotional and relationship problems of their clients are inevitably

used to understand the emotional and relationship problems of staff in the work milieu.

The clinical approach to professional distress is remarkably similar to the response of a family system to an acting-out adolescent. As the worker experiences a distress-related deterioration in performance, the organization recognizes the inappropriate behavior and attitudes of the worker (acknowledgment of deviancy). The problem is seen as emerging from the personality of the worker (diagnosis of psychopathology). The worker becomes a problem (identified patient) about which something must be done. The supervisor confronts the worker on his or her current level of functioning and recommends that the worker seek help outside the agency, or turns the supervisory relationship into a counseling relationship (psychological therapy). If the worker's behavior does not change, he or she is fired or manipulated out of the organization (the equivalent of institutionalizing the adolescent).

The clinical approach has been noted by a number of other authors. Ezra Stotland and Arthur Kobler, in their classic study *The Life and Death of a Mental Hospital,* noted the way in which key staff and consultants of a private mental hospital began talking about "treating" the board, "treating" the hospital staff, and "treating" the hospital, at a time that severe organizational problems were besetting the facility. Many of the problems were attributed to the "sickness" of key staff members. The large number of staff casualties that occurred during the demise of this particular hospital were viewed as problems of individual psychopathology and were not seen in the context of the tremendously high-stress conditions under which the individuals were working. The propensity to individualize organizational problems, and the accompanying failure to address major systemic problems in the organization and the organization's relationship with its outside environment, played crucial roles in the demise of the hospital studied (Stotland and Kobler 1965). Arthur Elstein, in his study of the service reorganization at the Massachusetts Mental Health Center, noted the tendency of administrative staff to use a psychological interpretation to explain conflict between particular staff and the administration. In one example from the study, a resident complained to the administration that his current job assignment was impossible to complete. "At first, his complaints were interpreted as reflecting personal psychological difficulties, but when he persuaded his supervisors to try the task themselves, they stopped talking about 'his problem'" (Elstein 1972).

Another variation of the clinical model is to define worker distress as a purely medical/health problem. The approach is often used when the worker affected by professional distress is suffering from one or more (distress-related) health problems. The organizational response is to refer the employee through the medical office or employee assistance program for medical/psychiatric treatment. Such intervention frequently includes the use of sedative and tranquilizing drugs. The approach, in essence, medicates the victim to increase the threshold of stress tolerance so that the worker can sustain his or her role performance. All the while, primary sources of distress within the organizational environment are ignored.

In summary, the clinical approach to reducing professional distress defines the problems of distress as psychological (and/or medical) and uses psychological (and/or medical) treatment of the worker as the primary means of remediation.

While distressed workers may truly need psychiatric and medical assistance, there are a number of disadvantages to the clinical approach to alleviating distress. This approach, like the authoritarian-moral and the cognitive approaches, individualizes what is essentially an interactional problem. The approach fails to address the need to modify the high-stress work environment. Perhaps most significantly, it stigmatizes the worker through the diagnostic process. In my interviews with distressed workers, it is clear that they frequently do not connect what they are experiencing to the work environment. Their greatest fear is that they are "going crazy." The clinical approach to professional distress inappropriately confirms these workers' worst fears. By focusing the worker's attention on his or her own emotional difficulties, the clinical approach decreases the worker's ability to mobilize external resources for support at the exact time he or she is in most desperate need of such supports. The definition of the problem as psychopathology increases the worker's feelings of isolation, paranoia, loss of control, and, in short, escalates the intensity of distress.

Employee-assistance programs have been established in many organizations to address employee problems that have resulted or could result in decreased performance. These programs can reflect the deficiencies of the clinical approach to the extent that they address only individual factors (psychopathology, medical problems) or factors outside the work setting (family problems, financial difficulties) that affect employee performance. It is much easier, for example, for an employee-assistance counselor to identify a problem of alcohol abuse and refer an employee to treatment than to report to management that an employee is using alcohol to self-medicate stress generated from intolerable conditions in the work environment.

2.4 The Training Approach: Professional Distress as Skill Deficiency

The training approach to helping distressed workers defines the problem as one of skill deficiency, particularly skills in the area of stress management. It is assumed that all employees will experience some degree of work-related stress and that some workers lack the skills to manage such stress. Remediation measures include providing stress-management training to increase the worker's level of stress tolerance and to increase the worker's repertoire of stress-management techniques.

The training approach also assumes that a significant amount of job-related stress occurs because of a discrepancy between the skills an individual possesses and the skills the individual needs to effectively perform his or her job. Skill training that enhances the worker's ability to perform role responsibilities thus becomes a primary vehicle for addressing professional distress.

The training approach should be an integral part of any organizational strategy to address distress. There are, however, some limitations to the approach. Training approaches that focus on deficiencies in stress-management skills may be used to immunize workers against stress generated by intolerable role conditions. Under these circumstances, the training approach might inadvertently distract the organization from the need to reduce role stress conditions and increase role supports for the worker, and may only prolong the onset of the distress-related deterioration in the worker's performance and health.

Training approaches that focus on skill development for improved role performance may be based on a misdiagnosis of the conditions that are responsible for inadequate role performance and the true sources of his or her distress. There may be, for example, conditions in the work environment that prevent the worker from effectively delivering those skills that he or she possesses. The problem may be one of unclear or outmoded organizational policies, a lack of role clarity, or excessive and contradictory demands on a worker's time, rather than adequate skills. Under these circumstances, skill training will neither improve role performance nor reduce the excessive strain experienced by the worker.

2.5 The Environmental Approach:
Professional Distress as Imperfections
in the Organizational Environment

The four organizational approaches to worker distress described so far all share one thing in common. They view the individual employee as the origin of professional distress, and utilize remediation strategies that seek to change the individual in some manner. The next approach ignores individual issues and defines the problem of professional distress solely as a malfunctioning work environment.

Many managers recognize distress-related problems in employees and see these problems as emerging from the structure or process of the organization. These managers are constantly tinkering with the organizational structure—altering roles, policies, and procedures, and continually creating and then casting off new work norms—all in an effort to discover the magical structure that gets the work done and makes everyone happy. Anytime an employee reports, "We've really got a problem with . . . ," this type of manager immediately jumps into action to manipulate the environment to address the problem.

During the years that my own management style tended to reflect this knee-jerk approach to management, much of my environmental tinkering aimed at reducing the distress of my employees actually increased their distress. It wasn't my resistance to change but my propensity for constant superficial changes that created an unpredictable and unstable work milieu.

Most managers want to be seen as capable decision makers, problem solvers, and innovators. Most managers, more than some would care to admit, want to be liked by those who work for them. It is discomforting to discover how such benign intentions can lead to inconsistent, rapidly changing, and stress-provoking conditions in a work unit. Some of the more common problems with this management approach are cataloged below.

Many managers who exemplify the environmental approach to worker distress fail to control the pace of change in their organizational units. Reflect back on the definition of stress as a demand for adaptational change, and it will be clear that we must gear the pace of change to the level of adaptational energy available to our employees. This is true even when we make changes in the environment to alleviate worker distress. There may be important changes that should be postponed or phased in slowly simply because employees have already experienced too much change in too short a time period.

"System tinkerers" also frequently neglect a basic principle of systems theory that we noted in chapter 1: A change in one part of a system inevitably provokes accommodating changes in other parts of the system. By manipulating the environment to reduce distress for one group of workers, we may inadvertently increase distress for other workers in the organization.

There is also a more fundamental flaw in the environmental approach to stress-management. The preoccupation with organizational structure and process may divert the manager's attention away from the individual worker who is experiencing some level of physical or psychological impairment. Such impairment may require immediate support or intervention.

2.6 The Systems Approach:
Professional Distress as Ecological Dysfunction

The five organizational approaches to alleviating burnout critiqued in this chapter all oversimplify professional distress by seeing it as caused primarily by a single factor. In this section, we will explore a more comprehensive understanding of professional and organizational distress.

The systems approach to professional distress advocated in this book defines such distress not as a problem inside the individual worker or as a problem in the work environment, but as a breakdown in the *relationship* between the individual and the organization. Such a breakdown also can reflect an even wider collapse of the relationship between the organization and its outside environment.

Biologists study the fragile balance, interrelationships, and interdependence among all living things. The systems manager must understand the ecology of his or her organization in a similar manner. I am indebted to the original work of Urie Bronfenbrenner and to Jerome F. X. Caroll for the development of this ecological perspective. Dr. Caroll and I collaborated on a paper more than fifteen years ago that set forth the major propositions of the systems approach, a perspective that views professional distress as a complex interaction among five layers of the professional ecosystem:

1. *Personal Vulnerability Issues*—personal factors that influence an individual's susceptibility to professional distress. We will explore these in depth in chapter 11.
2. *Microsystem Issues*—the prevalence of role stressors and the availability of role supports in one's immediate work unit. In

chapter 9, we will define thirteen role stressors that impair worker performance and health, and we will catalog a number of role supports that enhance worker productivity and health.

3. *Mesosystem Issues*—problems in the structure (mission core values, goals, and roles) and process (relationships, communication, problem-solving methods) of the organization. We will describe mesosystem problems that can cause professional and organizational distress in chapters 5, 6, and 7.

4. *Exosystem Issues*—turbulence in the organization's relationship with its outside environment and changes outside the organization that have a profound impact on the organization.

5. *Macrosystem Issues*—political, economic, and social changes in the world at large that alter the basic relationship between people and work (Carroll and White 1981).

The remaining chapters will demonstrate how each of the above factors are "ecologically nested within one another," and how managers seeking to understand and address professional distress must recognize and respond to the multiple and reciprocal relationships that exist between the factors. We will place particular emphasis on the first three.

The systems approach advocated in these pages is not without its own drawbacks. The model requires a much greater degree of knowledge and skill to implement as well as a high degree of organization. Within the systems approach, there is often a bias toward environmental interventions that can sometimes ignore the need for strategies to reduce the personal vulnerability of the individual worker and respond to individuals in distress. There is also the danger that managers facing the overwhelming number of factors contributing to professional and organizational distress may themselves be overwhelmed. Armed with our knowledge of these limitations, we will begin to outline the systems perspective in great detail.

⫸ 3

The Systems Approach to Professional Distress

This chapter lays out the theoretical map that undergirds the remaining chapters of the book. For those of you who benefit from and enjoy such cognitive maps, the chapter will provide a detailed presentation of the systems approach to professional and organizational distress. For those who tend to get mired in such maps—those who, like me, never read the directions to anything before attempting assembly—feel free to move on to chapter 4 if you find yourself getting bogged down. The principles set forth in this chapter are buried in all the detailed stories that fill the remaining chapters.

3.1 The Ecology of Professional Stress

In exploring the ecology of professional distress we will address a number of key questions. What factors can be used to predict one's vulnerability to professional distress? What roles do organizational structure and internal organizational relationships play in increasing or decreasing vulnerability to professional distress? How do forces outside the organizational setting influence the prevalence and intensity of professional distress?

Figure 3-A illustrates an ecological perspective on professional distress. In the figure, the worker is ecologically "nested" (like the center of an onion) in different layers or levels of social organization. The figure depicts the complex and synergistic relationship between individual and environmental variables that can result in distress. The elements of the worker's ecosystem are briefly summarized on the following pages in this chapter.

Figure 3-A
Factors/Relationships Affecting Individual Stress Response

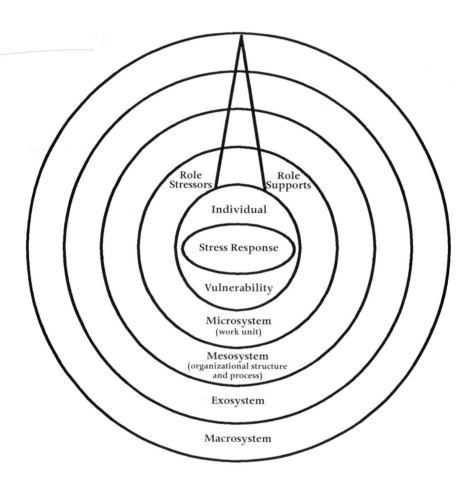

3.2 The Individual

When you began work in your current organization, you brought to the workplace a unique level of vulnerability to professional distress. This vulnerability was shaped by your body's inherited capacity to respond physiologically to excessive stress—a capacity potentially decreased through illness, physical trauma, poor self-care, and toxic habits; historically shaped style of stress management; level of technical knowledge; personal values; family relationships; degree of mastery of developmental tasks appropriate to your stage of life; capacity to initiate and sustain nurturing intimate relationships; expectations and motivations related to work; ability to assert needs and set realistic limits; feelings about your capabilities and self-worth; unresolved emotional pain (anger, shame, guilt); and need to devote adaptational energy to other life changes.

Many of these factors are mentioned in traditional stress literature as if they are fixed, isolated characteristics. What distinguishes the systems perspective is the idea that most of the characteristics are dynamic rather than static and begin to change as soon as you enter the life of the organization.

Let's consider, for example, what happens when you bring to a new work environment high levels of motivation and enthusiasm and high expectations for professionally satisfying and stimulating work, only to encounter a milieu of low productivity and negativity. Under these circumstances, a war of adaptation will begin almost immediately. Forces within the work unit will operate to pull your expectations and work values toward the group norm. The intensity of your enthusiasm, on the other hand, may begin to change the group norm. Such synergy marks the dynamic, reciprocal adaptation process between the individual and the organization; it can be described through numerous examples.

The self-concept you bring to a work setting can be confirmed or altered through feedback from the organization. As your self-concept is being affected by the organization, your self-concept is influencing the collective self-concept of the work unit. You could, for example, bring to a new work setting a history of stress management that relied heavily on self-medication with caffeine, nicotine, and alcohol. In this war of adaptation, the organization could reinforce your stress-management style through informal work norms characterized by the motto "when in doubt, drink!" At the same time, your propensity for self-medication could influence work-group norms so that other workers were more inclined to self-medicate to manage stress. Imagine how many times, in such a situation, you might say to a co-worker, "We've had a hell of a day! Let me buy you a drink before we go home." In contrast, the organization could diminish the strength of your self-medication pattern through values that inhibit psychoactive drug consumption and through mechanisms that provide healthier alternatives for managing stress.

The systems perspective dictates that we address not only characteristics in the individual and in the work environment that increase vulnerability to burnout, but also the special chemistry in the reciprocal relationship between the individual and the organization. The systems perspective demands that we look at what might be called the collective vulnerability of organizational members.

Collective vulnerability implies that the manager must ask the following questions. Are there shared characteristics of employees within a work unit or the whole organization that have special implications related to their vulnerability for professional distress? Might these shared characteristics suggest particular types of strategies to address professional distress? If we were to identify the stress management style of each member of the organization and then look at this data collectively, what style would dominate? What early-warning signs would best indicate a disturbance in the multiple relationships between these individuals and the organization?

3.3 The Microsystem

The microsystem is the smallest unit of organization in the work environment. It is the department, division, bureau, section, service, unit, or team. The microsystem is that unit of organization or group of people each individual interacts with most intensely in the performance of his or her role.

Several characteristics of the microsystem shape the organization's relationship with the individual worker and influence both the level of professional distress in the work unit and permissions and prohibitions on how such distress should be managed by the individual. These characteristics include the physical environment of the unit; the goals, objectives, and tasks of the unit; group sentiment (the emotional content in co-worker relationships); definitions of power, authority, and control (decision making and accountability); structure of the organization; group norms on how, when, and to whom one can communicate; the relationships between the unit and other components of the organization;

the management style and philosophy of unit leadership; and equipment and materials.

The microsystem is the primary unit in the relationship between the individual worker and the organization. No matter what values and ideals are espoused by the organizational leader, it is at the microsystem level that those values become reality or empty rhetoric. Many organizations ignore this principle when confronted with worker distress, internal conflict, and poor morale. They create new appendages (even other microsystems) to the organization, such as employee assistance programs or health promotion programs, but do nothing to change the day-to-day conditions at the microsystem level.

There are two basic challenges at the microsystem level, and how these challenges are met will, to a great extent, shape the quality of work life for organizational members. The first challenge is to organize the work of the microsystem—defining tasks, allocating resources, clarifying roles and accountability, defining methods of problem solving, establishing time lines and outcomes, defining transactions with other units and entities outside the organization, and supervising the flow of activity. The second challenge is to assess who can adapt to and perform microsystem roles, to assess how the microsystem will in turn be affected by each individual, and to develop group norms and values that are consistent with organizational goals and supportive of worker health. Examining structure issues allows us to determine how conditions in the microsystem environment promote or diminish employee productivity and health. Examining process issues allows us to assess and control the degree of harmony or disharmony in the worker/microsystem match. A mismatch of an individual with the wrong microsystem, or microsystem role, can have disastrous consequences both to the health of the mismatched individual and to the entire work unit.

While this special reciprocal relationship exists between the individual and the microsystem, both the individual and the microsystem are involved in broader transactions with the whole organization, here referred to as the mesosystem. Mesosystem transactions also involve structure and process issues. A critical function of the microsystem manager is to regulate such transactions and balance the need for healthy cohesion between microsystem members with the need for these same workers to identify with and support the organization as a whole. A balance is sought between the twin problems of, on one hand, the worker identifying passionately with his or her work unit but having no sense of affiliation with or support of the mesosystem, and on the other, the worker supporting the overall organization while undermining unit goals and leadership.

The management of internal boundaries between the microsystem and mesosystem has tremendous implications on the incidence and prevalence of debilitating professional distress. A major function of the microsystem manager is to sustain the availability of supports for workers in both the microsystem and mesosystem, while serving as a gatekeeper to control the pace of change (stressors) thrust on the microsystem by the overall organization. This notion of balancing role stressors and role supports will be addressed in greater detail in later chapters.

3.4 The Mesosystem

The mesosystem embraces all of the microsystems and constitutes all elements contained in the boundaries of the organization.

Factors in the mesosystem that can have a direct influence on the intensity and duration of professional distress include the clarity of the organization's mission, goals, and objectives; the efficiency and utility of the organization's structure in meeting organizational goals; the ability of the organization to adapt to changing conditions in the outside environment; the ability of organizational leadership to manage harmonious and complementary boundary transactions between the organization's microsystems; the nature of the organizational culture—beliefs, attitudes, values, and emotions that govern formal and informal relationships between organizational members; the ability of organizational leadership to generate hope, direction, control, and a vision that integrates the activities of the microsystem units; and the ability of the organization to distribute rewards in fair and consistent ways.

The systems perspective seeks to understand the chain of reciprocal relationships between the individual worker, the microsystem, and the mesosystem. Individuals influence both the micro- and mesosystems. The distress-related disruption of the behavior and health of a single worker increases stress on other workers in the microsystem and may compromise the ability of the microsystem to accomplish work objectives, which in turn negatively impacts other microsystems and the organization as a whole. Conversely, decisions and actions in the mesosystem have immediate ripple effects through the microsystems on individual workers. A mesosystem that has overextended itself by committing to objectives that surpass the levels of fiscal, technical, and human re-sources will inevitably overload the production capacity of the micro-systems and, in turn, lead to the stressful role-overload of individual workers.

Many classic studies on organizational stress and management have detailed the important aspects of internal structure and leadership ac-tivities in the mesosystem. Few, however, have focused on the relation-ship between the organization and its outside environment, and the impact of that relationship on worker health. In the coming chapters, we will emphasize that a critical factor in the cause of professional distress and intraorganizational conflict is the organization's relationship with its outside environment and the manner in which the boundary between the mesosystem and the exo- and macrosystems is being managed.

3.5 The Exosystem

The next layer of an organization's life space—the exosystem—contains all of the other ecosystems that impinge on the life of that organization and its workers. The exosystem can be divided into two areas for pur-poses of discussion: In one area are the exosystem factors that directly impinge on the organization; in the other are those elements of each em-ployee's life that constitute his or her nonwork ecosystem.

The organization's exosystem includes important variables such as the physical environment through which workers, clients, materials, and products are transported into and out of the organization; the availa-bility of an affordable labor pool with the desired knowledge and skill; regulatory agencies that govern conditions under which the organiza-tion must operate; the availability and costs of similar products or ser-vices offered by other organizations (competition); the availability of capital; allied professional agencies; agencies that govern the technical or professional certification of workers; consistency for the demand of the organization's products or services; professional organizations/ unions; and community attitudes and values that relate to the organiza-tion's products or services.

If we go back to our definition of stress as a demand for adaptational change, then an organization's response to the pace of change in the exo-system has a profound impact on the level of professional stress experi-enced by workers. The accelerated rate of global cultural change that has characterized this century—change driven largely by astonishingly rapid technological advances—has left most organizations operating in highly turbulent fields. If change unfolds too rapidly in the exosystem, organizations become reactive, and the focus shifts from identified objectives to merely adapting and controlling the demands and contingencies thrust upon the organization by the environment. Alvin Toffler, in his 1970 book *Future Shock,* accurately predicted the fragmentation and transience of organizational goals produced by accelerating change, which we are experiencing in nearly every sector of business and industry.

The acceleration of change in the exosystem has forced the acceleration of change inside organizations. The management of the mesosystem/exosystem boundary has become crucial in preventing a sudden demand for adaptational energy that can far surpass the capacity for change in the organization and its individual workers. In later chapters, actively controlling and managing the pace of organizational change will emerge as a major systems strategy in addressing both professional and organizational distress.

A second aspect of the exosystem is the personal nonwork ecosystem of each organizational member. This ecosystem includes such components as the family, the nonwork social network, the neighborhood, and the community. Turbulence in these ecosystems inevitably spills into the work environment just as high levels of stress in the work environment are brought home into the family and social network of the worker. This cross-boundary transfer has important implications to the impact of stress both in the work and home environment. Your vulnerability to distress increases as you simultaneously experience high demands for adaptational energy from your job and from your personal ecosystem. The family and social ecosystem can also serve as a source of replenishment from work-related distress. Later chapters will describe how closure of the organizational boundary reduces your ability to sustain access to such replenishment and increases the intensity of your distress inside the organization. Later chapters will also detail how work-related distress is carried as a disruptive force into our family and intimate relationships.

3.6 The Macrosystem

The macrosystem encompasses broader social, political, and economic forces that affect all of the previously described ecosystem components. The macrosystem forces that can have direct and indirect influences on occupational distress include

- the value attached to various professions as measured by cultural rewards such as money and status
- broad changes in technology that produce ripple effects throughout the culture
- turbulence, such as international conflict or economic crises, that creates shifts in priorities and the allocation of fiscal and human resources
- changing values and expectations related to work
- demographic factors such as changing life expectancies, birthrates, immigration, and mobility

It should be clear from the above that professional and organizational distress is a complex problem influenced by forces at all levels of the ecosystem. Strategies that seek to address the problem of professional distress must be sophisticated and target multiple levels of the professional ecosystem. Strategies that seek only to intervene at the level of the individual, or that seek a simple manipulation of one element of the work environment, are doomed to failure.

In the coming chapters, components of the systems perspective will be isolated for in-depth analysis. The next chapters will examine the tendency of many work environments to become "closed organizational families," and will explore the relationship of such closure to the professional distress of workers.

⟨⟨⟨ 4

The Organizational Family Continuum

4.1 The Organizational Family

The conceptualization of an organizational group as a family system is not new, particularly in the health and human services field. The history of child welfare is replete with models that show how to care for and re-habilitate children by re-creating the family system. Most of these models designate professional staff in parental surrogate roles. A wide variety of helping services—in which such catch phrases as "resocialization," "retraining," "reparenting," "normalization," and "milieu" are popular—use a family model to conceptualize the treatment of emotional disorders. Many private companies have thought of themselves as extended families and business leaders have often used the family as a metaphor for the kind of cohesion and loyalty they hope to instill in their organizations. In this chapter, we will push this analysis of the organization as a family system on the assumption that people sustain or lose their emotional health in organizations in much the same way they do in families. We will try to extract from our knowledge of families some lessons about professional and organizational health. First, we will look at the structure of the organizational family.

The term "organizational family" will be used throughout this book in an attempt to conceptualize the organizational group as a family system.

> *The* ORGANIZATIONAL FAMILY *consists of those people identified as organizational members and any other people who, by virtue of frequent interaction with members or influence on internal decision-making, constitute the organizational group.*

Those persons making up the organizational family will vary greatly from setting to setting. The organizational family may include paid staff, volunteers, consultants, interns, board members, clients, and, under certain circumstances, intimate partners of people in the above groups.

As with the nuclear families, one can also speak of an "extended organizational family."

> *The* EXTENDED ORGANIZATIONAL FAMILY *consists of the professional, social, and intimate relationships of organizational members that serve collectively to buffer and link the organizational family and the outside world.*

The extended family includes the most significant relationships between organizational members and individuals who reside in the organizational exosystem. It may include family, intimate partners, friends and relatives of organizational family members, board members, patrons, stockholders, key personnel from funding and regulatory agencies, and key individuals from allied organizations.

The use of family systems theory to understand organizational group dynamics begins with the premise that organizational problems, and in particular personal and interpersonal conflicts within a working group, can best be understood and resolved by looking at the operations of the total system rather than the functioning of the individual members of the group. Events that create ongoing conflict and disequilibrium in the system will inevitably affect the health of organizational members and their ability to adequately perform tasks crucial to the survival and health of the system. In this manner, individual health is inextricably tied to system health, and vice versa. Organizational families and nuclear families share many of the same problems. The organizational family contains the same kinds of triangulations, myths, projections, taboos, ghosts, heroes, and scapegoats found in the family system. Both systems can be examined in terms of the strength and flexibility of their structure, roles, and rituals. One of the most important determinants of system health in both families and organizations is the nature of the boundary transactions they make with the outside world. To better understand this, we must introduce the notion of open and closed organizational systems.

4.2 Open Versus Closed Organizational Families

Since Ludwig Von Bertalanffy described "open" and "closed" systems in the 1950s, family therapists and management and organizational specialists have applied the concept to their particular areas of concern.

An understanding of open and closed systems begins with the concept of a system's boundary.

> A SYSTEM'S BOUNDARY *is that "invisible circle" that encloses a system, separates it from its environment and distinguishes members from nonmembers.*

A boundary is the skin, or perimeter, that contains the organization and distinguishes it from its outside environment. It has both physical and psychological dimensions. A system boundary could be represented by lines on a map separating countries, states, or cities. It could be represented by the physical walls of a prison, or different groups by powerful social norms that separate different groups and restrict contact between their members. In families, a boundary may be defined by law, name, and blood, or it may be more loosely defined, say, by affectional bonds. In my own family, I had three blood sisters, an adopted sister, twenty-three foster brothers and sisters, and frequent drop-ins—a loose boundary definition, indeed. With organizational families, a boundary is the definition used by organizational leaders and members to determine who is and who is not part of the organizational family system. Like nuclear families, organizations can define this boundary very tightly (a closed guild) or very loosely (a rapidly changing ad hoc committee).

Organizational families differ not only in who is included within the boundary, but also in the quality and nature of the boundary itself. The latter difference includes what is called boundary permeability.

> BOUNDARY PERMEABILITY *is the degree of resistance encountered when attempting to move ideas, people, and resources into and out of the organizational family.*

Boundary permeability is what distinguishes open and closed systems. Closed organizational family systems tend to have very rigid boundaries, or low permeability, that restrict interaction with the outside environment. Open organizational family systems have very permeable boundaries, allowing members easy access to other people in the social environment.

Every organizational family manages and controls boundary transactions through gatekeepers.

> GATEKEEPERS *are those people who control, through their regulation of the physical and social environment, when, where, under what conditions, and with whom boundary transactions can occur.*

In most nuclear families, parents perform this gatekeeping function. In the organizational family, it is managers and their designees who control the frequency and intensity of boundary transactions. Figure 4-A illustrates the gatekeeping functions in an organizational family.

Figure 4-A
Gatekeeping Functions in the Organizational Family System

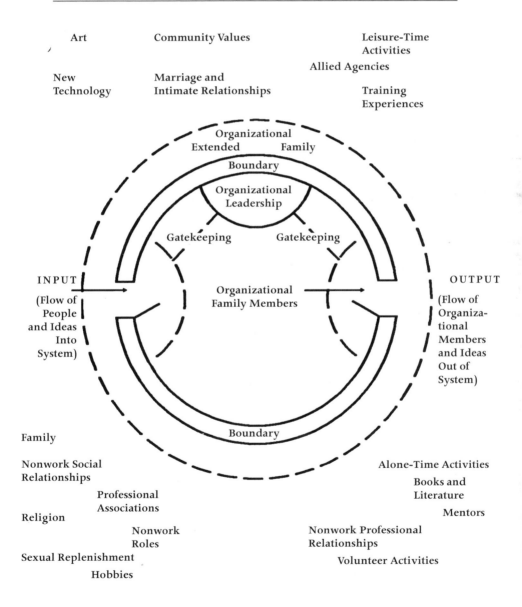

In organizations with low boundary permeability, gatekeepers aggressively restrict the flow of ideas and people into the organization, and restrict the ability of members to develop and sustain professional and social relationships and activities outside of the organization. Closed organizational systems are inherently conservative. In their drive to maintain system balance, they are defensive, reactive, and instinctively resistant to change. They seek maximum homogeneity in the system and tend to expel that which is different. The energy exchanges between the organization and the outside environment are reduced to the point that most organizational family member needs must be met inside the system. In summary:

> CLOSED ORGANIZATIONAL FAMILY SYSTEMS *are organizations characterized by low boundary permeability, aggressive gatekeeping, a rigid definition of values and behavioral etiquette, and a high degree of intimacy among members.*

In contrast, open systems have much less restrictive gatekeeping functions, which allows for easy interaction between organizational family members and the outside professional and social environment. At their extreme, open systems become porous, allowing untold numbers of ideas and people access to the organization. Such organizations can, however, be so porous that their own ideas and values leak out, leaving the system, if it can still be called that, virtually void of definition and defense. While there is nothing in the porous, open system that could be said to imprison workers, neither is there anything that could protect workers from internal or external threats. At their most positive, open systems struggle not for maintenance of the status quo, but for growth and the ongoing evolution of the organization.

> OPEN ORGANIZATIONAL FAMILY SYSTEMS *are organizations characterized by high boundary permeability, lax to nonexistent gatekeeping, minimal definition of values and behavioral etiquette, and a low degree of intimacy between members.*

Examining the variations between organizational families in boundary permeability and gatekeeping functions, one could construct a continuum of organizational family types based on their degree of closure. The following illustration borrows a couple of terms from family therapy literature to describe three types of organizations along this continuum.

Figure 4-B:
The Continuum of Boundary Permeability
In Organizational Family Systems

The Enmeshed Organizational Family	*The Self-Regulated Organizational Family*	*The Porous Organizational Family*
Low Boundary Permeability and Aggressive Gatekeeping		High Boundary Permeability and Lax Gatekeeping

4.3 The Enmeshed Organizational Family

The enmeshed organizational family represents the most extremely closed system on the continuum. Characteristics that typify this organizational family system include the following:

- Low boundary permeability, creating limited interaction between the organizational family and the outside professional and social environment
- Aggressive gatekeeping functions
- Excessive demands for time and emotional commitment to the organization
- A focus on group rather than individual activities and achievement
- Minimal internal boundaries that provide access to private space
- Extreme demands for loyalty ("It's us against the world")
- A management style reflecting belief that workers must be controlled by fear, force, or charismatic persuasion
- Control provided through tyrannical, authoritarian leadership or through manipulated consensus
- Harsh response to behavior deviating from norms (for example, scapegoating members to force them from the organization)
- Extreme levels of group cohesion and mutual dependence
- Implicit rather than explicit organizational family rules

While there are numerous variations in enmeshed organizational families, all such closed systems share an isolation from the outside environment and a high level of cohesiveness between organizational members.

Now there is nothing inherently wrong with a system being closed for a period of time. The epitome of family health is the ability to achieve temporary closure in the face of a threat to a member or the group, such as a member's injury or death. Families must achieve a degree of closure to take care of their infants. In a similar manner, organizations may need to go through developmental stages of closure, such as when the organization is being established or reorganized or when it is facing a crisis. Our concern here is what happens to a system that closes itself off and sustains such closure for an extended period of time, particularly when rapid changes are unfolding in the ecosystem in which such closure is maintained. We know from decades of psychiatric and family systems literature that the health of the family system deteriorates when the family remains closed throughout its life cycle. A similar process can occur in the organizational family. When we speak of "closed organizational family systems," or "closed systems" for short, our focus will be on organizations that maintain extreme positions of isolation for extended periods of time.

What kind of organizations are usually found at the extreme end of the closure continuum? Extreme closure occurs more frequently in smaller, less complex organizations. Organizations whose purpose demands isolation, such as prisons, security installations, or psychiatric hospitals, are very vulnerable to such closure. Aggressive entrepreneurs—successful self-made men or women—have a tendency to create closed organizational family systems around themselves. Professions such as law enforcement, the ministry, or medicine, in which high stress combines with high standards of personal conduct, tend to organize themselves into professionally and socially closed systems. Health and human services workers have a built-in propensity for organizational closure that may be related to both the intensity of emotional demands and the degree of stigma or discomfort attached to the clients served by the workers. A hospice unit may be more susceptible to extreme closure than a pediatrics unit. A residential program for sexually abused women may be more prone to closure than an educational program for displaced homemakers seeking entry into the job market. A community mental health center may be more prone to closure than a YMCA.

4.4 The Porous Organizational Family

The porous (open) organizational family represents the opposite of the enmeshed (closed) organizational family. As discussed earlier in this chapter, the high boundary permeability—at times the near absence of an organizational boundary—creates a high level of external interaction and a low level of cohesiveness among organizational members. Other characteristics often shared by porous organizational families include the following:

- No clear sense of mission or goals that bind members together
- High levels of rationality; low levels of emotional disclosure and intimacy
- Explicitly defined norms and rules
- Compartmentalization of work resulting in low levels of internal interaction and interdependence
- "Invisible" organizational family members who have been "retired on the job" by the removal of all significant responsibilities
- Low levels of organizational identity (the organizational family is rarely together in one place)
- Absent or sporadically involved leadership

The prototype of the porous organizational family system can be found in a large, complex, and aging federal, state, or county civil service agency.

As with organizational closure, there is nothing inherently wrong with a system being open. A sign of family health is the ability to progressively open up the system to let members out (adolescents) and bring new members in (foster children, in-laws). Some family crises may require resources from outside the family, and under such circumstances, the need to open the system and take in ideas, people, and resources may be essential to family survival. Our concern is with porous systems that are unable to maintain system integrity and member protection because they can't at least periodically move toward closure.

To underscore the differences between our two system prototypes, let's compare an extremely enmeshed family with an extremely porous family. The closed family may do a wonderful job raising children, but let's assume those kids are now fourteen, sixteen, and seventeen, and the family is as closed as it was eighteen years ago. Clearly, this is a family in trouble, and they may not even know they are in trouble until they send their eldest off to his or her freshman year of college. Most of us have seen what happens under such circumstances. The ability to define a structure at the same time we are loosening that structure is the essence of helping adolescents mature and find healthy guilt-free pathways of exit from our families. Closed families, in order to maintain closure and homeostasis, retard this maturity and developmental separation. Now, in contrast, the extremely porous system may not be able to provide for the safety and care of infants and children, or provide the structure needed to take adolescents through a healthy process of boundary testing. Whereas the closed system punishes severely for testing family rules, the porous system offers no rules to test and no consequences. System health and member health, for families and organizations, are most often found in the ability to flexibly move up and down our continuum from open to closed.

While our primary focus in this book will be on closed systems, we will return to a more detailed discussion of open, porous organizational systems.

4.5 The Self-Regulated Organizational Family

Enmeshed and porous organizational family systems have in common a fixed position on the continuum of organizational closure. Neither has the flexibility to move forward or backward on the continuum in response to changing needs. It's as if history and inertia have cemented these organizations on a fixed path that allows no deviation in boundary management.

Between the two poles on the continuum lies the self-regulated organizational family. This type of organizational family moves back and forth on the continuum, rarely staying at any point for an extended period of time. The self-regulated organizational family is like a living organism, constantly adapting in response to changes inside and outside the system.

The self-regulated organizational family is characterized by the following:

- Changing boundary permeability controlled by organizational leaders with appropriate input from members
- Regulation of gatekeeping functions that provides changing degrees of openness/closure
- An organizational climate that seeks balance between the smothering intimacy of enmeshed systems and the isolation and detachment of porous systems
- Decentralization of power and authority
- Organizational values and rules explicit but open to negotiation as needs and conditions change

The most important quality of the self-regulated organizational family is the flexibility to alter boundary permeability to change the degree of openness or closure. We will see in the next three chapters the profound impact this flexibility (or lack of it) has on the health, vitality, and sustainability of the organization, and the equally profound impact it has on the health of organizational family members.

4.6 The Organization with Mixed Characteristics

Before we proceed into a more detailed analysis of the impact of system closure on the health of the organizational family system and its members, keep in mind that some organizations have characteristics of both enmeshed and porous systems. Some complex organizations, for example, may be broken into departments or divisions, each of which could be described as an enmeshed organizational family. Yet this same organization when viewed as a total system could be described as a disengaged organizational family system.

This point has important implications for our later discussion of system interventions. Intervening in enmeshed and disengaged organizational families involves moving the organizations away from their polarized positions toward what we have described as the self-regulated family. This is accomplished by altering boundary transactions and increasing or decreasing organizational closure. In an organizational system with mixed characteristics, however, one may need a two-fold strategy, such as moving the overall organization toward more closure while moving the departments toward greater openness. Chapter 9 expands on this point.

4.7 The Role of Boundary Transactions
in Professional and Organizational Distress

The highest incidence of distress-related symptoms—staff casualties, in particular—occurs at the end of the organizational family closure continuum. A significant relationship exists between the frequency and intensity of boundary transactions and the health of the organizational family and its members.

One can find plenty of theoretical support for this relationship in the work done on family systems. There are times when closure in the family system is healthy and essential. The family system, however, that remains fixed at the extreme end of the closure continuum will become unhealthy as a whole and will be detrimental to the physical and emotional health of its members.

The same principle applies to organizational family systems. The closure required to successfully start an organization from scratch or respond to a crisis, if continued indefinitely, may undermine the health of organizational family members and sow the seeds of the organization's eventual destruction.

Family therapists have also noted the high rate of disturbance in the porous family system. Whereas pathology in the enmeshed family develops from too much intimacy and cohesion, pathology in the disengaged family emerges from too little cohesion and intimacy between family members.

Whereas the enmeshed family may thwart the growth and developmental separation of family members, the porous family does not provide sufficient bonding or boundaries to help family members in meeting intimacy needs, developing a value system, or mastering other key developmental tasks.

In a parallel vein, porous organizational families create a number of high-stress role conditions, yet offer few opportunities for relationships or supports to balance those stressors. The stressors that are most pervasive in porous organizational families will be described in chapter 9.

Although we have looked at the continuum from enmeshed to porous organizational family systems, the emphasis of this book will be on the dynamics of the enmeshed organizational family. To simplify terms, the enmeshed organization will be described as the "closed organizational family." "Closure" will be used to describe the movement of an organization toward decreased boundary transactions and increased intimacy among organizational family members.

4.8 The Incestuous Organizational Family

When I began consulting with troubled organizations in the 1970s, I was struck by the way interpersonal dynamics in these institutions bore striking similarity to what happened in closed, or enmeshed, families, as family-systems literature was calling them. It took no originality on my part to further compare these organizations with families in which incest had occurred. In fact, I was rather slow in realizing the deeper meaning behind the oft-heard phrase in my consultation interviews: "This place is so incestuous." The realization finally struck after an adult survivor of incest who worked for a disintegrating organization told me her personal history to emphasize why her sexual exploitation by the agency's executive director was so devastating. She concluded by saying, "It's just like I'm back in my family. It's like organizational incest!"

Studies of incestuous behavior in animals and humans indicate that incest occurs in those situations where the natural developmental separation of family members failed to happen, leaving the family unit as the sole arena for the expression of sexual behavior. One finds in the normal family a unique combination of social intimacy and sexual distance between family members. In contrast, the incestuous family combines social bonding (overconnectedness) with sexual intimacy between members. A significant amount of incestuous behavior can thus be viewed as one of the last stages in, and consequences of, the progressive closure of a family system (Hoffman 1976).

Incest is not merely an act but a progressive violation of intimacy barriers in a family relationship. This has several implications. Foremost is the understanding that it is the entire continuum of intimacy violations that is traumatizing, not simply the final and most physically invasive of those violations. Second, preventing incest and treating incest survivors requires an understanding of the continuum of boundary violations and the isolation of the closed family in which they occur.

The incestuous dynamic of some organizations parallels the incestuous dynamic that occurs in some families. Briefly, what the incestuous organizational family dynamic and the incestuous nuclear family dynamic have in common is the following: the isolation of members from outside boundary transactions, a preoccupation with system loyalty, coercive methods of monitoring and control, the loss of personal privacy, and abuses of power that involve the psychological and physical exploitation of vulnerable members. An incestuous organization is an organization characterized by these traits. Incest is a violent, abusive act that takes place within a larger process of family closure that has its own power to psychologically wound. There is an analogous process in organizations that we will explore in the next three chapters.

The individual distress of workers in a closed system can be a symptom of system dysfunction (progressive closure), just as incest can be a reflection of broader family system dysfunction. Closure can occur at multiple levels in an organization. When we speak of a closed or incestuous organization in the coming chapters we will be describing the following:

An incestuous organization is an encapsulated institution in which members increasingly meet their personal, professional, social, and sexual needs inside the boundary of the organizational family.

The next three chapters will describe the professional, social, and sexual closure that mark this incestuous dynamic. The highlights of the closure process are illustrated in figure 4-C. Concepts used in the coming chapters include the following:

- Workers can sustain themselves in high-stress work environments over time only through sources of support and replenishment outside the work setting.
- The closure of an organizational system increases stressors, reduces internal supports, and decreases workers' ability to develop and sustain sources of support and replenishment outside of the organization.
- Certain patterns of professional distress emerge out of and are symptomatic of the progressive closure of the organizational family system.
- Strategies to address professional distress and strategies to address the internal organizational problems of closed systems will fail unless they reverse the progression of organizational closure.

Figure 4-C
The Profession of Organizational Closure

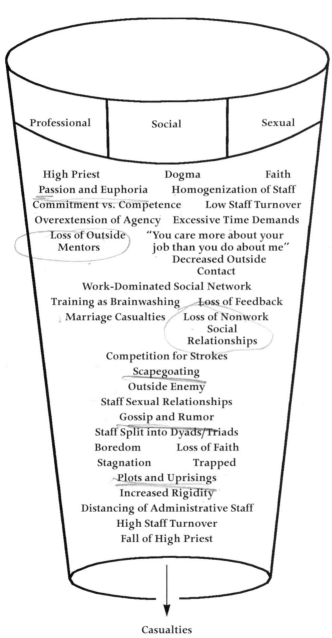

Professional   Social   Sexual

High Priest   Dogma   Faith

Passion and Euphoria   Homogenization of Staff

Commitment vs. Competence   Low Staff Turnover

Overextension of Agency   Excessive Time Demands

Loss of Outside Mentors   "You care more about your job than you do about me"

Decreased Outside Contact

Work-Dominated Social Network

Training as Brainwashing   Loss of Feedback

Marriage Casualties   Loss of Nonwork Social Relationships

Competition for Strokes

Scapegoating

Outside Enemy

Staff Sexual Relationships

Gossip and Rumor

Staff Split into Dyads/Triads

Boredom   Loss of Faith

Stagnation   Trapped

Plots and Uprisings

Increased Rigidity

Distancing of Administrative Staff

High Staff Turnover

Fall of High Priest

Casualties

Health Indicators   Relationship Indicators

Excessive Behavior Indicators   Attitude Indicators

Emotional Indicators   Value Indicators

⫷ 5

Professional Closure

In this chapter, we will further explore the idea that professional distress can be a symptom of system distress and that both types of distress can be caused or exacerbated by the closure of the organizational family. Professional closure begins with the assumption that all of the professional-development needs of the organization's members can and should be met inside the boundary of the organizational family. This closure is evidenced by reduced contact with people and institutions outside of the organization and by the onset of a highly predictable sequence of problems and experiences.

It is not unusual for an organization that is starting up, reorganizing, or confronting a crisis to close itself off from the outside world. Closure under such circumstances is often necessary for the survival of the organization and the emotional safety of its members. The boundary flexibility that can facilitate such timely closure, as we noted earlier, is a sign of a healthy, resilient organization. These same healthy organizations also can, when circumstances change, reopen themselves to increased contact with the outside social and professional world.

Some organizations find themselves unable to reverse the closure process. The organization takes on the tone of an overprotective parent sheltering organizational family members and the organization itself from what is perceived as a hostile and threatening world. An "It's us against the world" attitude begins to dominate organizational values as the fear and mistrust of outsiders become permanent components of the workplace culture. This closure process isolates staff from outside sources of replenishment, increases the physical and emotional demands upon staff, leads to a deterioration in personal and professional relationships, and, in short, sets the stage for severe individual and organizational distress.

There are both unique and common aspects to the process of organizational closure. Surprisingly, the common elements far outnumber the unique and can be seen unfolding in organizations from diverse professional arenas, in both the public and private sectors. The following pages will identify and describe these common stages of organizational closure.

There are two overarching dimensions of the closure process to be aware of. First, the onset and full development of these stages occur slowly over months and years. Second, the early signs of closure are often quite subtle—so subtle, in fact, that they are rarely recognized by organizational family members as crucial events in the life of the organization while they are occurring. It is this slowness and subtlety that can make the closure process both invisible and insidious. The transformation of the organizational culture is not observable because each step toward isolation is a small one, and the steps are interspersed with periods of apparent normalcy.

The stages of professional closure described in this chapter are noted here briefly. Professional closure is marked by

- the emergence of a rigid, unchallengeable organizational belief system
- the centralization of power in a charismatic leader and his or her inner circle
- the progressive isolation of the organization and its members from the outside professional world
- the homogenization of the workforce by age, race, sex, religion, or values
- the progressive escalation of demands placed on the time and emotional energy of workers
- a loss of learning and a growing sense of professional stagnation in the organization
- the identification of outside enemies as the source of organizational problems and/or the scapegoating and extrusion of organizational members
- the escalation of interpersonal and intergroup conflict to include staff conspiracies and coups against organizational leadership
- the emergence of a punitive, abusive organizational culture
- the rise of breaches in ethical and legal codes of conduct

- the fall of the "high priest/priestess"
- the potential demise of the organizational family

We will, in turn, explore each of these stages.

5.1 Dogma, Mythmaking, and Faith

The first stage of professional closure is the development of a rigid and unchallengeable belief system in the organizational culture. Every organization needs a philosophy that communicates the organization's mission, clarifies in broad terms how that mission is to be accomplished, and makes explicit the important values of the organization. The philosophy captures a vision of the needs of a world, a community, or a market and the organization's response to those needs at a fixed point in time. Successful organizations are characterized by a clear shared vision that is dynamically refined and redefined, sometimes on almost a daily basis. The vision is alive, constantly moving and adapting in response to internal feedback, changes in the external environment, and, in the case of service agencies, the changing needs of organizational clients. In contrast, the vision in closed systems has been concretized and is not open for redefinition or even reinterpretation. The move toward professional closure is almost always marked by the embrace of an unchallengeable doctrine.

A rigid belief system can take many forms. It can be reflected in a company's blind adherence to a single, progressively outdated product line. It can be reflected in the unquestioning acceptance of a particular theoretical framework for organizing professional activity. It can be seen in the fixation on a narrow marketing approach on which a company's survival depends. It can be seen in the bureaucratic system that is run on tradition and inertia rather than present needs and realities. It can be seen in any organization in which the philosophy or belief system takes on a life and power of its own, and can't be further challenged or changed by those who created it or those who inherited it.

In closed systems, organizational beliefs are transformed into a holy cause. Ideologies in closed systems are not just defined as true; they are defined as the Truth—one that is whole and fully evolved. Any proposed alteration is seen as a violation of its perfection. One's relationship to this truth is defined not as one of continuing investigation or interpretation but as one of honoring and defending. To suggest that this truth might benefit from modification or refinement is heresy. Whereas openness allows ideas to serve as ways to achieve the organization's mission, organizational closure elevates ideas to ends in themselves. Philosophy becomes gospel, gospel becomes dogma, and dogma is canonized in codified doctrine. Doctrine is encased in near-mythical accounts of its deliverance or discovery. This mytho-history is often framed in a language of destiny, callings, and spiritual visitations. The capacity to recite this history with great fervor becomes a requirement for organizational membership— a ritualized demonstration of faith.

How do otherwise reasonable adults become so vulnerable as to wholly embrace such rigid doctrines? The answer is that dogma emerges in organizations at times of crisis and vulnerability. It is my experience that socially isolated people experiencing great distress and uncertainty can be made to believe almost anything if the message is delivered in the context of a supportive relationship that promises immediate comfort and continued safety, security, and happiness. There may even be an illusion of freedom surrounding this growing control of ideas. Critique of oneself or the organization is permitted and even encouraged—but only within the framework of the organizational ideology. It is not that critical thinking is prohibited; it is that the criteria used to judge the self, the organization, and the outside world are dictated.

Various mechanisms are used to enforce adherence to dogma in a closed organization. Employees, volunteers, and board members are selected primarily based on the strength of their belief in the dogma. Information that would bring the organizational philosophy into question is not allowed to enter the system. Employees are discouraged from making contact with the outside professional environment, where they would be exposed to divergent viewpoints. "No-talk" norms emerge in the organizational culture that silence any potential challenges to the organizational philosophy. Members who challenge the ideology are extruded from the organizational family. Ideas are used to test loyalty in closed systems. They become litmus tests of inclusion and exclusion.

An organization has two dominant characteristics during its earliest years of closure: belief and passion. While these characteristics can contribute to its success, they can have more ominous effects that, as we shall see, can contribute to the organization's demise.

5.2 The High Priest / Priestess and the Inner Circle

The power in most closed systems becomes highly centralized in a charismatic leader and his or her inner circle.

When an organization becomes organized around a rigid ideology, the function of the leader changes from the role of systems manager to that of "high priest/priestess." The role of the high priest/priestess in a closed system is to instill and maintain faith in the ideology among organizational family members; provide rituals that test member loyalty and allow members to periodically recommit themselves to the organization and its philosophy; rally and lead organizational members during times of crisis; carry the "message" to the broader professional and social community; and serve, through the conduct of his or her personal and professional life, as the living embodiment of the organizational philosophy.

High priests/priestesses in closed organizations become objects of worship—targets of corporate idolatry. The deification of the high priest/priestess occurs through a process of projection. The greater the strength projected onto the leader, the greater the self-perceived weakness of the members. The glorification of the leader involves an unseen diminishment of self. Member self-esteem is derived from identification with the idealized leader and the organization as a whole. The essential message is "You are important because you are part of us."

How do we explain the emergence of this high priest/priestess role? There are many potential answers. Some leaders, based on their personalities, inevitably gravitate to such roles. Attraction to this role can come out of the best and worst in us—a desire to leave a positive lasting legacy or a megalomaniacal desire to have power and control over others. Closed systems can offer to leaders what they offer to followers: a chance to redeem what is feared to be a stained self. There are individuals who will always select, or create around themselves, closed systems and who will always gravitate to the role of high priest/priestess. There are some organizations that can only be formed by a high priest/priestess. Who else but a potential megalomaniac would take on such a challenge? Imagine a job description posted for someone to found Synanon: *Wanted: A visionary man or woman who can organize a thousand drug addicts, prostitutes, felons, and former asylum patients into a self-managed therapeutic community. The job will require twenty-four hours a day for the next ten years. The job pays no salary and provides no benefits.* Who would step forward to assume a job like that? The very characteristics needed to successfully launch an organization like that have within them the potential seeds for the leader's and the system's success *and* eventual self-destruction.

There are other people who end up in the high priest/priestess role simply by accident—a collision between character and circumstance. These individuals simply have personal characteristics that result in them being thrust into such roles during times of crisis.

Whether by intention or by accident, those in high priest/priestess roles are there in part because of an indefinable quality of charisma. High priests/priestesses of all types are frequently described with such words as "magnetic," "radiant," "mesmerizing," "spellbinding," "intoxicating," "captivating," and "hypnotic." While not all are spellbinding speakers, most have exceptional verbal skills, and all have a *presence* about them. All have a capacity to lead—a capacity for passionate action in the face of crisis. They have the ability to mobilize those around them, to articulate individual sufferings and aspirations and link those to a message of hope for the future. They have the ability to bestow on each of us a sense of power and shared destiny tied to collective action. Charisma plays such an important role in closed organizations that such institutions might be deservedly called "charismatic systems."

As we detail the typical saga of a closed organization, it will be easy to cast the high priest/priestess in a malevolent role. We will be tempted to see the high priest/priestess as a kind of psychopathic manipulator. While there are such individuals, most high priests/priestesses do not fit this profile, and for that matter, didn't even seek out the high priest/priestess role. What follows is not a simple story of what evil individuals have done to organizations and those who work in them. Most people become high priests/priestesses because there is a period of time in which the organization needs precisely this type of person. More often than not, the high priest/priestess role emerges out of the collective needs of the organizational family. When this role becomes fixed, however, there are ominous consequences both for the person in the role and for the organization. As we shall see, the high priest/priestess is also a victim of the process of organizational closure.

5.3 The Inner Circle

An inner circle inevitably evolves at the center of a closed system—a royal family of sorts that buffers the high priest/priestess from organizational members and the outside world. It is very hard not to be seduced by offers of inclusion in the inner circle. The elitism and sense of specialness derived from membership in a closed system are even greater in the inner circle. There are, as might be expected, special perks and privileges that accrue to those in the inner circle. An inordinate concentration of wealth at the top of closed organizations is almost universal—at least toward the latter stages of such systems' life spans. Salaries at the top may be many times that of member salaries. But the most important perk derived from inner-circle membership is special access to the high priest/priestess.

The inner circle of a closed system is usually filled with "little" high priests/priestesses who run around modeling the latest thoughts and behaviors of the high priest/priestess. Such identification can be quite complete. I have been in organizations in which members not only emulated patterns of thinking and personal tastes in music or literature, dress, and speech, but also took on a high priest's/priestess's rather unique, and somewhat bizarre, behavioral tics.

The primary role of the inner circle is that of system maintenance. This involves organizing daily life in the organization and responding to various organizational crises. But more important, it involves shielding the high priest/priestess and the general membership from feedback that would cast doubt on the validity of organizational dogma.

5.4 The Disciples

There are two key points about the members of closed organizations that will be further elaborated in a later chapter. The first is that any of us can be drawn into a closed system, or take a job in a reasonably healthy system that over time begins to close in around us. The second point is that some of us may possess particular developmental experiences or traits of character that make us particularly drawn to closed systems. Eric Hoffer noted in *The True Believer* that faith and devotion to a holy cause can serve as a substitute for a loss of faith in ourselves. Those of us who have come from closed families, who have experienced shame and stigma, whose selves have been injured may be particularly drawn to the promised structure and safety of the closed system. Both the strong and the weak who find themselves in such organizations will stay too long. As you proceed through the descriptions of closed organizations in the next three chapters, you might ask yourself why people don't just leave these systems. The answer to this question, which we will explore in chapter 12, is quite intriguing.

5.5 The Loss of Outside Contact

As noted earlier, systems become closed through a decrease in boundary transactions with their outside environment. Closed systems empower gatekeepers to protect the organization. Gatekeepers are those people in the organizational family who control who, when, and under what conditions outsiders enter the system, and who, when, and under what conditions those inside the organization may have contact with outsiders. Anyone who has had to work their way through multiple people to reach someone on the telephone has experienced gatekeeping. Anyone who has been discouraged by a supervisor from seeking outside training or has been cautioned about speaking to "outsiders" has experienced gatekeeping.

Gatekeeping functions intensify through the progressive closure of the organizational system. It gets harder and harder to get outside ideas into the system as it gets progressively more difficult for those inside to sustain relationships outside the organization. It even gets progressively more difficult to reach the high priest/priestess or other key members of the inner circle. The very essence of closure is decreased movement of people and ideas across the organizational boundary.

The decrease in boundary transactions takes many forms. Ideas from outside are shut off through decreased access to training and continuing education, and a discouragement of contact with outside professional associations and allied professional agencies. Outside agencies are vehemently criticized and contact with outside professional groups is seen as inherently corrupting. The high priest/priestess or members of the inner circle venture out to conferences and return to tell staff what's going on in the outside world. Such communication usually involves a filtering process through which any information that conflicts with program ideology is deleted. Some systems may be so closed that staff are not aware of the existence of outside professional organizations, and organizational leaders even sever most of their own contacts with the outside professional world. Professional development activities in most closed systems are moved internally and take on the flavor of indoctrination seminars and pep rallies.

The preferred stance of the closed system is one of progressive isolation. The extremes to which this isolation can go are quite remarkable. In my consultation work with health and human service agencies, I encountered two agencies that were so extremely paranoid of outside contact that the staff of these twenty-four-hour residential care facilities were given explicit orders that 911 could not be dialed in the case of a fire or other emergency without first calling to get permission from the agency director.

The effect of this isolation on workers is that all of their professional needs must then be met inside the organizational family. Lacking outside feedback and stimulation, stagnation is almost inevitable.

As the number of outside transactions decreases, the nature of outside relationships changes. Relationships are reduced in number to those essential to the survival of the system; the leaders of closed systems become quite adept at politically or personally seducing valued outsiders. Before the system approaches a further acceleration of closure, organizational leaders have usually strengthened ties with key outside sponsors and protectors. Outside relationships take on a highly manipulative quality. Leaders of closed systems begin to see the outside world as either gullible or hostile. People and institutions are to be used, manipulated, or attacked. When closed systems break up amid media exposure of breaches in ethical and legal conduct, it is sometimes surprising to find a long list of political and public figures who had continued to support these organizations long after they became isolated from the wider community. Political seduction and political intimidation are common ways closed systems relate to their external environment.

5.6 Homogenization of the Staff

As an organization closes, members begin to look more and more like one another. This "sameness" may be based on age, sex, race, or lifestyle but almost always entails the selection of staff members with homogeneous value systems—values that reflect a high degree of congruence with the organizational dogma.

Closed systems tend to keep out or expel that which is different. People in closed systems who are the only anything—only women, only people of color—are in high danger of becoming isolated, scapegoated, and extruded from the organization. Scapegoating escalates the closure process by eliminating those people who are most likely to inject new ideas and change into the organization. Sameness is reinforced by selecting only prospective employees, consultants, volunteers, and board members who share similar value systems; it is ensured during the latter stages of closure when almost all new staff members hired are from the professional and social network of the current staff. As the professional and social worlds of organizational members shrink over time, this homogenization may be intensified by the recruiting of new employees and volunteers primarily from the intimate family and social networks of the staff—particularly the family members of the inner circle.

Homogenization contributes to the further closure of the organizational family by shutting off the flow of new ideas and approaches that inevitably arise from staff members with diverse life experiences. During the early stages of closure, convergence of staff values and experiences may contribute to group cohesiveness and productivity. As time goes on, however, such convergence leads to the loss of learning, professional stagnation, and feelings of being trapped.

To an outside consultant entering a large number of closed systems, the "sameness" of these systems can be striking. People in closed systems speak a narrowly codified "systems vocabulary" that separates insiders from outsiders. They often use the same words, phrases, and voice inflections as though they've been programmed—which they have. Their mastery of this language and their deteriorating ability to communicate with a wider, outside professional community strengthens their ties to the closed system.

5.7 Euphoria

Not all of the stages of organizational closure are unpleasant and injurious. The most exhilarating professional experiences of one's life can be found in the closure required to build a new organization or program. The early months, and even years, in a closed organizational family system may be experienced more as euphoria than pain. The following remark from a taped interview with a casualty of a closed system (a counseling agency) illustrates the point:

> I was working sixty to eighty hours per week and loving it. I loved the adrenaline, the knowledge that I was essential to the program, the feeling of commitment, the fantasy that I was the program. . . . It was like a fix—I couldn't get enough or get free of it. I'd go to a movie and find myself making lists of what I needed to do the next day. I would be eating dinner and jump to the phone to handle some minor detail I had forgotten. I'd stop by and see other staff on an evening I had off, and all we would talk about was work. Nothing outside could compete with the sense of excitement I felt during this early period.

The early euphoria in closed systems is an intoxicating mixture of challenge, clarity of purpose, intellectual and spiritual fulfillment, and the experience of being unconditionally accepted and loved. People feel as if they are on fire with the intensity of it; nothing can compete with it. It is epiphany, ecstasy, and defining moment all experienced simultaneously.

At the heart of this euphoria is a sense of passion, the experience of commitment, and an incredible camaraderie that blinds one to the consequences of following the siren call of continued self-sacrifice.

Some of the most fulfilling periods of my life have been in these early stages of organizational closure. Even the healthiest of organizations need periods of such coming together. However, all of the conditions in the closed organizational family that produce euphoria have their darker side when the closure process continues over an extended period of time.

5.8 Addiction to Crisis

Closed systems and those who work in them can become addicted to crisis. My addiction metaphor here is intended to be taken quite literally. As with a chemical addiction, there is the phenomenon of building tolerance—it takes crises of greater frequency and magnitude to satiate the need. There is a predictable withdrawal period after things have been too quiet that features disorientation followed by a reactivation of crisis. And there is a compulsive quality to the crisis-seeking behavior, as if one or more key people are addicted to the adrenaline and endorphins the crises bring.

Closed systems seem to always exist on the edge financially and emotionally. They seem to always be responding to internal or external threats; there is always a new crisis to which members must respond. And there is always the promise that things will slow down when they get over this hump. Such crisis orientation is used to evoke ever greater levels of loyalty and commitment to the organization. The climate is one of great emotional intensity, and this is one of the payoffs for participation. Closed systems can provide us with a sense of participating in an intense, high-stakes drama—a sense that one is fighting valiantly on behalf of important issues.

The crises in a closed system can be real and can spring from the external environment. This may be, in part, why the system moved toward closure in the first place—for self-protection. But crises can also be internally induced as a way to keep the pot stirred and divert attention away from serious internal problems. Crises can be manufactured as a process of de-focusing, projection, and scapegoating. All organizational members can get needs met through such crises. Some are drawn to the intensity as an antidote to numbness. For those of us who feel numb, closed systems can make us feel fully alive—later, painfully alive.

High priests/priestesses and inner-circle members often receive the greatest personal gains from crises. It is in the middle of such threats that their power is both demonstrated and affirmed by organizational members. The problem with the unending cycle of crises is that each crisis drives the system toward greater closure. The history of many closed systems is a history of crises, each closing such organizations tighter, one concentric circle at a time.

5.9 Commitment and Loyalty

As the organizational family becomes increasingly closed, commitment to dogma takes on a higher value than competence in both the evaluation of existing staff and the recruitment of new staff.

As adherence to dogma becomes more passionately valued in the organizational family, there develops a no-talk norm concerning open questioning of the ideology. In some settings, this no-talk rule is even extended to the point that any criticism of the organization, no matter how constructive, is seen as an act of disloyalty and a personal betrayal of organizational leaders.

Initial euphoria, addiction to crisis, and the primacy of member commitment and loyalty is accompanied by increased demands on the time and energy of organizational members.

5.10 The Making of a Workaholic

One of the earliest consequences of the period of euphoria is simply the excessive allocation of hours to one's work life and the resulting strain on one's personal life. We will see in the next chapter how this type of overload sets the stage for the loss of one's outside-of-work social relationships and even a deterioration or loss of family and intimate relationships. People become simultaneously dependent on and worn out by the intensity of the closed system.

Role overload—the insatiable demand for time and emotional energy—is endemic to professionally closed organizations. When an organization is involved in an impassioned cause, there are few limits to the expectations placed on members. Most closed systems do not clearly define what they can and cannot do with available human and fiscal resources. Closed systems are notoriously overextended. Job descriptions are nonexistent or bear no relationship to reality. Promises for goods and services that surpass the reasonable capacity for production are routine. The hopeless overextension of the workers is a reflection of the overextension of the organization.

The personality of the overachiever has been extensively cited in the literature on occupational distress, but little recognition has been given to the organization's responsibility for promoting overextension of individual members.

Professional closure creates an atmosphere in which organizational interests and ideologies take precedence over human needs, and workers are used and expended in a no-deposit/no-return fashion. Professional closure initiates a chain of escalating commitments. While each of these commitments in isolation is insignificant, seen as a whole, they can absorb one's life.

5.11 The Merger of Personal and Organizational Identities

Most of us have a professional identity that transcends the particular organization in which we currently work. The development of such professional autonomy is retarded or progressively eroded in closed systems. The closed system consumes the psychological skin that distinguishes us as separate people from the organization. The identification is so powerful, the erosion of individual autonomy so insidious, and the meeting of personal needs inside the system so pervasive that there is quite literally a merger of personal and organizational identities.

Closed systems get inside you. You and the system become symbiotically merged. It's as if the system becomes your heart or your lungs. Separation is unthinkable. To leave is to psychologically die and perhaps even to physically die. The latter point may sound absurd, but let me share my speculations in this area. Many readers will likely be familiar with morbidity and mortality studies showing the high risk of sickness and death following the death of a spouse (particularly in highly dependent relationships) or, for some, professional retirement. Some stories are so common they border on the cliché. A couple spends forty years together and both partners die within hours, days, or weeks of each other. Or someone works a lifetime only to get sick and die right after he or she retires. While health or illness in retirement is most often depicted as a function of individual characteristics, perhaps the kind of organization people are leaving also figures into this equation. People who retire from open systems have a much easier adjustment because they have established an identity beyond the organization. In closed systems, however, one's whole identity has been rooted in the organization. People who have spent their lives in such systems are at risk of shriveling and dying when they leave.

5.12 Professional Closure and Marriage Casualties

I have been particularly concerned in my studies about the ways distress experienced in the work setting can spill over and begin to deteriorate the quality of intimate relationships outside of work. The overextension of workers and their overidentification with the workplace, both of which are parts of the dynamic in the incestuous organization, take their toll on intimate relationships. The incestuous dynamic produces a domino effect. Increased demands and commitment to the organizational family result in decreased energy available to sustain intimate and family relationships. Expectations of our partners and family members that we participate in their lives increases our feelings of inadequacy and may result in increased escape into the organizational family. The stage is then set for the development of social and sexual relationships between staff who provide each other transient respite from outsiders "who do not understand" them.

Most marriage casualties in closed organizations occur with little awareness on the part of those involved of how sources outside the marriage served to drive a wedge in the relationship. It was with a great deal of sadness that many of the people I interviewed looked back after many years finally to see that the conflict in their marriages was exacerbated beyond toleration by outside forces and not by the basic quality of the marital relationship. The frequently heard comment from workers' spouses—"You care more about your job than you care about us"—typifies the torn loyalties for time and emotional energy experienced by members of the closed organizational family.

Some closed systems promote close social relationships and even intimate relationships between organizational members as a way of strengthening the community and decreasing the need for external contact. In this sense we may have the organizational unit in direct competition for the time, energy, and loyalty of the person who belongs to an outside system. Closed systems, to enhance their position in this competition, consume the lives of their workers in a way that causes outside relationships to wither on the vine.

5.13 Insulation, Isolation, and Organizational Decay

The loss of outside contact produced by professional closure reduces the feedback available to stimulate personal and organizational changes. Professional and social isolation erode the flow of information to organizational members, preventing workers and the organization as a whole from accurately reading and adapting to changes in the outside environment. Feedback from outside the organization that could be used for self-correction is attacked, as are its sources.

Internal feedback is also reduced through the process of professional closure. No-talk rules about organizational problems become the norm. Information provided by members from inside that could be used for self-correction is negated by focusing on the sender rather than the message. The focus is not on what is said about the organization, but the alleged motivations and personal problems of the staff member offering the feedback. In service programs, a similar process is used to discount feedback from service consumers. Closed systems are notorious for their arrogant refusal to listen to the needs of their customers. Over time this even evolves toward an increasingly antagonistic relationship with service consumers. A closed system that believes it knows more about its customers' needs than its customers do sees customers not as the source of its existence but as problems and distractions. What these mechanisms have in common is that feedback is discouraged, discounted, rationalized, and distorted in ways that keep the organization from making needed adaptations. Closed systems might be said to suffer from a progressive deterioration in their capacities to see and hear.

5.14 The Competition for Strokes

A major premise of this book is that if people are to sustain themselves in high-stress work environments, they must have a network of personal, professional, social, and sexual replenishment separate from the work environment. The closed organizational family, by breaking down the boundary between workers' personal and professional lives, decreases their ability to get replenishment outside the organization. As organizational family members lose these replenishment networks, they become physically and emotionally depleted in the high-stress work environment. This depletion radically alters the availability, frequency, and distribution of positive relationships in the organizational family.

Relationships among replenished staff members in a relatively open system are characterized by reciprocity. Staff interactions are frequent and mutually supportive. When staff members feel good about themselves, it's easier for them to feel good about their co-workers, and it's easier to express those feelings. In contrast, depleted staff members in closed systems simply don't have the emotional energy to extend that kind of support to one another. Closed systems are stroke (support)-deprived systems. In the closed organization, strokes are competitive rather than reciprocal. Given the small number of available strokes, the acknowledgment of one person triggers jealously and resentment in others. The assumption is: If you are recognized, I won't be. Because the closed system shuts off external sources of physical and emotional support, the internal milieu often becomes cannibalistic in nature. As support becomes competitive rather than reciprocal, the system breaks into social and ideological camps competing for system resources.

5.15 Mirroring, Boredom, and Loss of Faith

The sustained closure of the organization leads to the erosion of the passion and commitment that marked earlier periods. Passion—the fuel of the closed system—is progressively consumed. It is depleted by loss of learning and by physical and emotional strain.

As professional boundary transactions with the outside world decrease, a process of decay begins. The loss of new information and ideas coming into the system leads to an impoverishment of learning. Systems in such a state are characterized by lack of imagination and creativity, sterileness of thought and language, and aversion to risk that presents itself in an almost robotlike uniformity of belief and style among members.

Loss of new ideas produces a phenomenon called "mirroring." The intense indoctrination of employees produces a group of people who tend to share similar ways of perceiving, thinking, and speaking. They, in effect, mirror one another. Most of us have experienced mirroring at some time in our professional careers. Have you ever looked at how members of your organization communicated on key issues and concluded that staff simply took turns spouting the organizational party line? Have you ever sat with a group of co-workers and felt you could predict almost word for word how each person would respond to any question? Have you ever looked back over a period of months and felt you were in a rut, speaking and performing like a robot with little creative energy or independent thinking involved in your work? Such experiences are common during this stage of organizational closure.

The loss of learning in closed systems leads to boredom and a mechanical approach to job performance. Mirroring and boredom often bring on personal and professional crises as individual workers begin to experience a loss of faith in the program philosophy. It's as if staff begin to see, for the first time, flaws in the philosophy and methods of the organization. Once this questioning of organizational philosophy breaks into the open, loss of faith can be a very contagious force in the organization.

Mirroring, boredom, and loss of faith mark a critical stage in the life of the closed organizational family. Some organizations use such a crisis as a chance to open the system and to clarify mission, goals, methods, and values, and to abort the closure process. Such organizations use the crisis to improve their overall health and vitality by opening and redefining their structures and processes. For organizations that do not utilize this crisis in this manner, loss of faith marks the beginning of increased internal turbulence and personal casualties.

5.16 Trapped

It is only natural when one experiences a loss of faith to think about leaving the organization. People come up against this situation all the time and often respond by changing jobs. This option, however, is more complicated in the closed organizational family.

There is no guilt-free way to leave a closed organizational family. Allegiance and loyalty issues are so powerful that leaving is viewed as a betrayal of the high priest/priestess and organizational family members. Many who express their dissatisfaction will be manipulated to stay in the system by promises from the high priest/priestess of forthcoming changes in working conditions and of economic rewards.

As staff members lose sources of replenishment outside the organization and experience the emotional depletion from excessive time and emotional demands, their confidence and self-esteem may deteriorate to the point that they question their marketability in other programs. This is complicated further if workers have been with the organization long enough that they find it difficult to get another job at a comparable salary. This is particularly true when family/financial obligations will not allow for a decrease in salary. Workers in this situation may feel like their very souls have been bought.

The inability of people to get out of closed organizational families is obvious by looking at turnover rates. There is a certain irony here because high staff turnover is often associated with high-stress work environments. I have been told repeatedly, "We don't have a problem of burnout here; our staff turnover is almost zero." The fact is, no turnover is as much an indicator of professional distress as excessively high turnover. Healthy organizations have a fairly predictable rate of staff change. Such turnover is desirable in terms of both the professional advancement of staff members and the introduction of new ideas and approaches into the organization through new members. In contrast, turnover in the closed system is extremely low until later stages of closure when there can be a contagion of staff turnover so high that it threatens the existence of the organization.

5.17 Xenophobia, Projection, and Scapegoating

We are at a point in the closure of the organizational family where workers begin to feel something has been lost in the life of the organization, and may start to verbalize feelings of boredom, being "trapped," and needing to "get out." Many of these feelings of disillusionment reflect a wearing down of the collective physical and emotional energy of staff due to reasons we have discussed. During this period of low morale, the stage is set for the selection of an outside enemy or the sacrifice of a victim from within the organizational family.

In the first case, worker dissatisfaction is projected onto and blamed on an outside person or organization. This outside enemy could be a funding source, a competing company, a regulatory body, one or more key board members, people who have been critical of the organization in the community, or even a political figure. The projection takes the form of extreme preoccupation, as indicated by an increase in the amount of time spent communicating about the enemy. This type of blaming helps diffuse some of the pent-up emotion in the organizational family, but it prevents the organization from accurately labeling and correcting the source of its difficulties. Instead, serious internal problems are denied and projected onto the outside enemy. At this stage of closure, xenophobia—the fear of outsiders—intensifies and becomes a pervasive quality of the organizational culture.

The organizational family may also discharge this pent-up emotion on one of its own members. In this situation, a member takes on the role of scapegoat in the organizational family, thus providing other members a needed diversion from much more threatening issues. As with an outside enemy, the organizational family can expend an enormous amount of time and emotional energy on the scapegoat. Where such pent-up emotion is excessive, the scapegoat may be painfully extruded from the organization. The exiled infidel becomes a pariah—an untouchable with whom all contact is prohibited. Any organizational member who sustains contact with the scapegoat also becomes suspect.

Following the scapegoat's extrusion, there is an aftermath of guilt in the organizational family as members slowly realize that many of the problems they had blamed on the scapegoat continue in the his or her absence. Since the organization won't allow mourning the scapegoat, the scapegoat becomes a ghost that haunts the organizational family ("If it happened to _____, it can happen to me"). It is my experience that this increased sense of personal vulnerability is a healthy warning sign. The early scapegoats are the first of what can become a long series of personal casualties in the incestuous organizational family.

Sequential scapegoating is marked by a long series of extrusions. It is not unusual to have these scapegoats drawn from the same role or unit. People actually can be recruited and hired for the scapegoat role during such periods. This happens when the organization unconsciously selects a series of individuals who are unlikely to fit into the already coalesced group. In the absence of such recruitment, people who do not have a natural affinity for the scapegoat role must be shaped to become the scapegoat through a group dynamic that sets them up for acting out.

One reason this casualty process escalates is that the system becomes even more closed following the scapegoating process. The scapegoats are often the most differentiated from the organizational family system. They are the staff most likely to introduce new ideas, challenge organizational family norms, and break no-talk rules. The loss of the scapegoats thus makes the group even more homogenous and decreases the probability that other staff will want to openly address problems or challenge family norms.

5.18 Fear and Paranoia

Scapegoating breaks the tradition of trust in the organizational family. Members begin to perceive themselves as potential victims and initiate acts of self-protection. This period, vividly described by people I've interviewed as "cover-your-ass time," is marked by such behavior as consciously lining up coalitions of support, writing memos to document situations, decisions, etc., in case such information is needed for one's defense, and decreased activity and decreased decision making due to fear of making mistakes.

Many of these fears are undefined but are reflected in worker comments such as, "It's like a sense of impending doom looming over our heads," "There's so much tension here," "I just feel like things here are going to explode one of these days," "I keep having this dream of needing to run away before something happens," and "It doesn't feel safe here anymore."

5.19 Plots and Conspiracies

The slow, subtle process of organizational closure described so far may have transpired over a number of years. In brief review, the program has organized itself around a rigid belief system, become increasingly iso-lated, gone through a period of almost euphoric missionary zeal, and workers have begun to experience disillusionment and a loss of faith. Staff members have become physically and emotionally depleted and are experiencing some increased conflict within the team. Much of the tur-moil in the system has existed as an undercurrent. We are now at a stage where this undercurrent is going to break into open conflict.

The organization is now like a bubbling cauldron. When we mix in such ingredients as personal turmoil over the loss of faith in the pro-gram, guilt over scapegoated members, loss of professional self-esteem, unresolved resentments, and all of the problems caused by social and sexual closure in the organization (described in the next two chapters), we have an organization ripe for revolution.

The no-talk rule related to serious organizational problems is finally broken and conflict breaks into the open. The shape this conflict takes varies widely from organization to organization. Some of the more com-mon variations I have seen include the following:

- A scapegoated (fired) organizational family member makes public countercharges against the organization and its leaders. Charges may range from embezzlement to gross incompetence to sexual abuse of clients.
- After months of whispered hallway conversations and secret meetings, a number of key staff members dramatically leave to create a new company that will be in direct competition with the parent organization. The history of many consulting firms I worked with in Washington, D.C., can be traced to such splits in closed organizational families. The source of the zeal that es-tablishes the new organization consists more of aggression and desire for vengeance than entrepreneurial spirit.
- The director (high priest/priestess) is scapegoated internally through open conflict, isolation, or sabotage.
- There may be efforts to overthrow the high priest/priestess—

most often taking the form of secret meetings with board members, funding and regulatory agencies, or the news media.

The high priest/priestess becomes a blotter onto which years of unresolved emotion are projected. The high priest/priestess, who has participated in the scapegoating of other organizational members, now becomes vulnerable to the same process.

5.20 Renegade Subcultures, Schisms, and Coups

Factions in the professionally closed organization can lie dormant for long intervals. During times of increased strain these factions can resurface both as vehicles of badly needed support and as forums through which aggression can be discharged. The fragmentation of the organization into subcultures is a serious sign of the whole system's deteriorating health. It's like an allergy: The organization's natural defense system goes to war against itself.

As systems move toward progressive closure, a split between the disciples and the heretics is inevitable. It is similar to a process of sibling rivalry, as the two camps struggle for crumbs of affection from the authoritarian parent. Even when the heretics and infidels are purged from the system, further splits continue as conflicts arise over which remaining faction represents the "true" disciples.

We will discuss a bit later in this chapter what occurs when the plots and conspiracies are successful in overthrowing institutional leadership. Whether such plots fail or succeed, the closed system is likely to be faced with loyalty tests and purges.

5.21 Loyalty Tests and Purges

While there are cycles of expansion (mostly to increase human labor and financial resources) and compression in closed systems, the long-term history is nearly always one of ever-tightening circles that drive out all but the most committed members. What begins as the scapegoating and extrusion of a few perceived malcontents often shows up later as wholesale purges. Purges often follow unsuccessful attempts to overthrow organizational leadership, but may simply be triggered by acts of heresy related to the core beliefs of the system. Each cycle of purges involves loyalty tests that demand an ever greater surrender of individual will by organizational members. The focus of purges is not so much the control or extrusion of a rebellious minority as it is keeping the majority within the emotional and financial bosom of the organization. Branding the renegade member as heretic, traitor, and pariah is not nearly as important as the recommitment of the member whose loyalty was wavering.

The most extreme example of loyalty tests in a closed system in my lifetime occurred in Jonestown, Guyana. In a ritual called "White Night," all of the members of the religious community led by Jim Jones participated in the enactment of a ritual mass suicide. In all but the final enactment, the liquid they drank contained only Kool-Aid. The White Night loyalty test was performed more than forty times before the final mass suicide at Jonestown. Less horrific versions of such loyalty tests occur every day in business: Is a worker willing to assume a new role, accept a transfer, accept overtime assignments, accept a cut in pay or benefits for the good of the company? Some loyalty tests in the business world involve pressure to take sides in a struggle for power or requests to move into gray areas of ethical conduct. Sometimes there are requests to involve oneself in illegal conduct, but the line separating legal from illegal conduct is usually approached one inch at a time. The last inch is hardly noticed, and then one's complicity ties one to the system. When the majority of employees have been so compromised, silence reigns because no one feels he or she can speak with any moral authority.

Purges are part of the cycles of contraction of closed systems: periods of minimal turnover followed by bursts of members fleeing or being extruded.

5.22 "The Infinite Dance of Shifting Coalitions"
The conspiracies and open conflicts create a tremendously high level of anxiety at a time when the staff has few supports to handle such tension. There may be constant pressure to choose sides as issues get polarized. There may be ruptures in long-standing personal and professional relationships. The staff may be confused by powerful feelings of ambivalence toward the high priest/priestess and other organizational family members.

As feelings of fear and personal vulnerability increase in this situation, the staff's self-protective defenses go up. One of the most common defensive patterns at this stage is the constant shifting of supportive dyads and triads in the organization, a pattern Gregory Bateson has described in nuclear families under conflict as "the infinite dance of shifting coalitions." This phrase graphically describes the constantly changing dyads and triads workers use to generate transient support and to exchange the latest rumors. One way to monitor the passage of an organization through this crisis is by watching the reduction in the turnover rate of coalitions, and noting the return to a more stable pattern of relationships in the system.

5.23 Increased Rigidity

As conditions become more turbulent in the closed organizational family, there is an attempt to administratively tighten the structure to get things back under control. Organizational leaders may take a punitive response to staff members they feel are undermining their authority and challenging basic tenets of program philosophy. Increased program rigidity may also take the form of adding new rules and policies governing staff behavior. This stage is exemplified by a comment shared with me during an organizational consultation: "The last act of a dying organization is a thicker rule book." The need for rules to control staff members marks a dramatic change in mutual respect, loyalty, and the esprit de corps that characterized earlier stages of organizational life.

5.24 The Distancing of the Administrative Staff

Through the process of closure, and particularly through the stage of open conflict, the high priest/priestess may be experiencing his or her own disillusionment with the organization and its members. It is a period in which the high priest/priestess is emotionally, and sometimes physically, distancing himself or herself from other staff members. It is the period during which administrative offices may be moved to a location separate from the main operations facility. More time may be spent by the high priest/priestess away from the facilities. The traditionally open door is more often than not closed. More middle-management positions may be created to serve as buffers between organizational members and the high priest/priestess. Informal verbal communication is replaced by more formal chain-of-command communication, a phenomenon one person I interviewed described as "memo-mania."

Where the early periods of organizational closure may have met everyone's needs, the organization has now reached a developmental stage in which few members' needs are being effectively met. The closed system has reached a critical turning point in its history.

5.25 Obsession with Secrecy

The rise in anxiety and fear that accompanies scapegoating and the breakup of formal communication channels breeds a system desperate for information. And yet secrets abound regarding what is truly going on in the organization. People in closed systems become obsessed with secrets. They create them, cherish them, disclose them, and spend enormous energy discovering them. The system has moved into this stage when a growing number of conversations between organizational members at all levels begin with a contract for secrecy—a contract always assumed to be morally and politically relative. Over time, it seems that such secrecy pacts have been generated on almost every issue relevant to what is really going on inside the organization.

The systems preoccupation with internal and external information control incites a frenzy of intelligence gathering that usually goes by the name "gossip." As the credibility of formal information channels declines, indigenous sources of information can wield enormous informal power in the organization. While the high priest/priestess of a closed system wields enormous formal power, a cook, receptionist, or janitor may wield enormous informal power.

The preoccupation with secrecy is even more apparent in the way the closed system tries to control the release of information outside the organization. Consider the closed system's relationship to the media. The relationship between closed systems and the press and television often is marked by extreme ambivalence. The high priests/priestess and other leaders are both drawn toward and repelled by these media. They glory in the adulation of manipulated media exposure because it fuels their vision of a world that will come to recognize their achievements. When adulation shifts to criticism, the system and its leaders are stung and further withdraw, having had the hostile intent of the world so clearly confirmed. Closed systems vacillate between attempting to manipulate the media and refusing to interact with the media.

5.26 The Organization as Chameleon

One of the earliest signs to outsiders that something is amiss in a closed system is the accumulation of conflicting reports on the nature of the organization. Closed systems become chameleonlike in their interactions with the outside world. They can speak one moment with passion about the most noble of values, exuding charm as warm as it is superficial, while simultaneously committing acts of incredible maliciousness or brutality. The messages sent to the outside world by closed organizations result from highly controlled processes of image manipulation and myth-making.

The veneer of the closed system is carefully crafted and polished. There is no such thing as an informal interaction with an outsider. Image is everything. Like many seriously troubled families, the worse things get inside, the greater the effort to project an image of perfection to the outside world. Public relations is elevated to highly sophisticated propaganda. To visit a closed system is to play audience to a perfectly executed drama. One is treated to the mythology of the organization's creation, its canonical history, its noble values, its unparalleled science and technology, its political sophistication, its financial acumen, and its marketing prowess. The pageant is impressive—but perhaps too impressive. One of the bitter ironies of this chameleonlike quality is that the beginning of the worst internal problems in the closed organizational family may coincide with the organization's greatest external recognition.

In late stages of closure, the pageant breaks down due to the system having lost touch with the outside world. It is not unusual at this late stage to see the emergence of a messianic quality on the part of the high priest/priestess, who becomes increasingly preoccupied with his or her own place in the history of the organization (or the world). When such high priests/priestesses are cornered in what they anticipate to be an irredeemable loss of face, the reactions can be quite extreme. Congressman Leo Ryan arrived in Jonestown, Guyana, in November 1978 to investigate allegations of abuses in Jim Jones's religious community. Perhaps Jones thought the pageant would work one more time. It seemed at first that it would, but then the pageant began to unravel with an outcome more tragic than anyone could have conceived: the shooting of Ryan and his entourage and the mass suicide of more than 900 people. More recent versions of this tragedy have unfolded in places like Waco, Texas.

5.27 Breaking Rules, Breaking Laws

Many closed systems, in their later stages, take on an essentially psychopathic character. In their elitist view of the world, they exist as sovereign entities for whom no external rules apply. Leaders of closed systems often espouse support of laws and rules as they apply to others, but believe special circumstances exist that suspend the application of those rules to themselves. This is how they can propose or defend a principle at the exact time they are violating it. Closed systems nearly always operate on the principle that noble ends justify questionable means. Evil done in the name of good is a common legacy of closed systems.

The evolution of rule-breaking in a closed system can be quite subtle. It begins with what might be considered minor indiscretions—a disregard for zoning and licensing regulations, a failure to adequately document financial transactions, or the fabrication of some piece of documentation. Organizational leaders and members always see themselves cutting corners in the name of some higher good. When caught in such indiscretions, they portray themselves as passionately committed humanitarians or honest entrepreneurs caught in the red tape of senseless and incompetent bureaucrats. In later stages of closure, grosser breaches of ethical and legal conduct occur as a result of the deterioration of the physical and emotional health of organizational members.

It is not unusual in closed systems to find that resources that once went to the noble cause are progressively reallocated to meet the needs of the high priest/priestess and members of the inner circle. Advanced stages of closed systems are noted by exorbitant salaries, large bonuses, large pensions, personal loans, and perks of inconceivable proportions: cars, airplanes, homes, clothing, servants, chauffeurs, bodyguards. Many closed systems have even used a service veneer to exploit their not-for-profit tax structure to subsidize extravagant lifestyles for the high priest/priestess and the members of his or her inner circle. Secret slush funds, fund diversion, and "creative accounting" are the norm.

In the end, the visionary goal is eventually sacrificed for the leader's appetite for power, recognition, money, or sensory gratification. Closed organizations are marked by a kind of moral disorientation that makes this corruption of founding values possible and rationally justifiable. Sustained isolation and the loss of objective, internal feedback means the absence of any moral or ethical gyroscope within the organization. What's amazing is not that ethical breaches or outright corruption are rationalized inside the system but that the rationalizations are believed by members for such a long period of time. Ex-members are left to ponder, "How could we have been there and not seen what was going on?"

Closed systems perceive and respond to ethical dilemmas very differently than more open systems. Basically good organizations, like basically good people, can make stupid decisions, suffer lapses in sensitivity, and commit harmful acts. What marks healthy organizations is their ability to recognize such lapses and correct themselves. There are two crucial elements here: a capacity for self-scrutiny and a capacity to initiate action to bridge the gap between organizational ideals and organizational performance. Closed systems suffer diminished capabilities in both of these areas.

In late stages of closure, leaks in the system escalate. Jealousy or anger fuel talk. Rumors and stories are carried out of the system by disgruntled ex-employees. Sometimes the evidence of the breaches springs from the very arrogance of the high priest/priestess. The most obvious case of such arrogance is the White House recordings made by Richard Nixon. Nixon was not alone among high priests/high priestesses in his narcissistic desire to capture his words in print and on tape. The writings and recordings of high priests/priestesses often show up as evidence when the closed system begins to disintegrate. There are always people from inside closed systems (like Alexander Butterfield, who disclosed the existence of the Nixon tapes) who will later call the world's attention to the fact that the sins of the system were meticulously recorded.

5.28 System Retaliation against Real and Imagined Threats

Internal plots and uprisings and increased criticism from the outside confirm the closed system's perception of the outside world's hostile intentions. Reports of everything from espionage and sabotage to imagined conspiracies to harm the high priest/priestess spark the emergence of a paramilitary aura in the organizational culture. Perimeters are defined and guarded. Outsiders have increasing difficulties entering the "compound." Contact between organizational members and outsiders is closely monitored through everything from facility searches to secret surveillance of mail and phone calls to a system of internally developed spies. The creation of an internal security force (and, in the extreme, the stockpiling of weapons), justified as a defensive maneuver, always signals a new and ominous stage in the development of any closed system.

It is ironic how such delusions of persecution become self-fulfilling prophecies. As the closed organization gets more and more out of control, there really are a growing number of people who pose a threat to the system and its leadership. It is in such a climate that everyone is taught to watch everyone within and without. Internal spy networks might even include spies to spy on the spies. Whatever connecting tissue or trust and respect that once existed inside the organization inevitably erodes in this climate.

Xenophobic delusions of persecution increase the risk of aggressive action by the organization. With the confluence of pent-up aggression and paranoia, lists of those who are perceived to threaten the survival of the organization can turn into hit lists. Closed systems are at risk to launch preemptive strikes, which they define in their paranoia as defensive actions.

Whistle-blowers who go public with system abuses become targets of intimidation. External watchdogs, such as representatives of funding and regulatory agencies or the press, often are threatened and, in some cases, harmed when they expose a closed system's questionable practices. The extremity of the response is justified by the worthiness of the system's cause and the portrayed evilness of its internal and external enemies. Personal safety should be a conscious consideration for anyone who could be perceived as posing a threat to a closed system.

5.29 Closed Systems in Collision

The growing prevalence of closed organizations in our modern world raises the distinct risk that the histories of two or more such systems will intersect with tragic and far-reaching consequences. Closed systems often incite the development of an equally closed oppositional force. We regularly see such closed systems conducting reciprocal surveillance of each another, sitting on opposite sides of a bargaining table, a court room, or, perhaps most dramatically, facing each other in an armed standoff. When we have closed, paramilitary-like subcultures squared off against each other, the results are often disastrous. Poor reality-testing, pent-up aggression, pressure for crisis resolution, ideological arrogance, unwillingness to call on outside resources, incapacity to listen, propensity to misread and misinterpret behavioral cues, delusional thinking— all of these, occurring on both sides, contribute to these disasters.

While such collisions between closed systems grab headlines, the more frequent pattern of aggression is that which is discharged internally in a closed system facing external threat. Unions, for example, in the middle of a bitter and prolonged strike almost always save their greatest animus not for replacement workers but for their own members who cross the picket line. Almost anything can be internally justified when a closed system perceives itself threatened.

5.30 The Breakup of the Organizational Family

On the heels of sustained closure, powerful forces build up and inevitably propel the organization toward a major crisis. It's as if the collective energy of the organizational family has been consumed and the system cannot sustain itself as currently constituted. Closed systems facing such a crisis often follow one of four potential trajectories: (1) organizational maturation, (2) the positive use of a near-death experience, (3) crisis containment and reclosure, or (4) organizational death.

Organizational Maturation. Many organizations move naturally through the early stages of closure described in this chapter without such dramatic long-term consequences. For them, closure was a healthy developmental stage that was shed as part of the natural maturation of the organization. Even though no one may have conceptualized the role of closure in the budding organizational problems, the direct confrontation of these problems sparked strategies that served to open the system. The organization defines more realistically what it can and cannot do. Outside resources are brought in to help with some of the problems. Staff members are given more access to outside training and professional development resources. The organization and its members evolve and adapt based on both their own needs and the changing threats and opportunities posed by the outside environment. Most organizations learn to recognize signs that indicate the need to shift the organizational character from a position of introversion to one of extroversion.

The Positive Use of a Near-Death Experience. There are organizations that have survived the process of extreme and sustained organizational closure. Many of these organizations underwent what might be called a transformative, near-death experience. They used the crises generated by closure to reevaluate and redefine organizational structure, leadership styles, and organizational norms. In short, the crisis forced a maturation and an opening of the system. Because of the pent-up emotion in the organization, this process can be highly volatile as members are brought together to address their problems and experiences in the organization. The collective release of anger, resentment, and guilt, although risky (there can be further casualties at this stage if this process is not handled carefully), often serves to break the organizational impasse. The organization uses crisis positively to redefine itself and renegotiate internal and external relationships. Such growth may create an even stronger organization that is fueled not by zeal but by the collective maturity and wisdom that have come from surviving the closure process. The overcoming of adversities induced by prolonged closure can strengthen the character and future resilience of an organization.

Crisis Containment and Reclosure. Rather than die, most closed systems go through episodic, crisis-induced ruptures in the membrane that separates them from their environments. During these brief openings of the system, some members escape or are extruded and new resources are brought in from the outside that can prolong the life of the organization. This process is clearly indicated by the pattern of employee turnover in closed systems. Closed systems alternate between prolonged periods of almost no staff turnover and brief periods of exceptionally high turnover. Decisions to leave the organization are almost contagious during these brief ruptures.

When the high priest/priestess survives the crisis, the organization often simply recloses around the same or slightly refined ideology, hires and socializes new members, and replicates the closure process described in this chapter. An alternative pattern often occurs when the high priest/priestess leaves or is extruded. In the absence of the high priest/priestess, the organization is vulnerable to reclosing around the same or another ideology, selecting a new high priest/priestess and continuing to replicate the stages of the closure process. Closed organizations may go through a series of crises, each of which conveys the illusion of change but which is simply a variation or chapter in the long-term process of closure—each chapter bringing the organization closer to its eventual demise.

Organizational Death. The organizational family may cease to exist. This might aptly be called a process of extinction. Closed systems most often die because of their overspecialization and their inability to adapt to a changing environment. While external events may precipitate the closed system's demise, such organizations may also simply implode. Decisions and activities crucial to the survival of the organization are simply not completed or are mismanaged.

There are many examples of the demise of closed systems. The rise and fall of Nazi Germany and the more recent breakup of the Soviet Union both parallel the dynamics described in this chapter. Closer to home, the fall of Richard Nixon and his inner circle could be described as the demise of a closed system. However, the horrible events at Jonestown, discussed earlier, remain the most dramatic illustration during my lifetime of a closed system's demise.

Closed systems remain stable only as long as the external environments on which they depend remain relatively stable. As soon as the external environment begins to change, the strain on the closed system increases, exerting enormous pressure inward on those inside the organization. When the environmental changes are extreme, closed systems die as a result of their inability to adapt.

A later chapter will detail some guidelines and approaches to intervening in closed organizational systems, but before we bring our discussion of professional closure to an end, we have a most significant item remaining: the fate of the high priest/priestess.

5.31 The Fall of the High Priest/Priestess

In open organizational family systems, family health is not totally dependent on the health of the leader. There are units and roles in such organizations that function autonomously, with little direct involvement of the leader. There are numerous sources of support for organizational members other than the leader. And there are checks and balances that limit the leader's ability to make decisions that could mortally wound the organization.

In contrast, the health of the closed system is entirely contingent on the health of the high priest/priestess. Because of the extreme centralization of power in the high priest/priestess role, transient or sustained disturbances in that person's health can have profound and immediate effects on all members of the organization and on the viability of the organization.

The high priest's/priestess's ability to function is progressively impaired by the closure process. The isolation of the organizational family also cuts off sources of support for the high priest/priestess. Given such a loss of replenishment and feedback, it is easy to see how the whole system can get twisted by the high priest's/priestess's manipulations to meet his or her own needs. Given the absence of internal and external feedback, it is easy to see how the high priest/priestess might be vulnerable to sudden and dramatic changes in his or her beliefs and values. The high priest/priestess in a system characterized by sustained closure who does not develop bizarre thinking and decision making is the exception. Considering that he or she often has little contact with the outside social and professional world, it is not surprising that his or her decisions increasingly reflect a divergence from prevailing professional and social values.

I have been particularly struck over the span of my career by the casualty process among leaders of newly emerging health and human service fields (hospice programs, addiction treatment centers, service programs for abused women and children, AIDS service organizations, for example). While sustained closure can be detrimental to the health of caregivers who work in these organizations, we may discover, in retrospect, that closure is even more devastating to the leaders of such emerging fields. The start-up of a health care field requires a particular kind of leadership, not unlike that seen in a private entrepreneur or a leader of a social movement. Such leaders are profoundly committed, seem to have unlimited supplies of personal energy, are exceptionally articulate, and engender a great deal of support through their personal charisma. They are organizers and revolutionaries who bring to us bold, new visions. How then do such leaders respond to their own stress during the years it may take to see their visions come to fruition? Over time, these leaders' professional and social worlds may become ever smaller. They may develop small cadres of converts who reinforce their beliefs and offer them support and adulation. The dissent-free environment of the closed system contributes to their failure to accurately perceive the internal and external environment. They may become increasingly disillusioned as they see "maintainers" coming in to stabilize and standardize a field that they themselves created. They may lose touch with the roots from which they came. Whether as an intellectual leader in the field or as a director of a service program, these leaders may create closed systems in which to insulate themselves. Cut off from outside sources of personal, professional, and social replenishment, the leader must rely on organizational members for support. Many things make it difficult for other organizational members to provide support, express affection, and give constructive feedback to the high priest/priestess. In such a state of isolation, it is little wonder that the leader's ability to function emotionally, socially, and professionally seriously deteriorates.

One of the most recently noted falls from grace in the health and human services field was that of William Aramony, who was president of the United Way of America from 1970 to 1992. Aramony was extruded (and later indicted for mail and tax fraud) in a widely publicized downfall that wounded the image of the highly respected agency. The charges against Aramony created an image of a man who used charitable resources to support a lavish lifestyle. Among the most serious charges were allegations that he provided his teenage mistress with housing, travel, and a salary for "consulting" services—all out of United Way funds.

There are debts we all owe to our intellectual and professional leaders. One method of repayment is to help the leader get "out of the role" to receive our personal respect and our constructive feedback. Such support may reduce the leader's need to seek shelter in a closed system that may prove destructive for us all.

5.32 The Curse of Icarus

The role of high priest/priestess is a very seductive one. For people who have filled such roles and who cannot refuse or move beyond the seductiveness of the role, the unfolding history is often a sad one. The high priest's/priestess's fall from grace can be mythologically described as the Curse of Icarus.

In the story from Greek mythology, Icarus and his father, Daedalus, were imprisoned in the labyrinth at Knossos. Daedalus used his powers to fashion wax-and-feather wings, which they used to escape. Icarus became intoxicated with his power to fly and flew toward the warmth of the sun. The increasing heat melted the wax wings, plunging Icarus to his death in the sea. Icarus is a symbol of the fate of the high priest/priestess whose self-intoxication transcends his or her personal capacities. It is sad to see people who have made enormous contributions leave organizations and professional fields in disgrace.

The pressured isolation of the closed system can, during different periods, elicit the best and the worst from each of us. We all have particular weaknesses of character awaiting only the right petri dish and growing medium. The centralization of power in the leadership role of a closed system can transform a minor quirk of character into a fatal flaw. There is buried in the role of the high priest/priestess a seed of recklessness, a seeking for risks and sensations that often takes those who fill the role to the precipice, if not over it. Unfortunately, the organization and its members are compelled to share the journey.

People close to the high priest/priestess, particularly those in the inner circle, are close enough to note a wide range of what outsiders will later call "obvious warning signs." To insiders, however, such variance in behavior is not viewed critically because the actions of the leader are viewed as unchallengeable. Such breaches are inconceivable in such a deified person. Later, such breaches may be noted, but silence is sustained in order to protect both the high priest/priestess and the system.

5.33 Professional Closure and Professional and Organizational Distress: A Summary

In the studies of professional distress I've conducted over the past twenty years, individuals' accounts were linked to a variety of organizational processes as well as to potential areas of personal vulnerability. In particular, high levels of professional distress were linked to the progressive closure of the organizational family system.

Sustained closure of organizational systems disrupts both the health of workers and the health and viability of organizations. Workers in a closed system are vulnerable to victimization just as the system itself is vulnerable to implosion and extinction.

Sustained organizational closure

- thwarts professional development by restricting workers' access to the outside professional environment
- constricts workers' professional identity to their experiences in the organizational family
- increases the time and emotional demands on members of the organization
- breeds interpersonal conflicts as members compete to meet their needs within the system
- leads to a distortion of personal and organizational values
- increases the frequency and intensity of abuses of power in the organization
- increases the number and severity of breaches of ethical and legal standards
- fails to provide permissions and procedures for people to get out of the system
- breaks down the boundary between one's work life and one's personal life
- sets the stage for the onset of problematic social and sexual relationships between organizational family members

This chapter described one aspect of an incestuous dynamic—professional closure—that can occur in an organization. The next chapter will detail how professional closure can begin to spill over and influence the social relationships of organizational members outside the work setting.

⫸ 6

Social Closure

Social closure is the stage in an organization's life in which members are meeting most, if not all, of their social needs within the boundary of the organizational family. Professional closure and social closure often emerge sequentially in an organization. In fact, by breaking down the boundary between one's personal life and work life, professional closure often sets the stage for social closure. In this chapter, we will describe the process of social closure and the impact it has on the health of organizational members and the organization as a whole. We will see how social closure encourages employees to develop a work-dominated social network, elicits an intense focusing on the personal and interpersonal problems of employees, and disrupts team functioning by injecting into the workplace problems between organizational members that typically arise only in outside-of-work social relationships.

6.1 Healthy Social Contact

The workplace has been, and probably always will be, an arena in which human beings meet social as well as professional needs. The quantity and quality of interpersonal relationships in the workplace are important indicators of organizational health and can provide workers with powerful incentives for continued identification with the organization. Most organizations strive to create a climate in which social relationships in the organization are both personally fulfilling and supportive of the system's overall mission. It is important that organizations provide rituals that allow us to socially recognize the entrance and exit of members from the group, celebrate our affection for one another, and recognize individual and collective achievement.

Given the above, it should be clear that I have no intention of suggesting that employee socializing outside the work setting is either undesirable or unhealthy. In many organizations, these social relationships have clear benefits to both the organization and the individuals involved. The concern is not with the existence of social relationships between workers, but with how the *diversity* and *intensity* of these relationships are changed in closed organizational families. The problem is not with the existence of work-related social relationships, but with their exclusivity. This chapter will demonstrate how the professional and social closure of the organizational family adversely affects the inner workings of the organization and increase the vulnerability of workers to professional distress by cutting off their sources of replenishment outside the work setting.

6.2 Professional Camaraderie and the Development of a Work-Dominated Social Life

As organizations become more professionally closed, members spend an increasing amount of time together away from work. This time, however, is forever fixated on work-related issues and personalities. No matter what topics of conversation arise, the subject is quickly pulled back to work-related concerns. These relationships and their fixation on work seem a natural extension of the camaraderie that develops on the work team.

Early stages of social closure are not experienced negatively by the organization or by those involved. Such social relationships affirm a sense of camaraderie among organizational members, fulfill needs for intimacy and social activity, and increase members' feelings of safety and security in the organization. Early stages of social closure seem quite benign: normal workplace cliques, car-pooling, occasional social gatherings at the end of a workday, shared recreational activities, migration to certain neighborhoods, shared apartments, joint private business-ventures, or shared vacations.

For workers who come to the organization with a small social network, social closure quickly fills the void with work-related relationships. The fact that the workplace has helped fill this vacuum heightens the value of the organization to the socially isolated worker. For workers who have an extensive social network, the process is more subtle. As professional closure reduces the time and emotional energy available to maintain nonwork relationships, they simply fade away without conscious decisions having been made to terminate them.

There are many factors that contribute to social isolation in closed systems. Social closure is often a product of role overload. Excessive hours and unpredictable work schedules inevitably erode outside-of-work social relationships. The lack of structured time at work for vital communications among employees often brings these same people together away from work to exchange information essential to the completion of their mutual responsibilities. In most closed systems, the status of being perpetually "on-call" never allows one to get "out of role" and frequently results in intrusions into nonwork social activities. The chronic fatigue and exhaustion produced by sustained overload creates a work force of people who have little interest or energy for nonwork socializing.

Another more ominous contributor to social closure is the pervasive distrust of outsiders that permeates closed organizations. As closed systems develop an us-against-the-world mentality, there are increased expectations of staff to participate in work-related social activities, and a growing discouragement of professional and social contact outside the organizational circle. As later stages of professional closure occur, the organization takes on the character of a jealous lover. Time devoted to outside relationships is viewed as a form of disloyalty to the organization. The elicitation of guilt feelings for outside-of-work interests and relationships evolves from the subtle to the blatant. Like the insecure, possessive lover, what closed systems ultimately want is all of us—our total, undistracted devotion.

6.3 Loss of Faith and the Highly Social Work Life

As organizations become progressively closed, work-oriented employee relationships begin to replace rather than supplement outside social relationships. Even where some contact is maintained with people away from work, it is the work relationships, by virtue of their frequency and intensity of contact, that are primary.

The number and intensity of these worker-worker relationships increases as distress heightens through the process of professional closure. Though it is only natural to reach out to co-workers for support under such circumstances, the result is often a work-dominated social network that is an extension and continuation of the distress we experience in the work environment. Bonding between employees in the midst of such turmoil can be quite intense (like that between soldiers in battle or disaster survivors), but there are two things such relationships can never provide: (1) a reprieve from the world of work and (2) objectivity related to the events unfolding in that world.

When such social closure overlaps the loss-of-faith stage of professional closure, the nature of outside relationships begins to change. There continues to be a high level of staff interaction away from the work setting, but the focus on work in these relationships begins to change as staff morale deteriorates. While there may be some continued focus on workplace personalities and politics, much of the interaction shifts away from work issues to the social activities of the organizational family. In fact, members spend less and less time inside the organization focusing on work due to the increasing focus on what members are doing with one another outside the organization. It's as if the purpose of the organization is to meet the personal and social needs of the staff. Cohesive team relationships, created as a means of enhancing the mission of the organization, themselves become the mission of the workplace.

Relationships in the organization become more social than professional, with an accompanying decline in worker productivity. As the number of staff members involved with one another socially goes up, interpersonal relationships among staff members can become so enmeshed that they spend more time talking about one another than about producing goods or services.

What occurs inside such closed organizations is what sociologists call "implosion." It is the inward collapse of a network of relationships. Imagine a network of personal relationships beginning with a core of the most intimate relationships moving outward in concentric circles, with each outer circle signaling a lessened degree of intimacy. Implosion is the reduction of one's social world to the inner circles. It is a simultaneous break with outside relationships and an intensification of the intimacy experienced in relationships inside the group. Gatekeeping intensifies following implosion as a way of sustaining the intensity of experience inside the group and protecting the group from outsiders. Social closure is a process of implosion through which the social networks of workers are reduced to one that consists only of organizational family members.

6.4 The Impact of Social Closure on the Individual

When one's primary social and work relationships become one and the same, one may suffer from (1) loss of replenishment outside the work setting, (2) loss of nonwork roles that help affirm one's self-esteem and identity, (3) distortion of personal values, (4) role confusion in one's personal/work relationships, and (5) painful role transitions in the organization.

The Loss of Replenishment. American workers in nearly ever sector of the economy report experiencing increases in the frequency and intensity of demands being made on them. To sustain such giving over time, each worker must have resources of physical, emotional, social, and spiritual replenishment outside the organization. Regularly replenished through these outside resources, the worker can continue to enter the high-stress environment and respond to increased demands. Lacking such replenishment, the worker will become physically and emotionally depleted. In a state of depletion, the worker is likely to respond in one of three ways. The first is to continue to meet the excessive demands—a sacrifice that will eventually produce serious symptoms of impairment. The second is to inadvertently exploit relationships in the work environment to address one's unmet needs. The third way is to begin to physically and emotionally detach from the work unit as an act of self-protection.

Loss of Nonwork Roles. In the last chapter, we described how professional closure increased one's vulnerability to distress by constricting one's professional identity to experiences one has in his or her primary workplace. Social closure escalates this vulnerability by cutting off the roles one performs outside the workplace. The increased amount of time staff members spend with each other decreases their participation in nonwork relationships and roles. It cuts staff members off from activities that affirm a sense of self outside the work environment. The resulting isolation can be particularly troublesome to workers who may later find themselves scapegoated in the organization.

Distortion of Personal Values. Some workers' face situations and experiences that can color their view of the world. The police officer, the doctor or nurse, the welfare worker, the teacher, and the rescue worker are just a few of the people who daily confront disease and disorder. Whether they must cope with the physical deformity of the diseased or injured, or the prolonged exposure to the victims of human neglect and violence, these workers must balance and reconcile the realities of their work with a broader perspective on life. When one's social network becomes totally work dominated, such perspective is lost. One's view of the world becomes increasingly distorted. The whole world begins to look screwed up, and one's life seems like a constant confrontation with craziness and pain. During professional and social closure, things can

begin to look hopeless as we lose our sense of how healthy people conduct their lives. Such isolation, along with the physical and emotional
exhaustion produced by organizational closure, may lead to radical
changes in one's personal values and beliefs.

Role Confusion. Social relationships with co-workers are natural and inevitable, yet in closed systems the boundary confusion between personal and professional relationships can create discomfort and pain.
When people in our social network also hold roles as co-workers, issues
or changes in the nature or intensity of those relationships can spill over
and influence our professional relationships. Conversely, problems in
work relationships can spill over and undermine the quality of social relationships outside the work setting. Given the dual nature of such relationships, confusion can occur on the exact nature of the relationships.

Painful Role Transitions. Dual relationships can also go through painful
transitions. There are numerous instances where social relationships
among co-workers are shaken by one of the individuals being promoted
to the role of supervisor over his or her peers. Such transitions leave the
new supervisor responding not only to the stress of the new professional
role, but also to the grief and isolation produced by the change in social
relationships.

6.5 The Inversion Process

An inversion process can occur during the social closure of service organizations in which the knowledge and skills that are channeled into
client services diminish and the process is turned inward by an intense
focusing on the personal and interpersonal problems of the staff. There
are numerous factors that contribute to this closure process. The sustained exhaustion of role overload may overwhelm the personal defense
structures of the most vulnerable staff members, producing symptoms
of severe distress. The extensive socializing between staff members can
exacerbate and further expose these symptoms.

This inversion process can also permeate the entire organization and
create what could be called a "personal growth" phase in the life of the
organizational family. This phase is characterized by staff growth
groups, process-oriented training, and the organization of the staff
around some well-defined growth ideology. Such growth ideology can
result in the organization taking on the emotional flavor of a religious

cult. While human service organizations seem to be particularly prone to this phenomenon, similar processes can go on in financial and manufacturing operations as an outgrowth of "team building" and "leadership development" exercises.

Marriage casualties are a frequent by-product of this "growth" phase. As members of closed organizations get caught up in the artificial intimacy of the closed organizational family, they begin to perceive their marriages differently and raise their expectations of those relationships. A growth culture unfolds with its own specialized vocabulary that serves as a code for inclusion or exclusion. The fact that the staff social group is closed provides little perspective on "nongrowth" oriented relationships. Marriages become work—a constant processing of feelings and issues. Expectations aren't adjusted when they can't be met; spouses are discarded (often with the support of the organizational family). Spouses are sacrificed so that the ideology and values of the organizational family will not be challenged. Such collective disillusionment with intimate relationships outside the organizational family also increases the probability of members developing sexual relationships with other organizational family members (for example, "our spouses don't understand us [we've outgrown them], but we understand each other, therefore . . .").

6.6 The Impact of Social Closure on the Organization

In a healthy organization, member status is related to the commitment, knowledge, skills, and day-to-day performance each person contributes to the achievement of the mission and goals of the organization. Social closure disrupts this process. Status and rewards in the organization become based on one's social relationship with organizational members outside the work environment rather than by one's professional contributions. Promotions, merit increases, preferences in time scheduling, choice of work assignments, and other rewards are given primarily to those who achieve favored status in social relationships outside the organization. Overall organizational productivity declines as more and more organizational members are embittered by such favoritism and see little relationship between organizational rewards and job performance.

Social Closure and Organizational Decision Making. To illustrate how social closure begins to complicate the organizational decision-making process, consider the following scenario.

An opening becomes available for a unit supervisor at a medium-sized company. Two employees, Robert and Jane, who work in the unit and who have relatively equal knowledge and expertise both apply for the position. Robert and his wife socialize regularly with the department manager who will make the hiring decision to fill the vacancy. Jane, on the other hand, has avoided much of the outside-of-work socializing.

If the department manager selects Robert, there is no way possible to convince Jane that the manager's outside-of-work relationship did not influence the decision. If the manager selects Jane, then there will be repercussions in the personal and social relationship with Robert.

A number of other organizational members watch this drama unfold. For them, the decision will communicate important messages about the organization and their future in it. A decision to select Robert for the position could reinforce social closure by communicating that one must cultivate social relationships to obtain upward mobility in the organization. Organizational members will make their own judgments about the roles the outside social relationships, gender, and other factors played in the promotion decision. These feelings will color their future relationships with the manager, Robert, and Jane. Even if Robert was chosen because he was the most qualified candidate, social closure undermines members' ability to trust in the objectivity of the decision. Robert, Jane, and other organizational members will act and generate feelings on their *perceptions,* not necessarily the *reality,* of how the decision was made.

When social and professional roles become enmeshed, organizational decision making becomes complicated and eventually corrupted. Social closure inevitably makes decision makers vulnerable to second-guessing and innuendos regarding preferential decision making. Social closure creates an organizational climate rife with hidden agendas, prejudices, personal favoritism, and secret deals that members believe govern the organization.

Loss of Direct Communication. Social closure escalates the loss of direct communication described in the preceding chapter. As conflict increases, an organization's staff splits into subgroups, and an increasing amount of communication related to the inner workings of the organization occurs in social settings away from the work environment. Gossip and rumor become staples of trade as members seek information to predict their level of safety and security in the organization.

Such loss of direct communication is most dramatic during the latter stages of closure we described earlier as being characterized by loss of faith, scapegoating, and rebellion. Many of us have witnessed the sudden scapegoating (extrusion) of an organizational member and the accompanying no-talk rules that ominously prohibited open discussion of how and why the person was no longer part of the organization. And yet such incidents are processed in excruciating detail in the social subgroups outside the work setting. People who are part of more than one social subgroup serve as vehicles to transfer information and misinformation from one subgroup to another. This frantic level of activity and information exchange in the work-dominated social network is paralleled in the interactions inside the organization by silences and whispers regarding the same event.

When no escape valves exist inside the organization, pent-up emotion may spill out in some unpredictable and potentially uncontrollable ways. Imagine the possibilities when we have such barely suppressed conflict and discomfort, and we bring all of the organizational members together for something like a Christmas party, and then add a drug such as alcohol that will lower the inhibitions and impulse control of many of those in attendance. One such event described to me occurred at an extremely troubled stage in the life of a professionally and socially closed organization. As the drinking altered judgment and loosened tongues over the course of the evening, the discharge of pent-up anger and resentment resulted in physical confrontations and serious destruction of property. Under other circumstances, it would have been sufficiently volatile to have warranted calling the police. In this case, however, those attending the party *were* the police.

6.7 Social Relationships in Open and Closed Systems

Social relationships among people who work together in open systems are established out of free choice and are based on common interests and the desires of those involved to share time and activities. Such relationships form out of individual preference and are not initiated or sustained by the dynamics of the organization. Such relationships are focused on personal interests rather than work issues. These work-related friendships serve to supplement our existing nonwork social network. In open systems, members have easy access across the organizational boundary and the freedom to develop and maintain social relationships both inside and outside the organizational family. Furthermore, the open system imposes no conditions that could inadvertently undermine nonwork social relationships.

Closed organizations possess a centripetal force that pulls workers further and further into the center of the organizational family. This type of organization strongly encourages the development of work-oriented social networks for its employees. Conditions in the work environment also serve to inhibit the development or maintenance of nonwork social relationships. Through the slow, subtle process of organizational closure, more and more time and emotional energy is pulled into the organizational family.

Social networks in closed organizations shrink until they might be said to shrivel on the vine. What's left of these networks is sometimes pulled into the system. This is arranged by hiring only from the existing intimate and social network of the current staff. Tremendous pressure can be exerted on intimate relationships as both parties are pulled into the system. This is done by incorporating the extended family of members into the boundary of the organization by getting them to visit regularly or by hiring or recruiting them as consultants, volunteers, or board members. The social dynamics in closed organizations dictate that an increasing number of organizational decisions be made based on the day-to-day intricacies unfolding in these work-initiated personal relationships.

When supervisors are asked to share day-to-day problems and concerns that arise in their work units, signs of social closure become apparent: Two workers do not want to work together anymore because of a problem in their outside-of-work social relationship. Two other workers, who normally cover each other's absences, now want to know if they can have the same time off because they plan to vacation together. Three workers are spending an excessive amount of time at work talking about an outside business venture in which they have all invested. Another worker is becoming increasingly withdrawn in response to his or her failure to be included in the outside-of-work social rituals. An increasing amount of workplace communication is filled with coded language and innuendo derived from the special knowledge acquired in extracurricular social activities. The language is not universally shared but reflects a splintering or cliquishness in what was once, or might have become, a team.

6.8 The Consequences of Social Closure

Social closure (the meeting of most of our social needs inside the boundary of the organizational family)

- increases the vulnerability of organizational family members to professional distress
- severs access to sources of personal and social replenishment outside the organization
- disrupts team relationships in a way that can interfere with the ability of the organization to accomplish tasks essential to its survival

There is another outcome of social closure. When a workplace becomes professionally and socially closed, the meeting of sexual needs inside the boundary of the organization is inevitable. Sexual closure, the third level of organizational closure, and the abuses of power and the disruption it can bring to the workplace will be described in the next chapter.

⫸ 7

Sexual Closure

It is hard to believe, when one looks at it objectively, that the brief joining of two sexual organs and a few subsequent muscular contractions could wreak such havoc in the life of an organizational group. But as we shall see in this chapter, sexual attraction and sexual activity among co-workers can flow out of an organization's aberrant group processes and, in turn, even more profoundly disturb those same group dynamics.

Throughout my early years as a supervisor and manager, I stuck firmly to the position that what my employees did away from the work setting was none of my business or the organization's business. I believed, particularly, that how, when, where, and with whom staff members expressed their sexuality (including with each other) away from the work setting was a personal and not an organizational issue. Any other position, it seemed, would be both a gross invasion into the private lives of the staff and the imposition of my personal moral judgments in an area in which I had no right to be involved.

While I still worry about the potential invasiveness of organizations into this territory, it is clear that sexuality can be more than an issue of private behavior and personal choices. Sexuality is always a dynamic in organizational families, just as it is always an issue in nuclear families. Whether unrecognized or consciously managed, sexuality has a profound impact on an organizational family culture and the interrelationships among organizational family members. This chapter will examine the impact of sexuality in closed organizational systems. We will place particular emphasis on the importance of managing sexuality in organizations providing services to individuals in the context of fiduciary service relationships, particularly within the health and human services arena.

Our concern with the social and sexual relationships among co-workers is practical rather than moral and can be stated quite simply as follows:

Social and sexual relationships among members of a closed organizational family create relationship dynamics that can (1) radically alter
team functioning, (2) increase the incidence of personal and relationship casualties, (3) lead to the painful extrusion of organization
members, (4) reduce the quality and quantity of services provided
to organizational clients, and (5) set the stage for the exploitation of
clients.

7.1 Sexuality as an Organizational Issue

Our culture in the last half of the twentieth century has done everything possible to move the issue of sexuality from the private to the
public arena. We have become a much more sexually explicit culture,
and yet there are dimensions of sexuality in our culture that remain virtually unexplored. With the exception of concerns about sexual harassment in the workplace, there is a marked absence of professional
literature on and discussion about sexuality as an organizational dynamic or a component of organizational culture. This chapter will explore this dynamic. It is my contention that the manner in which
sexuality is managed in staff-to-staff and staff-to-client relationships has
a profound impact on professional and organizational health.

Many of the examples in this chapter are drawn from my experiences
consulting with health and human services agencies. Sexual relationships between members of an organization are obviously not limited to
such agencies. We could explore this issue in almost any type of business or organizational setting. However, there are two factors that make
sexuality issues particularly problematic in this occupational arena.
First, by virtue of the fact that so much of the work of a human services
agency involves a focus on interpersonal relationships, the impact of
sexual activity in this setting may be magnified. There may also be
unique problems in this type of organization due to the types of people
drawn to the work. Some are drawn to the human services field not to
provide intimacy in the context of a helping relationship, but to find
and experience intimate relationships themselves. There are helping
professionals who have found that it is only in the emotional intensity of
dealing with extreme and tragic problems that they experience intimacy
and feeling. Many such paid helpers have had difficulties experiencing
and maintaining personal intimacy away from the profession, particularly in relationships that were sexual. It goes without saying that problems could easily arise as these people experiment with the intimacy

produced by close worker-worker and worker-client relationships in a closed organizational family system.

The second factor that makes sexuality a particularly important issue in health and human services is the incredible degree of personal vulnerability of the consumers of those services. Consumers of health and human services seek such services at a time in which they are physically, psychologically, and socially vulnerable. When sexual dynamics in an organization move from worker-worker to worker-client dynamics, the consequences can be devastating and enduring. Our focus in this chapter will be on sexual relationships between people who do not share equal power, and there are few relationships in which power inequity is greater than in those between providers and consumers of health and human services.

7.2 Sexual Cultures and Organizational Life

Every organization can be said to have a sexual culture. This culture may be developed through conscious planning, or it may evolve informally, shaped by the attitudes and values of organizational members and, in particular, organizational leaders. Sexual cultures vary widely from one organization to another. The differences in sexual cultures in health and human services agencies are reflected in the following:

- *Language:* Is there permission in the agency to talk about sexual issues? Is there a generally accepted vocabulary used to communicate about sexuality?
- *Artifacts:* What values about sexuality are expressed by physical objects in the organization's milieu: paintings, sculptures, photographs, books, magazines, pamphlets, posters, and clothes worn by the staff and clients?
- *Ethics and Values:* Are there clearly stated ideals for human relationships? What judgments are placed on the various forms of sexual expression? Does an ethical code exist governing relationships between staff members and clients?
- *Attitudes:* What methods of sexual expression in (and out of) the workplace are condemned? What attitudes about men, women, and sexuality are regularly expressed inside the organization? What values are reflected in the nature of sexual humor in the organization?
- *Relationships:* How is affection expressed physically and

verbally in the organization? How are adequacy, self-worth, and competence demonstrated in the work environment? What is the prevalence of sexual harassment and other abuses of power in the organization?

The sexual culture of an organization constitutes the milieu in which the staff and clients served by the agency maintain their self-esteem and adequacy. It shapes the interactions among staff members and between staffers and clients. The sexual culture defines the boundaries of client self-disclosure. Clients rapidly learn what, if any, areas of their sexual lives they may discuss. Some counseling agencies are blind to the sexual problems of their clients because the agencies' sexual cultures covertly prohibit the raising of such issues in a serious and straightforward manner.

There can be great incongruence between the sexual culture of an organization and the values expressed to clients receiving services from that organization. In cases where specialized services have been developed for women, for example, such services may exist in an overall organizational milieu that discounts the specialized needs of women, forces women into stereotyped sex roles in the name of clinical progress, and undermines the power and professional legitimacy of female staff members. Clients receive two contradictory messages from such an agency. Whereas the explicit message from the women's services specialist is sexually empathic, the implicit message from the organization's sexual culture is sexually insensitive and exploitive. Such contradictions may exist on a number of levels and include a broad range of issues. A professional counselor, for example, might articulately communicate to clients the need to slow down, relax, enjoy, explore, and share sexual intimacy, while addressing his or her own sexual needs like they were emergency appointments squeezed into a frantic schedule.

The sexual culture in any organization defines the response to the sexuality we bring to the organization. The sexual culture can also begin to change our own attitudes, values, and behavior related to our sexuality. The nature of the sexual cultures in open and closed organizational systems differs significantly.

7.3 Sexuality in Open and Closed Systems

I do not wish to imply that all sexual coupling between organizational members is somehow pathological, or that all sexual activity in a group results from what I will refer to as an incestuous dynamic.

Sexual relationships between members of open systems reflect the free choices of individual members, do not flow out of the process of the organizational group, and, in most cases, have very little impact on the organization. There is also, in most cases, no increase in professional distress for those involved in such relationships in open systems. This is particularly true when the jobs of those involved are not significantly related to each other, and when the personal relationship does not also involve a power relationship (for example, supervisor-supervisee).

When one superimposes sexual relationships on the stages of professional and social closure described in earlier chapters, one has a situation very different from that in a more open system. Sexual relationships in a closed system often flow more from the process of the group than from the free choice of the individuals involved. In the closed system, sexual activity flows out of and then back into the interpersonal processes of the closed organizational family. The knowledge of this activity, in turn, alters the organizational family. It is not the sexual relationship that is primary, but the meanings and feelings attached to that activity by members of the group. The incestuous dynamic occurs when something in the sexual relationship triggers primitive feelings among group members that the staff family has been violated, and that from that point forward it cannot be the same. It is a situation in which members' varying feelings of rage, hurt, jealousy, and loss of faith boil up and spill out, and begin affecting the relationships in the closed group.

The existence of sexual relationships, the problems they create for participants and other organizational family members, and the concurrent increase in worker casualties they cause, are all symptoms of broader distress in the organizational family system. Closure in the nuclear family creates an incestuous dynamic that sets the stage for the violation of intimacy barriers (including incest) and the acting out of this system dysfunction by individual family members. The process is replicated in closed organizational family systems.

7.4 The Incest Analogy

To those not familiar with the family dynamics seen in cases of consummated incest, my description of organizational dynamics as "incestuous" may be both confusing and offensive. The analogy was not chosen lightly. My contention is that the process of organizational closure described in this book directly parallels the family dynamics often noted in cases of incest. It was by comparing my clinical work counseling incest survivors and their families with my work consulting organizations that I noted the similarity in group dynamics. Below I have charted a number of these similarities, some of which will be explored in greater detail in this chapter.

AREA OF COMPARISON	INCEST DYNAMIC IN THE NUCLEAR FAMILY	INCEST DYNAMIC IN THE ORGANIZATIONAL FAMILY
Degree of closure	Family members prevented from making outside transactions.	Professional and social closure precedes sexual closure.
	Outside world viewed as evil and threatening.	Same
	Extreme control of family members (dating discouraged, hostility toward suitors).	Outside intimate partners of organizational family members may be treated with hostility and jealousy.
	Closure may be secondary to family stigma (alcoholic, psychiatric illness, etc.).	Organizational closure may be related to stigma (see chapter 8).
	Inherent message that all needs of family members can and should be met inside family.	Same
Family Image	Preoccupation with looking good on the outside.	Same
	No-talk rules; distrust talking to outsiders about family events.	Same
	Incongruence between external image and internal emotional reality.	Same
Timing of Incest	Father-daughter incest is often preceded by or concurrent with deterioration in husband-wife sexual relationship.	Sexual relationships between organizational family members often preceded by deterioration in outside marital/intimate relationships.
Type of Relationship	Father aggressor may try to establish pseudo-marital relationship with daughter (courting behavior, daughter's interest in boyfriends seen as unfaithfulness).	Pseudo-marital relations may be established as part of sexual relations. Problem in worker's outside intimate relationships escaped through, but replicated in, incestuous relationship in the organization.
Restraining Agent	Lack of an effective restraining agent (physical absence or illness of mother in case of father-daughter incest).	Lack of an effective restraining agent (absence of anyone with sufficient power to check supervisor as sexual aggressor).

AREA OF COMPARISON	INCEST DYNAMIC IN THE NUCLEAR FAMILY	INCEST DYNAMIC IN THE ORGANIZATIONAL FAMILY
Distortion of Sexual Culture	Violation of intimacy barriers.	Same
	Breakdown of sexual privacy and distance.	Same
	Consummation of incest last stage of this breakdown.	Same
Value System	Value system not sufficient to restrain sexual contact.	Same
	Where value system is present, there may be incestuous dynamic without consummation of incest.	Where value system is present, there may be professional and social closure without sexual closure.
Individuation	All aspects of incestuous dynamic violate the victim's need for individuation (having personal and sexual safety at home to begin the process of individuation; meeting needs and establishing identity separate from the family).	Adults may regress from the emotionally ingrown atmosphere of the closed organizational family, thus reversing their process of individuation; identity and self-esteem needs are all tied to the emotional life of the organization.
	Aggressor dominates life of the victim; causes emotional suffocation.	Same
Sequential Victimization	In father-daughter incest, sons may mimic the behavior of the father and also become sexually aggressive with the victim.	Sexual relationships in the closed organizational family rarely occur in isolation; the pattern usually involves multiple concurrent or sequential sexual relationships among organizational members.
Response of Nonparticipants	At first, denial— "conspiracy of silence."	Same
	Rage, shame, jealousy	Same
	Identification with aggressor or victim	Same
Extrusion	Incest increases the extrusion of individual family members from the family, e.g., runaway behavior.	Same
	A son who challenges the sexual supremacy of his father is extruded from the family.	Staff members who challenge the sexual supremacy of the supervisory/management staff are extruded from the organizational family.

The table on pages 100 and 101 notes just a few of the parallels between the incestuous dynamics in nuclear and organizational families that will be explored in this chapter. One comparison between incestuous dynamics in families and organizations is particularly important, and that is this: Sexual exploitation in both systems is the last stage in what has most often been a progressive violation of intimacy barriers. Whether we speak of incest in families or an incestuous dynamic in closed organizations, what is harmful is not just the sexual acts, which represent the invasive end of the intimacy continuum, but also the entire process of closure. Each progressive step in this incestuous dynamic can have powerfully debilitating effects on nuclear and organizational family members and the overall health of these systems regardless of whether sexual activity has occurred.

There are obvious differences between incest in nuclear families and the incestuous dynamic that can occur in the workplace. Most acts of incest in families involve a clear distinction between perpetrator and victim, the former often having power over the latter by virtue of size, age, maturity, and role-derived authority. Though, as we shall see shortly, many of these factors have parallels in the organizational family, problematic adult sexual relationships in the workplace can occur where no clear delineation of perpetrator and victim exists. Additionally, two co-workers can be involved in a sexual relationship—even one that generates significant problems for themselves and the organization—that does not warrant the designation "incestuous." Based on our understanding of incest as an event and a process, we will characterize sexual activity between organizational members as "incestuous" under two circumstances: (1) when the dynamics of the relationship mirror the dynamics of the incest relationship charted above and (2) when the relationship and its accompanying problems flow out of a sustained social isolation in which staff members come to expect that all of their needs will be met inside the organizational family.

7.5 Setting the Stage for Sexual Closure

When an organizational family has closed itself off professionally and socially, the eventual meeting of members' sexual needs inside the boundary of the organization is inevitable. But how can this happen? How can changes in the organization actually create conditions that will increase sexual activity among organizational members?

Most people use multiple roles to fulfill their personal needs. Our combined experiences in diverse roles reinforce our identity and allow us to address different needs in different settings with different people. We try to establish some boundaries between our roles to keep one or more of them from dominating our lives and restricting interactions through which we meet other important needs. Most people are able to meet a number of important needs in the workplace while maintaining a separate lifestyle through which many other needs are met. In short, there is a clear boundary between their work lives and their lives away from work.

One of the problems inherent in closed organizational systems is that they begin to progressively break down this boundary between our personal life and our work life. As noted earlier, the breakdown is often slow and subtle. Dramatic changes are often only noted when we look back over a number of years and perceive how work-dominated our life has become. Deterioration of boundaries can occur in the following manner. (The dynamics have been for the most part discussed earlier in other contexts, but they bear repeating here in the context of sexual closure.)

1. Excessive time and emotional demands in the closed organizational family reduce the number of roles workers participate in outside the work setting. As outside contacts are lost, identity and self-esteem are increasingly shaped by interactions in the work environment.
2. The spillover of distress from the closed system into our personal lives may place an unbearable strain on marital or other intimate relationships and lead to emotional escape back into the organizational family. Problems in outside relationships, by creating a high level of unmet needs, set the stage for the development of intimate relationships among organizational family members.
3. The loss of outside sources of replenishment leaves workers physically and emotionally depleted from the high-stress work environment. Given the conditions of low personal nourishment and high vulnerability, organizational family members may reach out to one another to meet needs that in the past were met outside the work environment.
4. The violation of intimacy barriers, produced by social closure of the organization, works to break down the emotional distance that usually distinguishes professional and personal relationships.

The above conditions set the stage. The reasons for the onset of sexual relationships among organizational family members can be summarized as follows: If the professional closure of the organizational family has restricted professional relationships to other workers in the organization, if social closure has resulted in nearly all social needs getting met with other workers, and if professional and social closure have slowly undermined the existence and quality of intimate relationships outside the work setting, then where else can one meet sexual needs if not in the organizational family? Meeting sexual needs inside a closed organizational family is a logical consequence of one of the premises of all closed systems: All needs must be met inside the system.

7.6 Sexual Dynamics and Professional Distress: The Metaphor of Impotence

The development of problematic sexual relationships among family members in closed organizational systems seems to occur as part of the syndrome of professional distress, and often occurs concurrently with other indicators of professional distress. The phenomenon should not be surprising if we revisit our examination of professional distress in the closed organizational family.

There are many parallels between the experience of professional distress in closed organizations and the experience of sexual impotence. The slow deterioration in outside sources of replenishment, and the increasing stressors and depletion of supports inside the closed organization, leaves one, above all else, feeling powerless. We may give in to passivity and helplessness or begin exaggerated attempts to reassert our potency in the work setting.

It is perhaps only natural that attempts to counter feelings of impotence in the workplace would include a demonstration of one's sexual potency. Why does this potency have to be demonstrated in relationships with other organizational family members? Because this is the precise arena in which we feel most impotent.

The metaphor of impotence may help us understand why during periods of excessive and prolonged stress we see an increase in sexual activity between organizational members, a preoccupation with titles, concern over comparative differences in salaries, conflict over the relative importance of different departments or professional disciplines, overt and covert struggles for power, and resentments over symbols of status such as office size and location. These all reflect attempts to counter feelings of powerlessness through exaggerated efforts to be recognized in the organizational family as valued, appreciated, and recognized on both a personal and professional level.

7.7 The Nonsexual Nature of Sex in the Closed System

We have looked at three separate points about sexuality and the experience of professional distress that on initial review seem blatantly contradictory. These points are as follows:

1. Two of the common symptoms of excessive and prolonged stress are a decrease in libido and varying levels of deterioration in the frequency and quality of one's sexual relationships.
2. The progressive closure of the organizational system results in the physical and emotional depletion of organizational family members.
3. In later stages of organizational closure, there will be an increase in the incidence of problematic sexual relationships between organizational family members.

There is an obvious question that if the experience of professional distress has such a devastating effect on people's libido, then why do we end up with an increase in sexual coupling? This apparent contradiction can be reconciled by pointing out that sexual relationships in closed systems have very little to do with libido. Sexual activity in closed systems has, in fact, very little to do with sex.

Below are some of the nonsexual functions sexual relations serve in the closed organizational family. Some of them are elaborated in more detail in the organizational case studies at the end of this chapter.

Sex as Power Dynamic. Sexual competition in some closed systems resembles primitive animal rituals in which the most dominant male gets sexual access to females. The human version of such rituals can be played by both sexes with an aggressiveness that justifies our continued placement in the animal kingdom. Sex in this scenario is more a demonstration of power and dominance over others than it is a function of affection or sexual release. In the closed system, the primary need being met through such manipulation may very well be the manager's need to have his or her power ritually affirmed through the submission of and homage paid by his or her subordinate. Sexual gratification may be secondary or inconsequential.

Sex as an Act of Violence. A case study at the end of this chapter describes the sexual relationship between an employee and his supervisor's wife during a time of conflict in both the supervisor's marital relationship and the supervisory relationship. Occurring in an incestuously closed organizational family, the sexual relationship was more an act of rage and violence toward the supervisor than an act of either affection or sexual gratification.

Sex as Risk Taking. Chapter 1 noted that increased risk-taking behavior can be a sign of professional distress. It was further noted that this behavior helped the victim create a transient escape from the emotional numbness produced by prolonged distress. High-risk sexual choices, the intrigue of arranging sexual meetings, the conspiracy to hide the relationship from other organizational family members, and the fear of being discovered all provide powerful emotional payoffs completely unrelated to the actual sexual relationship. In fact, it is not unusual that it is only through these other payoffs that the sexual relationship can be sustained.

Sex as Physical Nurturing. The loss of replenishment created in closed organizational family systems creates almost desperate needs for physical and emotional nurturing. The loss of outside relationships to provide such nurturing increases the probability that organizational family members will reach out to one another to meet those needs. In such cases, sexual gratification is of secondary importance to the need to be physically and emotionally touched.

Sex for Money and Position. When personal support in the closed system deteriorates to the point of intense competition for meager scraps of personal acknowledgment, sex may become a bargaining chip to get rewards of money, position, and recognition from organizational leaders. Sexual relationships simply become units of exchange for purchasing more important commodities in the organization. Such institutional prostitution is usually short-lived, as the arrangements can rarely be kept secret in the closed organizational family and are almost guaranteed to produce the eventual extrusion of participants from the system—usually as a direct result of the rage or envy of nonparticipants.

Sexual Partners as Co-Conspirators. Closed systems can create, sometimes quite quickly, very powerful relationship dyads. Two workers currently being scapegoat in the organizational family, for example, may quickly reach out to each other for support. They may almost enter a pact as co-conspirators planning defensive strategies and committed acts of organizational sabotage. Although the relationship may be sexual, it is completely work-dominated. One member of such a couple talked to me about this quality of the relationship in retrospect: "I remember the whole early period we were sleeping together. We would be having sex and all I could think about was 'If only _____ (supervisor)' could see us now." This sexual relationship emerged out of the process of the group, and it was literally as if they were having sex on a stage with other organizational members as the audience. The sexual relationship had little meaning apart from the organizational dynamics.

7.8 Internal Boundaries:
Predicting the Impact on the Organization

The impact of a sexual relationship between two organizational members can differ significantly depending on what roles the persons involved formally and informally perform in the organization.

One method of predicting this impact is to examine the internal boundaries within the organizational family. Figure 7-A graphically displays the key members of a small residential treatment center. This organization is four years old and has grown progressively closed professionally and socially over the past two years. The diagram shows three board members and a patron that have contributed to the program's professional isolation and who socialize extensively with other organizational members. The diagram further shows three management staff members (a director and two supervisors), twelve line staff members consisting of two three-person teams of counselors, one three-person team of house managers, two cooks, and a clerical position. The diagram also includes both current and former program clients. (We will discuss worker-client sexual relationships later in this chapter.) Interns, consultants, and ex-staff members also hold positions in the outer ring of the organizational family because of their involvement in the professional and social closure, but with a reduced degree of time and emotional involvement. Spouses are included because they have become a very visible part of this organizational family due to extensive staff socializing during the past two years.

Figure 7-A shows a number of levels that reflect formal power in the organization. These levels are separated by internal boundary lines that

demarcate units and roles. The double boundary lines that separate
clients reflect the special status of clients and the strength of the taboo
against worker-client sexual contact.

In general, we can say that the greater the number of boundary lines
crossed by those sexually involved, the greater the potential repercussions in the organizational family. We could speculate that the act producing the least reactions in the organization would be a sexual
relationship between two members at the same level whose daily role
functions are only minimally related. A sexual relationship between a

Figure 7-A
The Organizational Family: Internal Boundaries

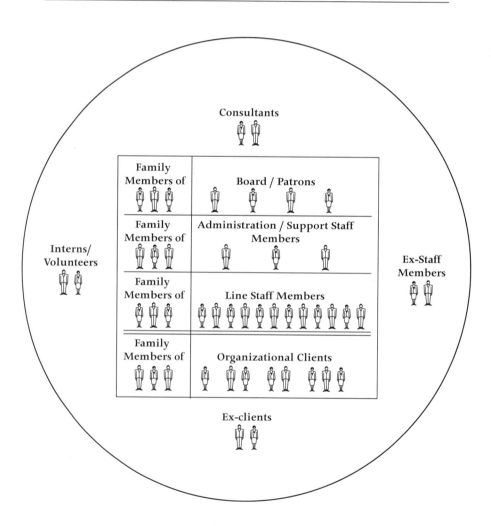

counselor and the secretary would have less repercussion than a relationship between two counselors working on the same team. According to our diagram, the sexual relationship having the most system repercussions would be between a board member, a manager, or spouse of one of the staff and a client.

Transactions across these internal boundaries reflect relationships between persons of greater power and persons with less power. The violation of internal boundaries tends to spark powerful feelings that alter the working of the group and alter the sexual culture of the organization. This is particularly true when managers or supervisors are involved in such relationships.

Another way to examine the potential repercussions of sexual relationships within the organization is to examine dynamically how family roles are replicated in the organizational system. This approach examines which people, by their personality and function in the system, most closely parallel the family roles of mother, father, uncle, child, and so on. A review of the incest taboo within families further illustrates this approach. There appears to be a continuum of the strength of the incest taboo. The taboo against mother/son incest is the most powerful, occurring mostly in situations where both mother and son are psychotic. The taboo against brother-sister and interfamilial (cousins) incest is the least powerful, with father/daughter incest falling in between (Lidz 1965, Lusting 1966, Frances 1976).

Much of this same continuum can be observed in organizations. For example, in the organization diagrammed in figure 7-A, there were several sexual relationships between organizational family members over a period of years. A relationship between two counselors eventually created some serious problems in their ability to work as clinical team members. The director's relationship with the secretary ended painfully in the secretary's resignation and a deterioration of the director's ability to supervise other staff members (who felt the director had used his position in the organization to sexually exploit the secretary). There was another relationship, however, that created the greatest emotional upheaval in the organizational family. The head cook in the agency was the ultimate earth mother. She was older than most of the other staff members and was extremely nurturing, often feeding, hugging, teasing, and chastising staffers to take better care of themselves. In the fourth year of the program's existence, the cook became sexually involved with a counselor who was almost twenty years her junior. According to our initial interpretation of the family diagram, the relationship should not have created a profound impact on the organization because both staff members operated on the same level and performed different functions. Such was not the case. The knowledge of this relationship horrified and almost emotionally paralyzed the organizational family. Organizational family members could not deal with the personal and sexual needs of the woman who was dynamically the family's mother. Both the cook and the counselor were scapegoated and eventually extruded from the organizational family. The episode marked one of the most disruptive and emotionally wrenching experiences in the organization's history.

7.9 Cultural Taboos and Sexual Dynamics

There are issues other than the participants' degrees of power and the participants' family functions that can influence the response to a sexual relationship in the organizational family. Staff members entering the organizational family bring with them personal and/or cultural attitudes that dictate the types of sexual intimacies that are considered acceptable or taboo. Taken collectively, these cultural taboos can have a profound impact on how organizational family members respond to a sexual relationship in the organization.

Where a wide age discrepancy exists, cultural values may add a further weight of condemnation, or at least ambivalence, about the relationship. Such can also be the case when the sexual partners are of different racial or ethnic backgrounds. Ageism and racism can intensify and exaggerate the organizational family's response to an incestuous relationship and may contribute to the extrusion of those involved from the organization.

Cultural taboos may also create a much more primitive emotional response if the relationship of concern is homosexual rather than heterosexual. Having listened carefully to the gossip and rumor mills triggered by the knowledge of such a relationship, it is clear to me that homosexuality can trigger a broad spectrum of feelings ranging from confused acceptance, to moral or religious condemnation, to aggressive homophobic outrage.

We have assumed in the above example that the sexual values of the culture at large and those of the organizational culture are the same. There are cases in which those values are incongruent. I am aware, for example, of a service organization in which all of the power positions were held by lesbians. Lesbianism was a very strong, if unstated, component of the sexual culture in the organizational family. The sexual relationship that proved the most disruptive to this organization was not any of the lesbian relationships, but the breakup of a lesbian relationship sparked by a heterosexual affair between one of the women and a male volunteer of the agency.

7.10 The Contagious Quality of Sexual Closure

Once the sexual intimacy barrier is violated in the closed organizational family, there seems to be an escalation in the meeting of sexual needs within the organizational boundary. The progressive closure of the organizational family often produces a contagion of concurrent and sequential sexual alliances.

The frequent socializing among organizational members sometimes requires only the inhibitions-reducing influence of alcohol (and other assorted psychoactive drugs) to dissolve the barrier between social and sexual intimacy. The early clandestine violation of this barrier may be followed by the more open, if not blatant, use of the organizational family to meet sexual needs. Such a transition marks a significant change in the sexual culture of the organization and produces increased permission (and sometimes pressure) for sexual intimacy in the organizational family.

7.11 Gossip and Rumor: Information as Power

The social and sexual closure of an organizational family displaces direct communication with gossip and rumor. The increase in gossip and rumor often happens concurrently with the division of the organizational family into the rapidly shifting dyads and triads described in the last chapter. As conflict in the organization increases and ever more work-related decisions are being made based on social and sexual intimacies, information about who's doing what to whom becomes an important source of power and self-protection in the organization. Social and sexual closure and the communication patterns that accompany them can rapidly turn a professional organization into a soap opera.

7.12 The Incestuous Relationship: Impact on Participants

The development of incestuous relationships in the organizational family can have profound repercussions on the system as a whole and on those participating in the relationships. Incestuous relationships in the closed organizational family undermine the personal and professional identities of those sexually involved, lead to the termination of outside marital and intimate relationships, and lead to the extrusion of members from the organization. The closed organizational family dramatically increases the personal and professional vulnerability of the participants of such intimate relationships.

When two members of a closed organizational family become a sexual dyad, it is not uncommon for one or both members to lose much personal and professional identity. The individuals become a couple. Decisions about their roles in the organization are no longer made independently. While the partners may seek to manipulate the work environment via work schedules and assignments to sustain their relationship, organizational leaders making decisions about one of the partners are forced to consider the impact on, and response from, the other partner. In my earlier studies, it was clear that women in these relationships suffered the greatest loss of identity. Many women who were interviewed noted that once they became sexually involved with an organizational member, other organizational members began to discount their professional knowledge and skills. Some women even felt they had been denied advancements because organizational leaders were uncomfortable promoting the women to positions in their organizations that were higher than their sexual partners.

We discussed earlier how professional and social closure decrease the time and emotional energy organizational members have available to sustain outside marital or intimate relationships. We have also noted that there are forces in the closed organizational family that will support members terminating outside marital or intimate relationships, particularly when the outside partner has remained aloof and unsupportive of the organization. Given such influences, married organizational family members who develop sexual relationships in the organizational family are at high risk of sacrificing their marriages. The incestuous relationship in the organization further drains the energy going into the marriage and may spark the final rupture of that relationship. The breakup of a marriage in the closed organizational family is rarely an isolated event. Extreme stages of organizational closure may instigate an epidemic of marriage and relationship casualties.

I remember with great poignancy the interviews conducted with couples whose marriages had failed during that process. At the time they split up, most of the couples felt there were deep, irreconcilable problems in their relationships. When interviewed some years later, many were still grieving the loss of their relationships. They had come to some awareness that much of the pain and conflict in their marriages were not caused by the basic relationship, but by the outside changes in their lives over which they had little control. Organizational family members looked back with bitterness as they realized that the loss of their marriages was only one part of the emotional turmoil produced by their tenure in a closed organization.

Sexual relationships in a closed organizational family increase the participant's risk of extrusion from the organization. Again, women who are involved in intimate relationships with co-workers are more likely to be extruded from an organization than are their male counterparts.

7.13 The Married Couple in the Closed System

There may be unique problems for the married couple in the closed organization. We noted earlier how people in the extended organizational family are eventually drawn into the core membership of the organization through professional and social closure. So, the married couple who both work in a closed system is not a rare phenomenon. Having observed couples in such systems for several decades, I would offer the following observations.

If the marriage occurred during the time the couple worked together in the closed system, one or both partners leaving the organization may provoke a crisis in the marriage. It's as if the marriage grew out of the process of the closed group and needs the closed-system group dynamic for continued sustenance.

The closer the functional relationships between the couple in the organizational structure, the greater the strain on the marriage. Power relationships may be particularly problematic as work issues spill over into the personal relationship, and personal issues get played out in the dynamics of work roles.

A major strain on marriages in a closed system is the inability of the couple to get "out of role" and maintain a separate life away from the work setting. The loss of nonwork replenishment in the marriage and in social relationships may result in increased conflict, emotional distancing in the relationship, and the eventual dissolution of the relationship.

7.14 A Redefinition of Sexual Harassment

I have had a number of people ask me during training workshops whether sexual harassment occurs during the sexual closure stage in the organizational family. The question is an interesting one and can be addressed by comparing the following two situations.

Mary was an administrative assistant to a supervisor of a large agency. She had worked for the agency for five years and had been quite happy with the position. Her contentment changed with the arrival of a new supervisor. About three months after the new supervisor arrived, Mary became uncomfortable with the supervisor's increasing comments on her physical appearance, questions about her personal life, and what came to be an almost incessant banter of sexual innuendo. Mary's attempts to communicate her discomfort with this situation had little impact. In the months that followed, the supervisor became very "touchy," increased his disclosure of problems with his wife (which generally centered on her sexual coldness), and began scheduling "working" lunches that Mary was required to attend. During the sixth month after his arrival, the supervisor's sexual advances became blatantly invasive. Mary's verbal attempts to rebuff the advances only resulted in the supervisor's implied rewards of money and promotion in return for sexual favors. When formal complaints produced no resolution of the problem, Mary resigned from her job rather than go through what she anticipated would be a long and emotionally humiliating process of administrative and legal redress.

The evidence that Mary had been subjected to sexual harassment is overwhelming. The sexual advances were unwanted. The advances continued in spite of Mary's request that such behavior cease. There were promises and threats used in an effort to coerce Mary's sexual compliance. Such blatant sexual harassment could occur in open and closed organizations, but there is another more subtle form of sexual harassment often seen in closed systems. Let's compare Mary's circumstances with those of another woman with the same role in a different organization.

Faye took a position as secretary in a community mental health center against the advice of her husband, who couldn't figure out why she would want to work around "crazy" people. Within three years, Faye's intelligence and organizational skills had got her promoted to administrative assistant to the agency director. During those three years, she'd found a whole new world of experience compared with her very sheltered upbringing and married life. Her work also changed her social life, as staff members socialized frequently away from work, which created problems at home because her husband couldn't handle what he viewed as the "weirdness" of most of Faye's co-workers. They reciprocated by applying a diverse range of diagnostic labels on Faye's husband. During Faye's fourth year of employment, the professional, social, and sexual closure of the organization intensified. Faye was given an opportunity to participate in staff growth groups that demanded a high level of emotional self-disclosure. As Faye got caught up in this process, the director and others commented on her natural counseling aptitude. It wasn't long before Faye was enrolled in college to prepare herself for a future career change. It was an exhilarating time for Faye, but also a time of conflict as her husband was coldly unsympathetic to her enrollment in school and her future plans. She increasingly sought support from the director as conflict in her marriage increased. The director became her trusted mentor, constantly providing encouragement and acknowledgment of her personal and professional value. Over the next year, Faye's escalating work and school activities caused increasing conflict at home—conflict further complicated by her progressive physical and emotional exhaustion. Partially through the counsel of the director, Faye separated from her husband and got an apartment of her own. Faye had heard, but didn't believe, that the director had been sexually involved with one of the counselors at the agency. The director had never made any sexual advances toward Faye, although there had been times that she wished he would. A month after her separation, she and the director began their sexual relationship—an act in which she was totally willing to participate. She was in love, a condition unchanged by her awareness of the director's wife and family. The relationship between the director and Faye continued and became common knowledge at the agency. Other staff members cooled their relationships with Faye, and she found herself increasingly isolated and dependent on the director. After four months, the director informed Faye in rather painful terms that he could no longer handle her demands for time, that she put too much stock in the relationship, and that it was over. Emotionally crushed, Faye never returned to the agency.

The only major details omitted from the vignette are that the director had been sexually involved with a number of staff members, and that other staffers had been involved in intimate relationships with one another. The use of sexual intimacy as a means of garnering emotional support had become increasingly prevalent in the organization.

In Mary's case, there was a clear aggressor and a clear victim. The sexual advances were clearly unwanted—a key issue in the traditional definition of sexual harassment. But what about Faye's case? The roles of aggressor and victim are less clearly defined. There were no "unwanted" sexual advances. The seduction process was slow and subtle compared with Mary's case, where the sexual advances were blatant and constant. Can Faye's case be considered a type of sexual harassment, or do we simply say that Faye was a victim of her own adult choices?

My contention is that a definition and understanding of sexual harassment in closed systems must include the phrase "manipulation of vulnerability." A supervisor, or other person with significant organizational power, can isolate staff members professionally and socially, overextend them in ways that deplete their physical and emotional energy, use his or her influence to undermine staffers' outside intimate relationships, and foster dependency by nurturing staff members who experience conflict in their outside relationships. If the supervisor then manipulates the vulnerability and dependency of a staff member to meet his or her own sexual needs, then the supervisor has committed a type of sexual harassment every bit as demeaning as the more blatant behaviors we associate with this term. Perhaps nowhere can this principle be better illustrated than in the sexual harassment scandals that have hit the U.S. military training bases in recent years. New military recruits are so vulnerable during their period of basic training, and the power of the drill sergeants so inviolate, that the very idea of "consensual sexual activity" loses its meaning in such a context. Closed systems in which power differentials are extreme are highly prone to abuses of power that include emotional manipulation and sexual coercion.

7.15 Worker-Client Sexual Relationships: Professional Ethics and Personal Needs

Periodically, there are headlines about a sexual relationship between a doctor and a patient, a counselor and a client, a teacher and a student, or a pastor and a parishioner. As citizens, and sometimes as professional peers, we respond with moral outrage and demand some level of retribution for the guilty party. We sit back believing such an act is reprehensible, and that only an emotionally sick or morally degenerate person could so exploit a helping relationship. While such moral outrage is understandable, it offers little insight into how such relationships can occur. The belief that sexual exploitation in helping relationships is committed only by unconscionable psychopaths, while providing a momentary fix of self-righteousness, does not explain the cases of such exploitation by people who have no such enduring character flaws. It is discomforting to discover that many professionals who have been involved in sexual relationships with clients also believed that such an act was ethically reprehensible and unthinkable right up until the time they found themselves in just such a relationship.

A doctor spends extended time talking with an attractive patient only to run the next series of uncomely patients through the office with assembly-line speed. A private therapist fails to terminate the wealthy client for another month because his or her patient load is down and the therapist needs the money. A socially inept counselor turns client relationships into friendships. A teacher devotes special attention to those students who worship his or her intelligence or charisma. A priest uses the confessional for his own titillation. In each case, the individual has manipulated the helping relationship to meet his or her own needs, and yet, each would be blind to the thin line that separates such behavior from overt sexual behavior between them and those they are pledged to serve.

In the framework of chapter 2, such behavior can be defined in terms of psychopathology or defects in moral character. While there may be some cases where those models are applicable, a significant number of people who become sexually involved with their clients are suffering neither from serious psychopathology nor from an underdeveloped superego. There are many factors, contextual as well as personal, that can contribute to such exploitation. For example, the same closure process that creates sexual relationships between organizational family members can also increase the probability and incidence of worker-client sexual relationships.

The exploitation of a helping relationship usually results from the conflict between professional ethics and personal needs. Inadvertent exploitation may spring from lack of clear ethical standards, but overt exploitation is more likely to occur when human needs block the application of standards. For example:

- I may have a strong ethical belief in marital fidelity and practice that ethic as long as my needs are met in that relationship. The longer needs go unmet in that relationship, however, the greater will be the difficulty in maintaining consistency between my ethical beliefs and my behavior.
- I may have a strong prohibition against stealing until my physical hunger and lack of money take precedence over my beliefs.

- The strength of the ethical prohibition against sexual relationships with clients is in direct proportion to one's ability to consistently meet sexual needs (directly or indirectly) outside of the professional helping relationship.

Participation in closed organizational families creates a broad spectrum of unmet needs and increases the incidence of exploitation of the helper-client relationship. If a program is closed professionally and socially (meaning the loss of professional and social relationships other than co-workers), a very narrow arena has been created in which all of the personal needs of staff members are to be met. Given that clients make up one part of the system in closed organizational families, they can quickly become targets through which staff members can fulfill their needs.

If there is a systems perspective, or recipe for worker-client sexual contact, it would include many of the following ingredients:

- Professional and social closure of the organization
- A physically and emotionally exhausted staff member
- An organizational structure that does not have built-in sources of replenishment to counter the high stress inherent in the helping process
- A work schedule leaving little time or emotional energy to sustain outside relationships
- A staff member's marriage or intimate relationship casualty
- A sexually permissive organizational culture
- A supervisory structure and process that exclude a review of sexuality in worker-client relationships (the lack of an effective restraining agent)
- A loose structure and boundary on worker-client relationships
- The lack of a clear and visible code of professional practice governing worker-client relationships
- The failure of the supervisory process to confront stages of overinvolvement that often precede worker-client sexual relationships
- The lack of resources to provide male-female co-therapists to work with high-risk clients

If service agencies are concerned about the sexual exploitation of clients by professional helpers, then we need to balance our talk of psychopathology and moral outrage with action to shape organizational systems that allow staff members to nurture and replenish themselves. We also need to provide supervisory mechanisms to inhibit the violation of intimacy barriers in worker-client relationships.

7.16 Organizational Case Histories

This chapter will close with a review of a number of case histories drawn from my studies and consultation experiences. Each case situation will be described briefly and then followed by an analysis utilizing the observations set forth earlier in this chapter. The cases are composites in which all names and identifying details have been modified. The seeming familiarity of any of the situations is a testament to the frequency with which they occur.

Counselor-Counselor Relationship. Jim and Rita had worked together for over a year in a residential child care center. Both were married, but, in each case, the marriage was in a very vulnerable position. Jim and his wife were experiencing stressful growing pains in their relationship, and Rita and her husband had just moved back together to attempt a reconciliation. Since it was early in their careers, Jim and Rita were attracted to the idealism and passionate intensity of the center's closed organizational family. The intimacy and self-closure they experienced working as co-therapists made a sexual relationship seem natural and almost inevitable to them. The sexual relationship lasted for about nine months. Toward the end of that time, serious problems occurred in the relationship that detracted from their effectiveness as co-therapists and their ability to work comfortably in their broader team assignments. When the relationship ended bitterly, Rita chose to leave the organization when working in the same facility with Jim became too painful.

ANALYSIS. The relationship followed a prolonged occurrence of professional and social closure in the organizational family. The closing of the social network coincided with sexual and interpersonal problems in the marriages of both counselors. The excessive time and emotional demands in the closed organizational family further undermined the stability of Jim's and Rita's respective marriages. The extramarital relationship allowed them to escape from, and yet play out in the work setting, issues they faced in their marriages. Jim and Rita's relationship became, in essence, a pseudo-marital relationship until its sudden termination. The staff response to their breakup was quite ambivalent, as a good deal of matchmaking had gone on to get the counselors together, in spite of the fact that both were married (subsequently divorced through the process). Although a good deal of staff time had been taken up by gossiping and judging, the strongest repercussion appeared to be staff guilt. While working for an agency dedicated to strengthening families, they somehow found themselves in a process by which one group member was painfully extruded and two marriages suddenly dissolved. The counselor who left became a "ghost" who haunted the group for some time to come. The feelings of the group were summed up by one member, who said, "We helped destroy two marriages for our own damned titillation and entertainment."

If we wish to test our incest analogy, we can compare the particulars in the example with Dr. S. Kirson Weinberg's classic description of incestuous family relationships.

A. The incest usually occurs in emotionally ingrown families.
B. Incest often coincides with difficulties in the marital relationship.
C. The incestuous relationship may take the form of a pseudo-marital relationship.
D. Nonparticipants may experience guilt as if they have promoted or failed to prevent the occurrence of incest.

Supervisor-Supervisee Relationship. Our next case involves a sexual relationship between Barbara, a counselor at a family counseling agency and her boss, Rex, the agency director. It was Barbara's first professional position following completion of social work training. The relationship began on a guru-follower basis, a stage not uncharacteristic of the early stages of supervisory relationships. When sex was added to the relationship and it became known to the staff, a number of complex dynamics began to occur. Supervision of other staff members deteriorated as the staff began to question the ethics and motives of the supervisor. Most believed that Rex had exploited the nature of the supervisory relationship. Barbara became extremely depressed when Rex withdrew his attention from her, and while distraught she threatened to expose him to his wife if the relationship did not continue. The blackmail went on for a short time, and then Barbara chose to leave the organization "for personal reasons." Although the supervisor continued in his position, much of his previous status and esteem within the group had deteriorated.

ANALYSIS. The relationship was what in incest literature would be called a "lust attachment." The isolation of program staff members from outside training and consultation made it easy for the supervisor to act out his acute case of "prima donna–hood" and sexually exploit the supervisory relationship. The supervisor's own professional and social isolation probably contributed to the breakdown of the usual professional ethics that would have precluded such a relationship. The deterioration of respect for the supervisor, and the daily soap-opera atmosphere that dominated the agency for weeks, all but destroyed the provision of services by the team.

In both cases reviewed, there is clear confirmation of how the incest dynamic increases the risk of members being extruded from the organization—particularly women partners in sexual relationships.

Supervisor-Supervisee, Nonconsummated Incest. Peg was a middle-aged counselor who had been traditionally trained and had worked in a highly structured work situation until she took a job with a youth program. The majority of her new employer's staff members were in their twenties, were sexually active with a number of partners, and expressed vocally their feelings about the limitations of traditional marriage. Peg's supervisor, Dennis, was a very attractive young man who had sexual involvements of varying intensity with a number of young women on the staff, and responded in an equally seductive manner to Peg. A number of staff members joked about how long it would take before Dennis would get Peg into bed, and it became something of an unstated goal of the group to "convert" the new counselor. Peg, confronted by new ideas, a lack of "professional" structure, the seductive behavior of her supervisor, and her own response to that seductiveness became conflicted over her values, her marriage, and her work. When the anxiety became too great, she turned in her immediate resignation and left quite distraught.

ANALYSIS. Though rather extreme, the example illustrates that the incestuous dynamic may produce extrusion of staff even when no sexual act occurs. Here we have a homogenous group that had become increasingly closed professionally, socially, and sexually. Again, there was no effective restraining agent (in fact, quite the opposite), and we see the organization's values were so distorted that it could turn the seduction of a new counselor into an entertaining game.

It is not uncommon to find an incestuous dynamic occurring in the families of runaway girls. In such a situation, running away may be a very healthy mechanism on the part of the adolescent girl to protect herself from what is vaguely experienced as a fear of impending involvement with a father, step-father, or perhaps, a mother's live-in paramour. In the above case example, the organizational family produced a middle-aged runaway through the same kind of incestuous dynamic.

Counselor-Supervisor's Wife, Incestuous Dynamics and the Extended Family. Our next case occurred in an organizational family in which the social and professional relationships were indistinguishable. For nearly two years, staff members (and their spouses) had extensively socialized with one another. The development of a sexual relationship between Larry, a counselor, and Jan, the wife of his supervisor, David, coincided with difficulties in David and Jan's marriage and intense conflict between David and Larry. Both Larry and Jan later admitted their sexual relationship was more an act of violence against David than it was a mutual attraction for either of them. The staff knew of the relationship long before David did, and a large amount of time was consumed by staff members in gossip and rumor. The staff was divided into dyads and triads to secretly share the latest event in this ongoing soap opera. When David discovered the relationship, he went to the board and demanded that the counselor be fired ("It's him or me!"). As might be guessed, the counselor was discharged. David filed for divorce and subsequently left the job and the community. His sense of humiliation and his anger toward co-workers who had known about the relationship but had not informed him made it next to impossible for him to stay at the agency. That the program was left in shambles for months should be evident.

ANALYSIS. The case illustrates and emphasizes a number of points we discussed earlier in this chapter.

   A. Again, the incestuous sexual relationship was preceded by closure in the social relationships of the organizational family.
   B. Sexual relationships may develop out of the organizational process as an act of anger at one or more members rather than as sexual attraction.
   C. Rumor and gossip play important roles in the closed organizational family.

D. Social and sexual closure inevitably breaks the organizational family into numerous cliques, dyads, and triads and results in what Gregory Bateson has called "the infinite dance of shifting coalitions" (Bateson 1967).

E. Sexual dynamics can rapidly get turned into power dynamics and result in the sudden extrusion of staff members.

What was not included in the above case study, but easily could have been, was the potential for violence. As an organization's intimate relationships become more intertwined, the potential for emotional destabilization of the whole system and individual acts of violence increases.

Switching Partners: The Saga of Synanon. The history of Synanon is not confidential. It has periodically made newspaper and magazine headlines since its founding by Charles Dederich in 1958 as a therapeutic community for the treatment of drug addiction. As Synanon's organizational family began to close, it evolved from a drug-abuse treatment agency to a closed alternative community to a religious cult. Nineteen years after founding Synanon, Dederich—the recovering alcoholic who was hailed for pioneering a new approach for treating addicts—was arrested in a state of extreme intoxication and charged with conspiracy to commit murder and solicitation of murder. Investigative reporting and court-seized tape recordings penetrated Synanon's closed system and revealed many of the company's internal practices and changes. Anyone interested in closed systems should study the literature on Synanon (Yablonsky 1965; Mitchell, Mitchell, and Ofshe 1980).

The focus here will be on the period in Synanon history from 1975 through 1977. As Synanon moved closer to the status of a cult, Dederich introduced a series of conformity and loyalty tests that drove out all but the most committed Synanon members. The tests included requirements that all members shave their heads and undergo vasectomies or abortions. In late 1977, all of the couples living together in the Synanon community were ordered to "change partners."

ANALYSIS. The Synanon story shows how the sexual culture in a closed organization can become distorted and create a wide breach between societal and organizational values. What is amazing in this story is not Dederich's demand that members change partners, but that over seven hundred Synanon members complied with his request. Isolated from the outside world, closed organizational systems have indescribable power to shape the values and behavior of organizational members. The greater the degree of closure and isolation, the greater is that power.

Counselor-Client Sexual Relationship. The following three case studies illustrate the way in which the professional, social, and sexual closure of health and human services agencies can corrupt the relationships between professional helpers and their clients.

Don, a counselor (and recovering alcoholic) who had been hired as the first paraprofessional at a community mental health agency, was discovered to be sexually involved with a female client. Within forty-eight hours of the discovery, Don was fired and left the community. Knowledge of the event leaked into the community and affected the agency's reputation for a number of years, as the client involved was a minor. The organizational process in this case is illustrative and not unlike one seen in family systems with acting-out adolescents. Don was immediately identified as the organization's problem (the identified patient), defined as pathological (we're okay, he's not okay), and extruded. All conversations among organizational group members focused on Don's character. Staff morale suffered severely not only because of the community's suspicion of the agency, but also because each staff member had some vague feeling of responsibility for the matter.

ANALYSIS. What was left out of the above description was that Don had been working for months without any supervision in spite of his minimal training, and had risen to the status of mythical folk hero among his clients and co-workers. No other staff exerted any effort to "keep his feet on the ground." Don's meetings with clients alone at their homes at night was known and approved by the agency. All organizational members were aware that Don had no outside-of-work outlets to meet social and sexual needs. Other staff members were receiving vicarious pleasure from Don's "hero" status, unorthodox methods, and his seemingly inextinguishable energy.

The vague feelings of guilt and responsibility experienced by the agency staff are remarkably similar to Nathan Ackerman's description of a similar process in the family system. Ackerman noted that, when a family member is made a scapegoat and becomes dysfunctional, other family members experience a contagion of guilt and a fear that, in retribution, they will experience the same fate (Ackerman 1966).

Again we see the consequence of an organization having no effective restraining agent to prevent the incestuous relationship.

Key Board Member–Client Relationship. The sexual relationship in our next example grew out of the chance meeting of a counseling agency board member and a client at the agency. Knowledge of the relationship among the staff produced feelings of anger and lowered morale, as it seemed the mission of the agency had been tainted. As the counselor who was seeing the client began pointing out the destructiveness of the relationship to the client, word began to filter down to the agency staff that the board member involved was suggesting that a staff cut might be necessary due to recent financial setbacks, and that he felt the counselor treating the client he was seeing was the one who should be cut. When the counselor's supervisor became aware of the complexities, she directed the counselor to transfer the case to another agency, and she took the information to the director and recommended that the board member be confronted. The confrontation did not occur, and the supervisor chose to leave the organization shortly after the episode.

Staff morale suffered severely because of the ethical issues they felt were violated, the organization's failure to confront openly what had happened, and the loss of a very competent supervisor.

ANALYSIS. The relationship occurred in an organizational family that had been closed socially for roughly a year and a half and was already seeing the development of sexual relationships among some members and extended family members (board members, spouses). Although many staff members were morally outraged at the behavior of the board member and the administrator's failure to confront the issue, none saw that the board member's behavior was merely an extension of a process nearly all of the staff members had participated in for some time.

The treatment of the counselor by the board member is reminiscent of Weinberg's observation that sons who challenge the sexual supremacy of their fathers (in incestuous families) are treated harshly and may be extruded. Staff members who confront the incestuous behavior of administrative or supervisory staff members in closed organizational families are often treated similarly.

High Priest–Client Relationship. Many of the people interviewed as part of the research for this book remarked that the severest organizational disruptions occurred when an organizational leader became sexually involved with a client, or in some cases, a series of clients. A number of the reviewers of my early papers on incestuous organizations also noted the importance of this phenomenon. One reviewer commented:

> It is very different from the examples of counselor/client sex you discuss in that dissonance noted is far greater. . . . In one instance, the person at fault was the director of the clinic, and the clinic was even named for him. Staff, who had guessed he was sexually involved with clients, and board members who knew of this, found themselves unable to really confront the situation.

The occurrence of sexual relationships between an organization's director and its clients often follows a prolonged period of professional and social closure of the staff group, and occurs at a time when a number of group members are already experiencing professional distress. The prolonged isolation of the director from professional peer feedback and accountability contributes to the development of such relationships.

7.17 Sexual Closure: A Summary

In summary:

1. There are significant differences between the impact of sexual relationships in open organizational systems and the impact of those in closed systems.
2. When an organization has become closed professionally and socially, the meeting of members' sexual needs inside the organization is inevitable.
3. A sexual relationship between two organizational members can be seen as not merely the isolated behavior of two individuals, but an act that flows out of the process of an organization.
4. A sexual relationship between members of a closed organizational family may have very little to do with sex, but may be a means of acting out other feelings and needs.
5. The greater the degree of organizational closure, the greater the impact of sexual relationships on an organization.
6. The closer that sexually involved members are to the perceived source of power in an organization, the greater the repercussions in the group.
7. Sexual dynamics in closed systems parallel the dynamics surrounding consummated incest in nuclear families.

8. Though often flowing from the group process itself, sexual relationships among group members alter the group process and increase the likelihood of disruptive interpersonal relationships.
9. When members of an organizational group become sexually involved, the rate of extrusion of those involved increases dramatically (particularly for the women involved). Sexual dynamics can rapidly become power dynamics and result in the sudden extrusion of staff members.
10. Sexual relationships among organizational members increase the casualty rate of marital and other intimate relationships and contribute to the further closure of organizational families.
11. Sexual closure severely affects on organization's mission by breaking the staff team into cliques and by displacing direct communication with rumor and gossip.
12. Problematic sexual relationships among organizational family members can emerge out of professional distress in closed systems and are usually concurrent with other signs of professional distress.

8

Why Closure?

The last three chapters described the professional, social, and sexual closure of the organizational family and the consequences of such closure for individual workers and the organization as a whole. Before addressing how we can prevent or manage the more destructive aspects of this organizational dynamic, it might be helpful to examine why such closure occurs.

In the past twenty years, I have spent considerable energy pondering this issue. Questions such as the following continually surfaced as I reviewed my work:

- Are there predictable periods of closure in the life of an organization?
- Are there organizations or professions that are particularly vulnerable to closure?
- What environmental factors work to instigate or enhance closure?
- Are there characteristics of organizational leaders or organizational members that tend to promote closure?

This chapter will set forth some tentative answers to these questions.

8.1 When Closure Is Necessary

Throughout most of this study, I've described closure as a negative process. In fact, there are times when closure is essential to the health and survival of an organization. Closure, in general, produces reduced transactions across the organizational family boundary, increased bonding and intimacy among organizational family members, and an affirmation of and commitment to organizational goals and values.

A period of closure may be essential to creating a new organization or program, successfully accomplishing a reorganization, or facing an internally or externally produced crisis. Closure is an appropriate short-term means of maximizing internal organizational resources. Closure is essential to launching internal change or defending the organization and its members from external threats. The passion and cohesiveness characterizing the early days of new organizations or social movements is indicative of very functional closure. New organizational leaders may need a period of closure to redefine the organizational family and its values. A company facing radical changes in technology may need a period of closure to plot its response to new developments. A company in a life-threatening fiscal crisis may need a period of closure that transcends the historical split between management and labor. A hospital facing a three-year accreditation site visit may need a period of closure to prepare itself for this critically important event. An organization buffeted by rapid and overwhelming change may need a period of closure for the health of both the organization and its family members. An organization being investigated by a regulatory agency may need a period of closure both for defensive purposes and for a period of self-assessment.

All of the above situations may represent appropriate movements toward organizational closure. Problems occur when closure continues beyond the point of crisis or beyond the time that closure is needed. Many organizations begin the closure process appropriately, but later are unable to reverse the process. Most are unaware that the process that saved the organization can also destroy it if it is continued indefinitely. This principle will be crucial in a later chapter when we begin to define the role of organizational leaders as boundary managers who move the organization back and forth along the closed-to-open continuum in response to changing internal and external needs.

So our first answer to "Why closure?" is that organizations move toward closure because it is a healthy and essential response to a developmental crisis. It is not closure itself that breeds injury, but enduring and irreversible closure.

8.2 Geographical Isolation

Geographical isolation can contribute to incestuous dynamics in organizational systems in the same way geographical isolation can contribute to incestuous dynamics in family systems. Isolation severely limits the boundary transactions (movement of people and ideas in and out of the organization) necessary for a relatively open system. Some organizations, such as prisons, psychiatric hospitals, or military schools, are designed for closure, with both physical and procedural barriers that limit boundary transactions. Organizations, from those in remote rural areas to those in impoverished inner-city areas, may face major geographical, cultural, racial, and language barriers that shape and sustain their closure and isolation.

8.3 The Personality Needs of Organizational Leaders

There are organizational leaders who inevitably create closed, incestuous organizations wherever they go. This often reflects a blending of their personality needs and leadership styles.

Such leaders isolate their organizations out of their own feelings of insecurity and needs for power and control. Their ego needs are fulfilled in the role of charismatic leader surrounded by followers who seek to lose themselves in a holy cause. Many of these leaders have histories of successful organizational leadership in situations where external checks and balances existed to keep the leader's personality needs under control. Lacking such checks and balances, the most destructive aspects of these leaders' personalities are magnified in closed organizational systems.

Leaders with paranoid personalities will inevitably create closed systems with radical beliefs that fuel fights against real or imagined enemies. In the paramilitary organizations of the right and left, in religious sects, and in the single-issue political action groups of the late twentieth century, one can see closed organizational systems that reflect the personality needs of charismatic leaders.

When the distorted personality needs of leaders and followers intersect in a closed organizational system, individual pathology can become organized into social or political pathology through such extreme acts as terrorism or mass suicide or, more typically, breaches in ethical business practices.

8.4 The Personality Needs of Organizational Members

Is it possible that certain types of people are attracted to work in closed organizational families? Few would question that there are irrational forces that influence our choice of intimate partners. Is it not possible that some of those same forces could influence our choice of work settings?

People of every personality type can find themselves caught up in the destructive forces of the closed organizational family. Many who work in the most extremely closed systems do, however, share remarkably similar backgrounds. A high percentage of such individuals come from very closed family systems. Many come from families that are closed because of geographical or social isolation. Many come from families touched by the stigma of moral or criminal misconduct or the presence of chronic disabling illnesses.

Some individuals in toxic organizations have long histories of involvement in closed systems. It is quite possible that they unconsciously seek out organizational settings that replicate their own family system experiences. They may also seek out roles in closed organizational families that parallel those they performed in their closed nuclear families.

8.5 The Role of Stigma

As I reviewed my experience consulting with a diverse group of closed organizations, a central question was what characteristics did these organizations share that could have contributed to the closure process. One intriguing possibility was that many provided services to stigmatized clients. They were organizations that worked with stigmatized issues and stigmatized people. They worked with criminals, alcoholics and addicts, the mentally ill, the developmentally disabled, the physically disfigured, the aged and infirm, the sexually abused, and the dying. I was intrigued because, while a great deal of attention has been given to the impact of stigmas on *clients,* little attention has been given to the impact of stigmas on *caregivers.*

Stigma can play a major role in promoting the process of organizational closure. Consider, for example, how stigmas can promote the development of a work-dominated social network.

Several years ago, I discussed with a group of hospice nurses how their work affected their social relationships, and why they spent most of their social time with one another. One of the nurses responded for the group as follows:

> Imagine yourself at a social gathering, and as people introduce themselves and ask what you do, you respond by saying, "I provide care for dying patients." Talk about uncomfortable! Nobody wants to look at death! If I tell people I'm a nurse, they want medical advice. If I tell them I'm a hospice nurse, they run away. With each other, we don't have to deal with any of that!

Those of us associated with issues, behaviors, or illnesses that are misunderstood outside our fields, and to which powerful stigmas and fears are attached, may find barriers to the development of nonwork social relationships. To encounter us is to encounter aspects of life that produce fear and discomfort in most people.

Imagine the social isolation of a person with AIDS in the late 1980s. Would not the same fears and stigmas that socially isolated those with the disease also isolate those who worked with people with AIDS during that period? Wouldn't such stigmatization promote the closure of an AIDS service organization, and the development of a predominantly work-oriented social network for those who worked in such an organization?

8.6 The Role of Status

Status also can work to promote organizational closure. Status and success can produce a loss of privacy that encourages one to retreat into the safety of a closed organization. Status and success can also spawn personal or professional arrogance that shuts off the flow of people and ideas into the organization.

There was a physician group practice that achieved an international reputation for its pioneering surgical techniques. The group's success produced a progressive professional, social, and sexual closure that would result in the self-destruction of the practice some eight years after its creation. The organization's demise caused shattered friendships, serious stress-related health problems for some key organizational members, and a string of marriage casualties.

Political and/or economic power can produce a level of closure that has far-reaching ramifications. A study of the Nixon White House years is illustrative. Such a study would reveal the progressive closure of the White House staff as an organizational system; the lack of reality testing and reduction of boundary transactions; the development and persecution of outside enemies; the scapegoating of members who challenged the ideology; and a twisting of values that placed the White House staff, in its eyes, above the law. In this ideological bubble emerged a belief that any means were justifiable in light of the holiness of the cause. The degree of closure is indicated by the length of time and amount of energy it took to penetrate the organization and unravel the saga that came to be called Watergate.

The disintegration of the organizational family and the fall of the high priest that accompanied Watergate shook the foundations of our government. But consider a more terrifying alternative that could have happened in such a closed system. Suppose the outside enemy of the organizational family was not the Democratic Party, but the then–Soviet Union. The closure process would have prevented reality testing, restricted the flow of objective information to organizational leaders, and scapegoated members who proposed more reasoned approaches to foreign policy. The escalation of conflict emerging from a standoff between two closed political organizations that also happen to possess nuclear capabilities has horrifying possibilities.

8.7 Xenophobia and Organizational Culture

Some organizational families have a built-in fear and distrust of outsiders as a permanent and major thrust of their cultures. Such xenophobia can play a major role in maintaining the closure of the organizational family. Examples of such systems include most military organizations, security or intelligence operations, or, at a local community level, most police departments.

Fear of outsiders also can build in people of whom we have high and rigid role expectations. The police officer, the minister, priest, or rabbi, the school teacher, or the local public official may develop a closed system around himself or herself as protection from public scrutiny. The fear that private behavior may not meet often unrealistic public standards can fuel the closure of such systems. Such closure helps hide the flaws of our public role models. When in public, these people are always in role. When with other organizational family members, they can relax and be human.

Our expectations of people in such public roles also extend to their family lives. Professional and social closure help form a wall of protection around the police officer whose son is involved in petty crime, the minister whose daughter is acting out sexually, the psychiatrist with a troubled kid, or the marriage counselor experiencing turbulence in his or her own marriage.

The issues identified in this chapter may enhance an organization's movement toward closure. Understanding which factors are at work is essential to developing strategies for opening the closed organizational family that has become toxic.

⑨

Porous Organizations and Their Leaders

In chapter 4, we looked at three prototype organizations: closed organizations, porous organizations, and self-regulated organizations. We saw how and why closed and porous organizations breed a high level of worker distress. Subsequent chapters described the professional, social, and sexual closure of organizations and the effects of closure on the health of an organization and its members. While the focus of this book is on closed organizational systems, let's briefly examine the nature of porous organizations.

There are books and articles galore on the rise and fall of closed organizations because people feel passionately enough about them (both negatively and positively) to invest time in documenting their histories. In contrast, there is little written about the life and death of porous systems. The demise of these organizations is often preceded by long and insidious processes of decay. As a result, there is simply no one left inside or outside such organizations who cares enough to tell their stories. And this perhaps marks the beginning of our comparison: The stories of closed systems are about the perversion of passion, whereas the stories of porous systems are about the absence or loss of passion. In the next section, we will introduce the porous organization by comparing and contrasting it with the closed organizations we have already described.

9.1 Porous Organizations and Closed Organizations: Comparison and Contrast

To detail the difference between closed and porous systems we must revisit and expand our discussion of organizational boundaries and gate-keeping. Most human systems are open in that there is a regular flow of people, products, services, ideas, information, and feelings exchanged back and forth across the boundary separating the system and its outside environment.

Self-regulated systems maintain a margin of transactions that allows an organization to remain in harmony with its environment without being overwhelmed by that environment. Closed systems prevent transactions from occurring and remain isolated from their environment. Porous systems, because of a lack of boundary integrity, can't retain their technical and human resources, and can't protect themselves from environmental threats. Porous systems tend to get overwhelmed and absorbed by their environment.

Closed systems don't receive data—information is checked at the boundary or is allowed in only after it has been filtered. Filtering involves the deletion or distortion of information likely to induce system instability. Porous systems receive information easily across their perforated boundaries. The problem is that there is so much information coming in, there is no capacity for discriminating which data are relevant, no capacity for data analysis, no ability to draw relevant conclusions, and no capacity to initiate timely responses. Porous organizations also suffer from an inability to contain data. The skin of open systems is so porous that critical information bleeds out into the environment, where it may be used, in turn, to wound the organization. In a similar manner, porous organizations can be overpowered by the speed at which outside information and people can move in and reshape the organizational culture.

Whereas closed organizations are built around a dogmatic belief system, porous organizations lack any guiding vision or beliefs. Whereas closed systems have a consistent appetite for charismatic leadership styles and a centralization of power, leaders in porous systems are more likely to be invisible, ineffectual, and transient. Power in porous organizations is not so much decentralized as diffuse. It is often actually hard to find the locus of power through which significant system action can be initiated in the porous organization.

Whereas the staff in a closed system tends to be homogenous in age, race, religion, and values, the staff in a porous system is characterized by great diversity—a diversity not balanced by mutual identification and loyalty. What porous systems lack is a definition of any *shared* values or *shared* identity. Porous organizations are filled with "I's," but lack any shared sense of "We."

Whereas workers in closed systems might be said to be suffering from too much intimacy, workers in porous systems suffer from too little intimacy. Relationships in closed systems become progressively invasive; relationships among workers in porous systems are so distant and detached as to often lack the most basic levels of mutual support and recognition.

Closed organizations are known for their volatility of emotion. Aging porous organizations, in contrast, might be said to be clinically and chronically depressed. Porous systems are filled with overwhelmed workers, many of whom present themselves as passive, helpless, and hopeless. Workers in systems in the latter stages of closure maintain a love/hate relationship with their organizations; workers in chronically porous organizations have a hostile/dependent relationship with their organizations. There is actually a pervasive subclinical depression that interferes with professional performance and organizational viability in porous organizations. Workers in such organizations consistently exhibit a lack of energy, an incapacity for pleasure, and a sense of hopelessness regarding the resolution of organizational problems. There is a contagious quality to such feelings that can rapidly devour the energy and optimism of new workers, leaders, and consultants who enter the organization.

Closed organizations have a propensity for action—what we earlier described as an addiction to crisis. Porous organizations, in contrast, have a bias toward inaction. They study, meet, discuss, and meet and discuss some more, but rarely initiate decisive action. Closed systems relish risk and conflict; porous systems minimize risk and conflict by introjecting the dominant values and beliefs in any situation. Whereas closed systems abuse their power, porous systems often lack power to effect their environment. Whereas closed systems scapegoat and extrude employees, porous systems lack courage and muscle to provide consequences for behavior regardless of its effect on the organization. The Achilles' heel of the porous system is the lack of personal accountability—a direct consequence of the lack of organizational direction. In porous organizations, system-enhancing behaviors are no more rewarded than are system-disrupting behaviors punished. Problem employees are pacified or retired on the job rather than confronted. The most incompetent and unproductive employees often feel invincible in a world where no one is accountable, let alone fired. And the most competent workers tend to feel overextended, unappreciated, and guilty by association. Porous public bureaucracies established as community service institutions are increasingly vulnerable to the charge that they have become middle-class welfare institutions that exist primarily to support those who work in them.

Porous systems, like closed systems, can generate incredible no-talk rules. Like the most dysfunctional of families, corporate etiquette prohibits labeling out loud the problem that everyone knows exists. The prohibition against public truth-telling on certain issues is so strong that saying out loud what everyone knows to be true is one of the few things that can get one extruded from the porous organization. Porous systems are institutional ostriches that operate on the belief that problems unseen and unheard don't exist.

Workers in closed and open organizations alike suffer from problems of self-esteem. The problems are masked in the closed organization by an aura of professional arrogance and feigned elitism. The wounded esteem in the porous system comes in part from workers seeing repeated evidence of organizational ineffectiveness and from a broader stigma attached to public service today. The whole mix contributes to a kind of malaise that erodes professional self-esteem and unit pride.

The death of a closed system is often a public spectacle; such systems rarely die quietly. In contrast, a porous system often just disappears, its demise being acknowledged no more so than was much of its existence.

9.2 How Organizations Become Porous

Organizations become porous due to a number of conditions. Some organizations are born but never achieve the kind of closure necessary to construct a sustainable organizational identity. Most of these organizations die within a few years from what might be medically called a failure to thrive. Lacking skins to contain and protect themselves in a predatory environments, such organizations are often mortally wounded before they reach maturity. Their human and technical resources leak into and are absorbed by their outside environments. Organizations also become porous during periods of ineffectual or absent leadership and sometimes merely from institutional aging. Some of today's porous organizations are the remnants of once-closed systems. Closed systems can become porous following the fall of the high priest/priestess and the high member turnover that usually follows that event. This parallels what happens when closed families suddenly break up.

Most healthy organizations drift in episodic cycles toward the closed and porous ends of our organizational family continuum. Healthy organizations move themselves toward closure or greater openness by need and design, and rein themselves back toward the middle when they remain at either end of the continuum for too long. Managers of such systems open or close the organization as needs dictate in the short run and try to achieve some degree of balance and system stability for the long run. The major challenge to achieving such balance, and the major factor in the rise of porous organizations in the United States, is the incredible acceleration of change in the environments in which organizations pursue their destinies.

9.3 Organizations in Crisis

Throughout the United States, organizations large and small describe themselves as being in crisis. Even large public service bureaucracies that historically viewed themselves as immune from the life-and-death struggles faced by private sector companies are today characterizing themselves as being in crisis. Much of this crisis talk reflects the strained ability of organizations to respond to rapid and turbulent changes in their operating environments. Public service institutions, for example, are facing increased performance expectations at a time when the problems they are responsible for addressing are rising exponentially and their resources are diminishing. Organizations are being held accountable by a much more critical consumer. Organizations that viewed themselves as only getting larger are facing downsizing, reorganizations, and forced mergers. Such changes have led to an acceleration of turnover among organizational leaders and key technical staff and an erosion of morale among the mainstream work force. The sheer speed and intensity of environmentally driven change is creating an increasing number of porous organizations. In the rest of this chapter, we will discuss some of the aspects of the crisis facing porous organizations.

9.4 The Loss of Vision

Every organization needs a vision. That vision is a synthesis of a clearly defined mission, a view of the evolving threats and opportunities in the organizational environment, a set of core values and professional/ethical standards that can drive organizational decision making, and a set of strategic goals to focus organizational activity. Let's compare how our three organizational prototypes respond to the need for vision.

If a porous organization has a vision it is so nebulous it arouses little passion and cannot be operationalized into production and performance goals.

The vision of a closed organization, while exceptionally clear, has been concretized and is not open for redefinition or even reinterpretation. There is a mustiness and nostalgia to the vision articulated in closed organizations. Porous and closed systems alike are notorious for shifting their visions from one of service to an external constituency to one of service to the institution and its members. Workers in self-regulated organizations share a clearly defined vision, but it is a vision that is dynamically refined almost daily. There is vision, but it is alive—it moves and adapts in response to internal feedback and environmental turbulence. No vision, deified vision, and dynamic vision—that's the continuum we are talking about.

There are many factors that contribute to the lack of shared vision in the porous organization. The sheer size of many porous organizations sometimes makes it difficult to consistently instill shared vision and values. Such systems are often highly de-centralized both functionally and geographically, making it difficult for each worker or unit to see the "big picture." One of the organizations I have worked with has 14,000 employees scattered across more than 100 service centers. Imagine the difficulties of instilling a single vision and a shared set of core professional values in a work force that large and that dispersed. Porous systems also have difficulty defining the big picture because their vision, their goals, and their priorities seem to be constantly changing. The changes stem from the multiple mandates placed on these organizations—a condition that makes them inherently reactive. Whereas the challenge in the closed system is to unfreeze the vision so that it may naturally evolve, the challenge in the porous system is to create a viable, durable organizing vision.

9.5 Invisible and Transient Leaders

Leaders of porous systems face incredible demands. They are asked to take responsibility for systems that have grown almost too large to control. They are operating in an increasingly hostile political environment. They must make decisions in a fishbowl of public scrutiny. Their time is torn between managing the interface with this turbulent environment ("putting out fires") and seeing to the internal needs of the agency. Such leaders are vulnerable to being politically scapegoated and extruded or to collapsing from overextension before they have fully implemented their personal visions for their organizations. The professional life expectancy of leaders of porous systems is rapidly decreasing. The transience of leaders in itself becomes an obstacle to effectively implementing a coherent organizational vision. Staff members in such organizations have been buffeted by such constant change that they take few proclamations from the top seriously. Highly institutionalized workers figure they have outlived the previous leaders and will outlive the latest one. Such attitudes create a sense that there are no enduring goals or values that make up the organizational character. The lack of a sustainable vision, and the inability of the organization without such a vision to fulfill its responsibilities as defined by politicians and the public, produces continued demands for change in the system. The focus of change is most often in one of three areas: (1) organizational leadership, (2) internal organizational structure, or (3) the merger of two or more organizations into what are being called in the public sector "superagencies."

9.6 The Rush to Reorganize, Downsize, and Merge

America spent more than a century building a prototype organizational structure that fit manufacturing and business enterprises operating in reasonably stable environments. The prototype was the pyramid—a hierarchical structure that provided an enormous amount of predictability, control, and efficiency. Workers entered at the bottom of the pyramid and spent a professional lifetime working their way up through the organization. It was not uncommon for leaders and workers alike to retire having spent thirty to forty years with a single organizational hierarchy. The pyramid proved so successful in the private sector that it was almost universally adopted as the desirable organizing structure for public (federal, state, county, municipal) institutions. What the pyramid provided was a clear chain of command and a clearly defined scope of organizational activity. These activities were organized in three- to five-year strategic plans that outlined goals, objectives, and personal responsibilities for nearly everyone in the organization. The pyramid marked the zenith of America's quest for productivity and efficiency.

Problems in the pyramidal structure emerged from two sources. The first problem concerned the sheer size that some organizations were reaching. While the hierarchy produced a high degree of decision-making control, what it didn't provide was decision-making speed, particularly when the number of levels in the chain of command increased with the growth of the organization. The hierarchy's effectiveness broke down in the face of two critical questions: (1) How long does it take an idea or piece of information (regarding a potential threat or opportunity) to get from the bottom of the organization to the top? and (2) Is the integrity of the idea or information maintained as it moves through the organization? Growing numbers of organizations found their structures failing these viability questions.

The second problem occurred when the speed of environmental change rendered much of the traditional technology of strategic planning obsolete. Growing numbers of organizations began to discover that their carefully crafted five-year strategic plans were irrelevant within months of their completion. This occurred not because of flaws in how they had planned but because the plans were based on faulty assumptions about the external environment. The escalating pace of change—much of it virtually unpredictable—has created the need for new approaches to planning and a different type of organizational structure. The pace of change has also been a challenge to organizational hierarchies because of their inability to quickly respond to suddenly emerging environmental threats and opportunities. Pyramidal structures served us well in reasonably stable markets and when work involved millions of repetitions of specialized tasks. But those structures are deadly in turbulent environments in which workers at all levels must anticipate and recognize problems and opportunities, and think and act—all with incredible speed and independence.

The trend everywhere seems to be the slow dismantling of pyramidal hierarchies, the de-centralization of power via the flattening of organizational structure, and the delegation of decision-making power to integrated teams and individual workers. Such restructuring is being accompanied by two other trends in porous systems: downsizing, masked by such titles as early retirement, reengineering, or restructuring, and by an increase in organizational mergers.

Downsizing is a euphemism for reducing the size of an organizational work force without reducing its production goals. The intensity of downsizing efforts is evident in figures documenting the number of workers laid off from various companies during the early 1990s: IBM (85,000), AT&T (83,500), GM (74,000), Sears and Roebuck (50,000), GTE (32,150), Boeing (30,000), Bank of America (28,930), and a long list of companies that laid off between 10,000 and 15,000 employees (including Proctor and Gamble, Philip Morris, Xerox, Eastman Kodak, Aetna, GE, and Ford) (Downs 1995). The process was repeated in smaller, less recognizable companies around the country.

Again, the primary goal of downsizing is simply to produce the same or more with fewer human resources. The goal is most often achieved by paring down the number of workers, particularly middle managers and those deemed support personnel. Many downsizings are based on the view that the problem with agency functioning is one of size rather than of organizational structure or process. It is assumed that reducing the number of employees will reap financial gains and some degree of heightened efficiency. Follow-up reviews two to three years following such efforts are calling into question the validity of both assumptions.

What seems on the surface to be an opposite trend is the growing tendency of organizations to merge with, or acquire, another or others. The trend is driven by the yet-to-be-tested perception that larger organizations will have a greater chance of survival in increasingly turbulent market environments than will smaller organizations. Generally, an organization hopes the merger process will broaden its technical knowledge, enhance its capital base, and improve its political or market position. Since the 1980s, we have seen a flurry of mergers and acquisitions in almost every sector of the economy: aerospace (Boeing-McDonnell Douglas), railroads (Union Pacific-Southern Pacific), airlines (Pan Am-Carnival), agribusiness (Tate and Lyle-Staley Continental), petroleum (Chevron-Gulf), communications (Turner Broadcasting-Time Warner), healthcare (a flurry of hospital mergers and acquisitions), insurance (Aetna and U.S. Healthcare), banking (Chase Manhattan-Chemical Bank), pharmaceuticals (Sandoz-Ciba-Geigy), tobacco (Philip Morris-General Foods, R. J. Reynolds-Nabisco), electronics (General Electric-RCA), computer engineering (Cray-Silicon Graphics), department stores (Macy and Company-Federated Department Stores), office supplies (Staples-Office Depot), and unions (United Steelworkers of America-Aluminum, Brick and Clay Workers International) (Adams and Brock 1989). This same process can be seen outside the business arena in movements to consolidate federal, state and municipal governmental agencies, school districts, and local human service agencies. There is a growing trend toward the creation of what are being called "superagencies." The State of Illinois, for example, is in the final stages of merging five of its state human service departments into a single agency that will have an annual budget of more than $4.3 billion and more than 20,000 employees.

We are moving through an era of mergers and acquisitions, takeovers (friendly and hostile), and participation in newly configured joint ventures, partnerships, and consortia—all occurring alongside parallel processes of organizational restructuring, divestiture, breakup, and demise. The speed of this trend and the breadth of the organizations touched by it are unprecedented. Historical relationships are being rapidly and radically reconfigured. Organizations that were bitter competitors a few years ago now find themselves involved in frenzied courtships and marriages, some of which might aptly be called shotgun weddings. Mergers and downsizings increasingly are being combined — a marriage of seemingly conflicting positions: bigger is better and smaller is better. The rush to merge and downsize organizations raises important questions about the optimum size of particular organizations, and equally important questions about the long-term effects of the processes used to achieve these changes.

For many organizations, there seems to be a critical relationship between mission and mass. There is an ideal size at which the achievement of an organization's mission can be maximized, and when the organization moves below or above its optimum size, that ability is compromised. What is even more interesting is that optimum size is not static, but dynamically evolves as internal and external environmental contexts change. Many organizations, believing success is measured by accelerating growth, expand themselves beyond the range of their ideal mass. They then face the dilemma of looking successful at the very time everyone in the organization knows something essential has been lost. Such growth could, in fact, be the very thing that turns a reasonably healthy self-regulated organization into a problem-plagued, porous organization. The lesson of such expansion is that growth at the periphery of one's mission may mask erosion at the core of that mission. What some organizations perceive as great opportunities turn out in retrospect to be wasteful diversions from the organization's primary mission.

Porous organizations may also move themselves toward even greater levels of system disintegration by the processes they use to implement downsizing and mergers with other organizations. While downsizings and mergers are said to arise from the noblest of intentions, the processes used to effect such changes may have unanticipated side effects that can seriously and, in some cases, mortally wound an organization. These processes all too often lead to the abandonment of organizational elders and the dilution and corruption of the organizational culture.

9.7 The Abandonment of Elders and the
Dilution of Organizational Culture

During recent years, many organizations have targeted senior employees through reorganizations, work-force reductions, and aggressive early retirement programs. Increasingly, workers between forty-five and sixty-five years of age are being pushed out of the American workplace. Many of those workers are being extruded from the only workplace they have known. The goal of such targeting is the elimination of people with higher salaries in the organization whose roles are perceived (some would say misperceived) to be expendable or who are seen as replaceable by workers commanding lower wages. The cuts are made in the name of cost containment and increasing efficiency. Little thought, however, has been given to the effects of such forced extrusions on the employees effected or to the long-term effects of such practices on the health of organizations.

There are stories emerging today that would have been unthinkable only a few years ago. Consider the following scenario. A fifty-six-year-old man who had worked for a company for eighteen years is sitting at his desk working when the personnel director enters his office and informs him that his job is being eliminated, that he will be immediately escorted by security guards from the building, and that the personal belongings in his office will be shipped to his home along with a severance check. He is further asked not to speak with other employees as he leaves the building. The man had not a single inkling that such an event was possible in a company to which he had given most of his professional life.

The rationale for the above "reduction in force" is financial crisis. The rationale for the despicable manner in which the employee was discharged is that he worked in a sensitive position and could have, during an extended termination period, sabotaged productivity, stolen proprietary information, and negatively affected the morale of other employees.

Such forced retirements wreak havoc on the individuals who lose their jobs, but they also wound the organizational culture. What's often left in their wake is a silent but pervasive sense that all workers are vulnerable—that workers can be used and manipulated with promises until they are discarded like pieces of used equipment. Whether senior employees are extruded or given "desk duty" (a desk, chair, and no responsibilities in the hopes they will voluntarily exit), all employees recognize at some level that this could be their own fate one day. What organizations fail to realize is that the way they end a relationship with *one* of their employees can redefine their relationship with *all* of their employees.

I also find in my consultation work that there are invisible victims in these forced-exit processes. People of conscience who must enforce the extrusion edicts are themselves wounded by what they must do. They suffer losses of honor and integrity in the eyes of those they have led and whose loyalty and sacrifices helped fuel their own rise in the organization. They suffer a loss of self-respect. They suffer enormous survival guilt. They are forced to emotionally numb themselves to survive. When people of conscience leave, when supervisors and managers trade their consciences for personal survival, and when the human and ethical sensitivities of the work force have been desensitized, the organization acquires a greater capacity for future evil. That capacity is most often actualized through breaches in ethical and legal conduct and a predatory pattern of exploiting everyone and everything touched by the organization.

9.8 The Changing Covenant between Workers and Organizations

What we have called the abandonment of elders is part of a broader change in the implicit covenant that has existed between American workers and the organizations in which they have toiled. The changing of the covenant is, in turn, part of a change in the function of the workplace itself in our society.

Through most of this century, men and, more recently, women left home each day to pursue a vocation. The workplace provided a source of income and, for some, a means of pursuing special interests and passions, but one's identity was to a large degree still linked to broader family and community relationships and activities. As the power of nuclear families, extended families, and cohesive neighborhoods to transmit values, shape identity, and provide emotional and social support dissipated over the past several decades, the workplace took on a much greater importance in many people's lives. The workplace began to assume first the historical functions of neighborhood and extended family, and more recently more of the traditional functions of nuclear families. It was in this context that a growing number of workers began to see their commitments to a particular company as more than a source of income. The workplace became their identity, a second (or first) family. At the same time, many organizations perceived themselves in a kind of maternal/ paternal relationship with their workers, and referred to the company in family metaphors. As a result, there was a sense that one's covenant of loyalty to the workplace was inviolate and, in many cases, more enduring than one's social or marital relationships. There was an unstated commitment of lifetime employment in many industries.

The mutual covenant of loyalty between worker and organization is rapidly turning into a contract of temporary reciprocity. Personal relationships are being replaced by a transience of functions. When Manpower, Inc. is placing some half a million temporary workers per year and is becoming one of the country's largest employers, something is shifting in the American workplace. The whole world is taking on a transience—an "ad hocness"—that is unprecedented. When one considers the 1990s layoff figures presented earlier in this chapter, one might wonder if we're not all at risk of becoming itinerant workers. Even for those workers who survive the latest corporate purges, the historical covenant with the organization no longer remains. Such workers are plagued by survival guilt, excessive demands, manipulative reminders of the tenuousness of their positions, and a pervasive sadness over the loss of what once could have been truly called an organizational family.

Covenants are being broken with groups of workers as well as with individual workers. Union members working with no contract, union members locked out and replaced with lower paid workers, workers working under threat of plant layoffs or plant closings, workers getting no salary increases while managers draw exorbitant bonuses and golden parachutes—all are part of the changing covenant between organizations and workers. A stunning illustration of this changing covenant is that in the fourteen companies named earlier in this chapter each laid off between 10,000 and 85,000 employees, the average annual salary of the CEOs of those companies at the time of the layoffs was over $6 million (Downs 1995).

The changes in the unwritten rules are affecting nearly every aspect of the individual and collective relationships between workers and the workplace. Let's consider, for example, just one issue, the growing problem of workplace violence, and see what insights might be provided by examining the problem under the lens of our "systems" perspective.

9.9 Perspectives on Workplace Violence

There are many things that contribute to the growth of violence in our places of work, and many of them have nothing to do with the nature of the workplace. But one of the more significant factors related to the increase of violence must surely include the growing perception by individual workers that they have been betrayed and abandoned by companies they have loyally served.

Violence can spring from the perception that the covenant between the worker and the organization has been violated. Violence can be incited by the perception that the company has betrayed its historical commitments to loyalty, trust, and fairness. The consequence of such perceived abandonment may be crystallized in a moment of explosive violence, but a more common effect is the overall erosion of the organizational culture—the disintegration of cohesive support into a competition for survival. Acts of interpersonal violence can be provoked by the experience of emotional and economic violence against the work force. In family-system terms, it is the retaliation of abused and abandoned children against their parents. Interpersonal violence can be a horribly misguided response to what are, rightly or wrongly, perceived to be acts of institutional violence.

While an after-the-fact analysis of workplace violence is nearly always presented as a psychological history of the current or former employee who became violent, a rigorous investigation would include questions like the following:

- Are individuals with increased propensities for violence drawn to certain types of organizations or roles? If so, what screening procedures might be used to enhance workplace safety?
- Are there objective environmental conditions or actions by managers and supervisors that have incited or exacerbated acts of workplace violence?
- Are there organizational processes that can activate latent propensities for aggression in a worker?
- Are there organizational processes that can elicit violent acts from individuals who had no propensities for violence?

Exploring the above questions is not a way of helping those who have committed acts of violence escape responsibility for their actions. Rather, it is a way of suggesting that there are cases in which responsibility may need to be shared by multiple parties. Exploring such questions further suggests that strategies to prevent workplace violence require influencing the workplace environment as much as influencing who is employed to work in that environment.

It is helpful to look at violence on a continuum, to see and understand gradations of violence that include nonphysical modes of violence that may help incite the behaviors more obviously associated with this term. Let's recall the earlier example of the employee who, having been led to believe he had a secure position with a company, was terminated without notice and led past his peers out of the building by armed security guards. Let's say the employee returns hours, days, or weeks later and violently assaults the person or people he views as responsible for his extrusion. Now the latter act will clearly be labeled violence, but what about the acts that preceded it? Does such unannounced extrusion of a long-term employee constitute a form of personal and economic violence? Does the manner of treatment— suffering the humiliation of being led by armed guards past one's peers—constitute a form of psychological or emotional violence? Acts that demean and humiliate exist on the same continuum on which are found acts of physical violence. To suggest this is not to attempt to justify what people describe as retaliatory acts of violence. It is to posit that violence-prevention strategies must be based on an understanding of this entire continuum. You can't prevent acts on the end of the continuum without stigmatizing the whole continuum of disrespectful, demeaning, injurious actions.

9.10 The Psychopathic Company:
The Question of Organizational Character

Every organization may be said to have a unique personality or character. The personality of a police department would be predictably different from that of a credit union or a day-care center. Ten police departments might have some shared personality dimensions, but each would also have its own unique subtleties of character and temperament. Organizational character as a whole is profoundly influenced by broader changes in our society. Organizational cultures might be said to be sponges that absorb and integrate broader environmental themes into the construction of their institutional characters.

A fundamental change is occurring in the character of many American organizations. They are becoming, in characterological terms, increasingly psychopathic. They are losing their capacity for empathic identification, their capacity for sustained relationships, and their capacity for value-mediated decisions. They are becoming increasingly impersonal, mercenary, and predatory in their internal and external relationships. They attribute hostile intent to their environments and enter internal and external relationships from an adversarial posture. They are becoming increasingly arrogant and grandiose while losing their capacity for self-observation and self-correction. They have a marked propensity for aggression, impulsivity, and risk taking. They are unable to postpone gratification of their immediate desires. They lack the cognitive abilities to effectively plan, solve problems, and project the long-term consequences of their actions. They are, increasingly, incapable of guilt and remorse following the disclosure of breaches in ethical or legal standards. They are, in short, becoming institutions without heart or conscience.

To suggest that a growing number of organizations have a psychopathic character does not just mean that we have particular organizational leaders who exhibit such character traits. It also means that there are deeply ingrained traits that become so pervasive in some organizational cultures that they can elicit psychopathic behaviors even from individuals who have no such proclivities. We have always had individual leaders scattered through business and industry who were psychopathic, but it was much rarer to have entire organizational systems take on this type of character. That more systems today are doing just that is what marks a significant change in the American organizational landscape.

Evidence of psychopathic organizational character can be found in many quarters: exposés of the exploitive practices and moral shortcomings of several televangelist organizations; reports of how the predatory behavior of savings and loan institutions led to the federal bailout of that industry; stories of corrupt judges (in Chicago) and police officers (in New Orleans); and the weekly accounts on television news programs of all manner of institutional scams designed to cheat the public. The issue is not that organizations have a few corrupt individuals, but that major portions of whole systems have become corrupt. There are long lists of companies that raped the environment in their struggle to reach the top, and who undermined public health in the name of institutional profit. Such far-reaching actions were not the product of one person but of attitudes and practices that had become endemic to those organizations. The predatory orientation continued even as the faces changed. Nowhere is psychopathic character more evident than in the tobacco industry—an industry that has systematically suppressed its own research about the harmful effects of tobacco while massively promoting a commercial product at home and abroad that for many will be as lethal as it is addictive.

Organizational character is being raised here because both closed and porous systems are vulnerable to taking on psychopathic characters. Closed organizations are vulnerable to psychopathy because of the kinds of people drawn to high priest/priestess roles and the sustained emotional depletion that occurs in such systems. Porous systems are vulnerable to developing exploitive characters because they lack strong countervailing value systems.

9.11 Team Building:
In Search of the Organizational Family

What porous organizations lack that closed organizations have in excess is cohesion. Porous systems are by definition splintered and fragmented. It is wrong to even refer to these collections of individuals as either organizations or teams, for they are neither organized nor cooperative. The prevalence of porous systems today is indicated by the number of organizations that begin a request for consultation services with a discussion of lost direction, interpersonal dissension, deteriorating staff morale, poor motivation and productivity, and high turnover of the best and brightest personnel. It is equally indicated by the number of organizations that request help in communication and conflict resolution, team building, and creating a work milieu that is positive and uplifting. Porous organizations ask consultants time and time again for two things: the first is help defining the overarching elements of an organizational culture, including mission, vision, core values, strategic goals, and standards of ethical and professional conduct; the second is help defining these elements through a highly participatory process that enhances interpersonal relationships, enhances team identity and loyalty, and improves team functioning. What porous organizations ask us to do is help take a diverse, often conflicted group of individuals and turn them into what everyone in America seems to want: a family. In these cases, an organizational family.

9.12 Organizations with Mixed Characteristics

The problem with any model is that it is only an approximation of reality—a helpful starting point that requires care and caution in its application. We have described two types of organizations—closed and porous—that generate excessive levels of professional distress among their members. But many organizations will appear to have mixed characteristics. Such systems have some units that are closed, some that are open, others that are isolated, and still others that don't relate to each other internally but have a high frequency of outside interaction with people and organizations. One of the most common configurations is a large, complex system that is easily characterized as porous at the mesosystem level. Leadership is weak and invisible to the vast membership of the organization. There is no clear sense of mission, no shared goals, no core values held in common by members of the organization. But if we went to the divisions, departments, bureaus, or units of such an organization, we might be shocked by the level of closure that characterizes its microsystems. (See figure 9-A.)

Figure 9-A
A Porous Organization with Closed Microsystems

In the organization pictured, we have a porous system characterized by invisible leadership and a weak organizational culture, and by closed microsystems with strong unit leaders and strong unit cultures. Worker loyalty in the system is not to the CEO or the company but to the microsystem manager and the microsystem team. The microsystems compete, often quite viciously, for system resources, and define outsiders not as those outside the corporation but as those outside the unit. What do you think would happen to this organization if it found itself in a life-threatening crisis that required each member of each unit to sacrifice unit interests on behalf of the whole company? The situation happens every day in America, and many such companies die, not from the outside threat but from their inability to come together internally as an organizational family.

Leader-directed, consultant-guided interventions into systems with mixed characteristics require considerable sophistication and subtlety. In the organization depicted in figure 9-A, for example, the strategy would involve increasing closure at the mesosystem level and strengthening mesosystem culture while opening the microsystems, weakening microsystem cultures, and broadening the professional identity of microsystem members.

Organizations undergoing major transitions often have characteristics of both closed and porous systems. It is not unusual to have a leader who knows that he or she needs to move from an autocratic management style to a participatory style of decentralizing power and decision making, but who, in making the transition between the two styles, gives employees contradictory messages. He or she might, for example, in the midst of implementing the new management philosophy, relapse to the old style of autocratic decision making on an issue that should have been opened up for staff review and participation or even completely decided at a lower level of the organization. Such relapses can sabotage the change process and lead to employee distrust in, and the physical and emotional disengagement from, the process.

More detailed discussions of such strategy development are contained in chapters 13 and 14.

9.13 The Risk of Renegade Subcultures

We have noted the propensity for porous organizations to breed closed subsystems. The risk in such situations is that one or more of the subsystems can take on the status of renegade subculture, with values and practices highly incongruent to those of the parent organization. Renegade subcultures usually emerge in systems that fail to define, indoctrinate, or enforce their norms. All three of these elements are often present when organizational members are isolated from those people who transmit and enforce system norms. Those members least connected to the core culture of the organization, lacking any primary system support, tend to cluster for their own self-protection and self-support. This is why we tend to see unique cultures emerge among those who work on night shifts, those who work in remote field or satellite offices, and those who work part time.

Let me illustrate the renegade subculture concept with a story. A few years ago, a large human services system called to schedule several days of consultation. At the time of the initial call, one of the items on the agenda was a request that I provide consultation to some supervisors on various "problem employees" with whom they were encountering difficulties. In a later call to finalize the agenda, the director noted that the item had been deleted as it seemed the problems "had solved themselves." I asked him how the problems had been resolved, as it was my experience that "problem employees" rarely experienced a spontaneous surge in productivity and positiveness. Lacking details himself, the director told me he would investigate and let me know. He called back a few days later to tell me what he had discovered. The problems might have seemed to have solved themselves, but a look at the whole system revealed a potential new problem. Over a number of months, a variety of problem employees had transferred into a particular program and were all working under the direction of one night supervisor, who had himself been moved to nights because of conflict with other workers. Needless to say, we spent considerable time exploring how to intervene in what was quickly becoming a renegade subculture. A cursory investigation revealed abuses that were already beginning to unfold on this shift.

9.14 Cautions on Organizational Intervention

Some important implications for intervening in organizations emerge from our comparison of closed and porous organizations. Intervening to improve the health of a closed organization requires strategies quite different from those used to intervene in a porous organization. Whereas closed systems need to increase their interactions with the outside world, diffused systems need to decrease such contact and define themselves internally. Whereas closed systems need a decentralization of power and decision making, porous systems require the emergence of a more visible and potent leadership. Whereas interventions in closed systems require strategies to weaken the connectedness among organizational members, interventions in porous organizations require strategies to increase relationship-building activities among members. Whereas closed systems need to soften their application of philosophy and core values, porous systems need to develop a clear sense of mission, a guiding vision, and a set of core values. The processes through which one intervenes as a leader or outside consultant in these very different types of organizations also differ significantly. We will explore this point in greater detail in chapter 13.

9.15 Porous Systems and Worker Distress

We should not end this discussion of porous organizations without defining the relationship between inadequate boundary management and the level of professional distress experienced by workers in such organizations. Whereas closed systems block members' access to supports outside the organization, porous systems prevent the development of supports inside the organization. Porous systems lack the very things that attract workers to closed systems: a clear and worthy vision, team cohesion, role clarity, and a predictable and consistent work milieu. Whereas the wounding of workers in closed systems (by scapegoating, for example) is often sudden and dramatic, the wounding in porous systems is often subtle. Recently, I heard the following comment regarding an individual's long tenure at a quite porous federal agency:

> It is so sad to see what happened to him. He was one of the most dynamic professionals I've ever seen, but he just stayed there too long. Somewhere he passed a point that he could leave—passed a point where he still believed he had things to offer another organization. It's like the agency sucked out the best within him and broke him. He'll never leave now, even though the agency has shuffled him off into a corner to do work that is as insignificant as it is unfulfilling.

Closed and porous systems share two things in common. First, they are characterized by an acceleration of role stressors on most workers. Second, they prevent the development of, or speed the erosion of, role supports. In the next chapter, we will define thirteen role stressors associated with the worker casualty process in closed and porous systems.

⫻ 10

Role Conditions and the Worker Casualty Process

Earlier chapters explored how broad organizational processes directly and indirectly affect the health of workers; this chapter will focus on the workplace microsystem—the smallest unit of the organization that surrounds each worker on a daily basis. We will focus not on the organization as a whole but on the department, the project, and the role expectations of each worker. There are many aspects of the microsystem that can contribute to professional distress. We will begin with a discussion of the physical environment of the microsystem and then examine the relationship between professional distress and the level of role stressors and role supports in the microsystem.

All activities and relationships in the department, section, or project team take place in the context of a physical environment. The qualities of that environment can have a profound effect on the level of distress experienced by workers. Some of the most important environmental concerns include the amount of physical space per person, the layout of physical space, lighting, ventilation (particularly in settings where materials or processes may produce noxious odors), temperature, noise level, cleanliness, including that of restrooms and eating areas, and the quality and quantity of equipment and materials available to the worker to successfully perform his or her job.

A key word in our study of the microsystem is *harmony*. When workers are in harmony with their environment, very little adaptational energy is required to respond to physical stressors, and energy can be devoted to the work objectives of the unit. Disharmony occurs when conditions in the physical or social environments undermine the health and comfort of the worker, lowering the energy available for high-quality performance.

The work environment represents the most basic element of the relationship between the organization and the worker. Conditions in the work environment convey the most primary message of respect or disrespect to the worker. Speeches and philosophy statements by organizational leaders expressing compassion and support for workers fall on deaf ears when the environment of the microsystem reflects a lack of respect.

10.1 Role Stressors and Role Supports in the Microsystem

This section will outline a model for understanding important dimensions of professional distress in the microsystem by examining the role stressors and role supports that surround each worker in the microsystem. The model is illustrated graphically in figure 10-A.

Figure 10-A
Managing Distress in the Microsystem

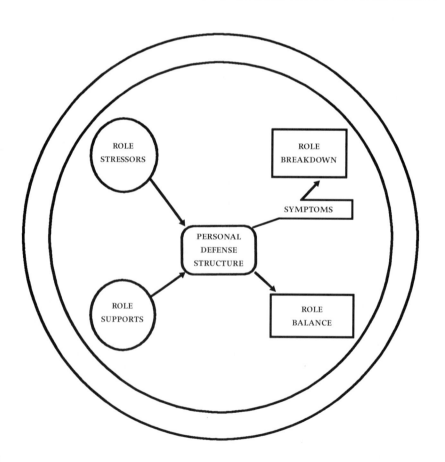

As an individual enters and works in a particular organization, there exist numerous role conditions that affect his or her physical and emotional health and productivity. The relationship between those conditions and the worker can be summarized through the use of the following terms.

> ROLE STRESSORS *are the number and intensity of conditions in the work environment that interfere with our ability to successfully perform assigned responsibilities and simultaneously decrease our self-esteem.*

Role stressors escalate the demand for adaptational energy and place a strain on the relationship between the worker and the organization. Such conditions frustrate us, irritate us, and trigger thoughts of escape or aggression. Examples of role stressors could include safety hazards, excessive work demands, isolation from other workers, or confusion over performance expectations.

> ROLE SUPPORTS *are the number and intensity of conditions in the work environment that increase our ability to successfully perform assigned responsibilities and simultaneously increase our self-esteem.*

Role supports neutralize our experience of role stressors in the work environment. Examples of role supports include compensation that is directly linked to our productivity, the availability of high-quality equipment and materials to perform our roles, and technical and personal support from our supervisors. Numerous role supports are cataloged in the last two chapters of this book.

> *The* PERSONAL DEFENSE STRUCTURE *is each individual's preferred pattern of thinking, feeling, and behaving when confronted with distress.*

Our personal defense structures represent our degrees of personal vulnerability to distress and own unique styles of managing personal and professional distress.

All of us experience both role stressors and role supports regardless of our occupation or type of organizational setting. Stressors and supports alike are filtered through our personal defense structures—a fact that makes each person's experience of the work environment different. This is why two people may respond so differently to a similar level of stressors and supports in the microsystem. Those factors that make up the personal defense structure will be detailed in the next chapter.

> ROLE BALANCE *exists when individuals are able to filter role stressors and role supports through their personal defense structures in a manner that allows them to sustain role performance and personal health.*

Our personal defense structures operate constantly to maintain this balance. When equilibrium is maintained, we can do our jobs without experiencing any stress-related disruptions of our physical or emotional health. In short, we function without symptoms.

> ROLE BREAKDOWN *is a deterioration in performance and personal health resulting from either changes in the levels of role stressors and role supports in the microsystem or changes in the strength of our personal defense structures.*

When we simultaneously experience an increase in role stressors and a loss of role supports, our personal defense structures are stretched beyond their capacities for adaptation. When this occurs, we develop distress-related symptoms that serve as warning signs of disharmony. (See chart of indicators in chapter 1.) These symptoms interfere with our individual work performances and can disrupt the surrounding health of our work teams. Distress-related deteriorations in the work performance of key individuals can threaten the very existence of an organization.

The model we have just outlined illustrates three levels of microsystem intervention that can be utilized to reduce the incidence of role breakdown and the toll of human casualties that accompany such breakdowns.

1. We can build programs and services into organizations that increase the strength and flexibility of members' personal defense structures, (for example, employee assistance, health promotion, and stress-management training programs).
2. We can manipulate the work environment to reduce the frequency and intensity of those role stressors over which we have control.
3. We can manipulate the work environment to increase the availability and variety of role supports.

Thirteen role stressors are identified in the following pages; these stressors can lead to role breakdown and to deterioration of the physical and emotional health of workers. Dr. Lennart Levi, in his seminal work on preventing occupational stress, noted that workers have amazing powers of adaptability, but that they can also become deformed (injured) when workplace demands transcend their powers of adaptation (Levi 1981). Organizations that sustain the role stressors described in this chapter prove Levi's point. The role stressors we will discuss include role-person mismatch, role-assignment misplacement, role conflict, role-integrity conflict, role ambiguity, insufficient role feedback, role underload, role overload, role safety hazards, role insecurity, role-connectedness problems, role deprivation, and role-termination problems.

10.2 Role-Person Mismatch

Role-person mismatch is the incongruence between

(a) an individual's *knowledge and skills* and the knowledge and skills required to perform his or her role responsibilities.

(b) an individual's *level of stress tolerance* and the stress endemic to his or her role in the organization.

(c) an individual's *style of stress management* and the methods of stress management officially and informally sanctioned by *the organization.*

The wider the incongruence in these areas, the greater are the demands for adaptation and the greater the likelihood that the individual worker will experience role breakdown.

A major portion of the responsibility for this mismatch can be found by examining an organization's screening and hiring procedures. An inadequate screening and hiring process can result in the hiring of a person for a role in which the skill demands far exceed the skills of the new employee. When the worker is then unable to perform at an adequate level, responsibility (blame) for the problem is attributed to the worker and not to the organizational procedures that led to his or her misplacement.

Common examples of such misplacement include the following:

• Hiring for a match with the team or organization rather than a match with a particular role (The applicant may have skills that

could be used by the organization but not in the role in which
he or she is placed.)

- Hiring based on scoring on objective tests in which the knowledge tested has little relationship to the knowledge and skills
  required to perform day-to-day role responsibilities
- Mistaking commitment for competence (High passion and motivation to do a good job don't, in and of themselves, guarantee
  that a person has the knowledge and skill to do the job.)
- Making assumptions that people with certain educational degrees can perform certain tasks

Misplacing workers in the wrong roles can also occur in employee role
changes. The most common example is in the promotion of staff members in technical roles to supervisory positions for which they may be
constitutionally unsuited. The Peter Principle, which observes that in a
hierarchy everyone eventually rises to his or her level of incompetence,
is in many organizations all too often true (Peter 1969).

The level of distress experienced by the misplaced worker escalates
as the discrepancy between assumed and real skills becomes painfully
evident to all microsystem members. It is quite common for the misplaced worker to overcompensate for the low quality of his or her performance by increasing the quantity of hours committed to the work
environment—a strategy that further taxes the limits of his or her adaptational energy.

The phenomenon of the misplaced worker is an excellent example of
the systems principles elaborated in this book. The misplacement of a
worker can thus produce a synergistic effect: It affects the misplaced
person, his or her co-workers, the total functioning of the microsystem,
the relationship of the microsystem to the larger organization, and, potentially, the health and viability of the whole organization.

Another type of mismatch involves an individual worker's history
of stress management and the level of stress inherent in the particular
role he or she is hired to perform. Numerous examples exist in which
role-person mismatch led to a serious deterioration of a worker's
health, not because of skill deficiency, but because the demands for
adaptation inherent in an assigned role surpassed the worker's capacity for adaptation.

Imagine the demands for adaptational energy placed on those African
Americans who broke the color line in various professions and organiza-

tions. Most commentators agree that Jackie Robinson was the perfect choice to break the color barrier in professional baseball. He was the perfect choice not simply because of his extraordinary skills as a baseball player, but because his level of distress tolerance and style of handling distress sustained him and prevented his self-destruction when confronted with some of the most shameful examples of racism in the history of professional sports. There must be a reasonable fit between our level of distress tolerance and our style of handling distress and the organizational milieu. The fit, or chemistry, between the individual and the organization is an inherent part of the stories of both superperformers and casualties.

10.3 Role-Assignment Misplacement

ROLE ASSIGNMENT MISPLACEMENT *is the movement of a person with excellent skills in an interior organizational position to a boundary position in the organization, or vice versa.*

Workers who hold interior positions in an organization interact primarily with other members of their teams, units, or departments. Workers in boundary positions interact frequently with other microsystems in the organization and/or have multiple transactions with systems outside the organization.

Role-assignment misplacement constitutes a special type of role-person mismatch. The mismatch often occurs when organizations reward successful performance in an interior role by promoting a worker to a boundary position, assuming the knowledge and skills are transferable. The fact is that boundary roles usually require significantly different skills than interior roles, and often require different levels of distress tolerance and different styles of stress management.

For example, a hospital unit supervisor, who provided other unit personnel with day-to-day leadership to ensure patient-care services, was promoted to a department head. The new position required a great deal of time interacting with other hospital departments and marketing department services outside the hospital. Rather than focusing on patient care, the new department head was thrown into a world of interdepartmental politics, budget battles, hospital committees, and special task forces to generate new money-making ideas to compensate for a decrease in patient numbers. In short, the technical patient-care skills were not applicable to the new role. The new role demanded areas of knowledge and skill foreign to the worker. The high level of interaction with other departments and the community proved highly stressful. The personal reward of participating in the healing of injury and illness was lost in the new position. As demands for adaptation escalated, the new department head resigned her position to accept a supervisor of patient care position in another hospital. The worker's role-assignment misplacement took not only its personal toll, but also resulted in the hospital losing a highly skilled employee.

The worker had established a record of successful performance in an interior role in the organization. The worker discovered in the boundary position new role stressors and a loss of old supports, and experienced a progressive deterioration of her self-esteem and growing frustration and dissatisfaction in her new role. As a result, she suffered distress-related deteriorations of role performance over time.

10.4 Role Conflict

ROLE CONFLICT *is the experience of incongruous demands from two or more simultaneously held roles.*

Have you ever been simultaneously accountable to two or more bosses and received contradictory messages as to your primary duties and priorities? If so, you've experienced role conflict. Role conflict is probably one of the most frequently described conditions in the literature on organizational stress. Role conflict places the worker in a no-win position. Incongruent and contradictory expectations from multiple roles mean that to meet the expectations of one role is to fail to meet the demands of another role. There are numerous examples of role conflict: the worker with two bosses who don't like each other, the employee filling two half-time positions that are in conflict with each other, or the shop steward caught between his or her status as a company employee on the one hand and his or her role representing union members on the other. Since so much of this book focuses on how work-related distress spills into our personal lives and disrupts our abilities to sustain intimate and family relationships, it would be appropriate to discuss conflict that can arise between our roles as employees and the roles we perform in our outside-of-work intimate and family relationships.

Most of us have roles to perform both at work and outside of work. Role conflict occurs when the nature of the demands from these roles are such that they cannot be met simultaneously. The units of exchange in all of these roles are time and emotional energy. There are some obvious conditions in the work environment that create role conflict. We may work for a company that places excessive demands on our time and availability. Some of us may work on an "on-call" status that renders every planned family activity tentative and contingent on the silence of the beeper or telephone. We may be involved in a pattern of shift work that means we see very little of our families, or that significantly interferes with our ability to attend social events, school activities, or athletic events in our roles as mothers or fathers. Our jobs may require excessive travel that makes it difficult to sustain strong family and outside-of-work social relationships.

There are also conditions in the family system that can exacerbate role conflict. These include any conditions or events that strain a worker's personal adaptational energy, such as the (high distress) career of a spouse or intimate partner, disabling illness or injury, marital or family problems, excessive needs of a child, aging parent, or other dependent, or single parenthood.

Many of the distress-related marriage casualties I've studied occurred when role conflict grew to the point that either the job or the family had to be sacrificed.

10.5 Role-Integrity Conflict

ROLE INTEGRITY CONFLICT *is the incongruence between one's personal values and beliefs and the values and beliefs inherent in the work environment.*

Workers bring values and beliefs with them when they enter the life of an organization, and these values and beliefs may evolve over time through experiences in the organization. The organization also has explicit and implicit values and beliefs that evolve over time through the influence of its members and through interactions with the outside world. When the values of the worker and the organization are divergent, stress results from the worker's need to bring the organization's values into conformity with his or her own values. At the same time, forces of homogenization in the work milieu seek to bring each worker's values and behavior into congruence with organizational norms. This battle of adaptation, and how it is resolved, may have a significant impact on the health and self-esteem of the worker.

The list of such value conflicts is almost unending: the nurse and physician confronted with hospital administrators more concerned with profits than patient care, the civil service worker fighting cynicism about the political distribution of government contracts, the construction worker concerned over materials and designs that could pose a future safety threat, the professional who encounters gross incompetence among his or her peers, the alcoholism counselor who must deny an alcoholic admission to treatment for lack of financial resources, and any worker who becomes privy to illegal or unethical conduct in an organization.

The above list is a bit misleading, as it pits apparently ethical individuals against more malign organizational forces. The fact is that role-integrity conflict doesn't include the issue of whose values are right. Stress is not a seeker of truth. It concerns only the degree of discrepancy between individual and organizational values. The degree of discrepancy dictates the amount of adaptational energy the individual will need to sustain his or her beliefs and attempts to influence the organization. Each individual, whether healthy or sick, right or wrong, will seek, at some level, to reshape the organization in his or her own image—which means bringing the organization's values into congruence with his or her own. Many conscientious organizations have implemented safety policies demanding that all workers wear hard hats, not consume alcoholic beverages on the job or during the lunch hour, and rigorously follow safety protocol. Some have also implemented ethics policies that rein in the misuse of company resources and define appropriate relationships between employees and the company's contractors (prohibiting the acceptance of gifts, for example). Employees not agreeing with such policies experience a degree of distress over what they perceive to be ill-conceived and intrusive regulations. The issue here is not who is right, but the degree of fit between personal values and organizational values.

The issue for the organization is to determine to what degree it will allow its values and beliefs to evolve and what the role of organizational members will be in shaping this evolution. To the degree that this process is open to participation, distress is reduced as values tend to move toward the center of the collective beliefs of organizational members. To the extent that the organization closes off participation and evolution of beliefs, distress is escalated by the divergence in individual and organizational values. The escalation is particularly intense when an organization maintains rigid adherence to dogma at the same time it engages employees and volunteers who bring with them new and conflicting ideas and personal beliefs.

10.6 Role Ambiguity

ROLE AMBIGUITY *is a worker's inadequate knowledge of (1) role expectations, (2) task priorities, (3) preferred methods of task completion, (4) whom he or she is directly accountable to, and (5) rewards and punishments related to superior or inadequate performance.*

Role ambiguity is a highly stressful condition for workers. It usually occurs in organizations that lack the management expertise to effectively organize work activity, or in organizations going through periods of such rapid change and turbulence that role clarity has been lost altogether.

The following comments typify the sentiments of workers who experience role ambiguity:

- "Look, I can play the game; I just need somebody to tell me what the rules are!"
- "I'm not completely sure who my boss is, and the only way I know what I'm supposed to do lately is when somebody tells me I forgot to do it or did it wrong."
- "I can't win. If I ask her how she wants me to do it [job tasks], she says I ought to know. If I don't ask her, then she comes by and tells me I did it the wrong way. Either way, I look like a fool."

Role ambiguity is often a sign that an organization has lost a clear sense of mission and strategic goals. This lack of clarity at the top ripples down into a majority of the roles in the organization. Role ambiguity can reflect a holding pattern or loss of direction in an organization, whose operating motto might well be stated as, "We won't know where we're going until we get there."

Role ambiguity leads to a loss of security and predictability in the life of the worker. How, he or she might ask, can I evaluate my own performance in an undefined job? How can I be accountable when I'm not sure whom I'm accountable to and what I'm accountable for? Role ambiguity can trigger behaviors as diverse as angry confrontations and an attempted withdrawal into invisibility.

10.7 Insufficient Role Feedback

INSUFFICIENT ROLE FEEDBACK *is the lack of regular feedback on (1) the adequacy of role performance, (2) the methods of*

*improving role performance, and (3) the adequacy of adjust-
ment to the work milieu.*

The lack of adequate feedback is a frequent complaint when workers
from diverse occupational groups are surveyed about what they most
dislike in their current jobs. Each of us needs feedback and acknowledgment to sustain our performance and self-esteem in any role, whether it
be a family or organizational role. When role feedback is absent, we
begin to disengage emotionally and seek out new roles that provide self-
affirming feedback.

Feedback can come in many forms—salary increases, bonuses, symbols of status, written acknowledgment, awards, verbal praise, a pat on
the back (meant literally), or through very objective measures of excellence. The quantity and variety of feedback in the work environment
has an important relationship to the experience of professional distress.
If we define stress as the demand for adaptational change, feedback is
the essential data that helps us shape, modify, correct, or experiment
with behavior to efficiently accommodate this demand. Feedback that is
affirming of the person, and specific enough to allow for refined improvement, helps reduce the movement from stress to distress. Feedback
that combines criticism and vagueness can be devastating. Examples of
the latter include the following types of supervisory remarks:

- "I'm really disappointed in you. I was relying on you, but quite
  frankly your performance just isn't up to par." (This comment
  indicts the worker as a person, seeks to elicit guilt, and provides no specific data on what the worker needs to change.)
- "You haven't quite got it yet. Why don't you try again." (The
  boss doesn't know what he or she wants but will know it when
  he or she sees it.)

Feedback communications can be supportive of worker health and productivity when they enhance the self-esteem of the worker, provide
data to support and improve role adequacy, and serve as an early warning of professional distress. Feedback, such as verbal praise, may be crucial in occupational areas where more objective measurable feedback is
unavailable, or where the nature of the service guarantees a negative
outcome. It is easy to conceive of feedback in such measurable terms as
sales, profits, production achievements, advances in student achievement scores, deadlines met, or number of crimes solved. But what kind

of feedback do we provide the manager in a declining industry where even the best management practices may show year-end losses rather than profits? What kind of feedback do we provide the physician and nurses caring for a terminally ill patient? What kind of feedback do we provide the rescue workers who are called to the horror of a plane crash in which all of the passengers are dead? In such situations, when effective mechanisms of social/emotional support and feedback are not present, highly competent and caring workers can become casualties of professional distress.

10.8 Role Overload

ROLE OVERLOAD *occurs when there are excessive expectations concerning the quantity and quality of work to be completed in a given time frame.*

Role overload can have a rapid and profound impact on the incidence of professional distress in an organization. The excessive demands for physical and emotional energy inherent in role overload sap the worker's capacity for adaptation and lower the body's resistance to disease and injury. Role overload also decreases the strength and flexibility of each worker's personal defense structure. Role overload decreases the emotional energy and the time available to a worker to seek sources of personal and social replenishment outside the work environment.

Role overload, one of the most frequent role stressors in organizations today, reflects the need to do "more with less" that seems to pervade nearly every sector of our economy. Companies are cutting the number of their employees, but not their production quotas. Companies are cutting corners by laying off workers (to decrease benefit costs), while increasing regular overtime for those workers who remain. Organizations are overextending workers in an effort to "get over the hump"—the "hump" being everything from a break into profitability to the discovery of new revenue sources. All of these trends confirm the point that overextended workers are often merely a reflection of the overextension of the organization. Given our understanding of distress, it is inevitable that these trends will affect the quality of organizational services and products, the health and vitality of the organizational culture, and the physical and emotional health of individual workers.

Much of the overload is due to turbulence in our organizational ecosystems. Nowhere is this more evident than in the health care industry, in general, and hospitals in particular. Radical changes in the organization of health care in the United States, sparked in part by dramatic changes in systems of service reimbursement, have changed hospitals from stable into highly volatile organizations. Similar transformations are occurring in many business and professional arenas. My point here is that the overload experienced by workers is irresolvable without an understanding of the overload whole systems are experiencing as they adapt to rapid changes in their environments.

10.9 Role Underload

ROLE UNDERLOAD *is the degree of tedium produced by too few responsibilities or by the organization of work into mechanical, repetitive, and nonstimulating tasks.*

Whereas role overload produces demands for adaptation from excessive stimulation, role underload produces demands for adaptation from too little stimulation. Monotony and boredom can be as wearing on health and self-esteem as the experience of excessive and unachievable role demands. This is also true for collective health. It is common for organizations to experience high levels of conflict when overall demands are at either their highest or their lowest. There are also roles, particularly those in which the level of demands changes dramatically with the seasons, that cause alternating cycles of overload and underload.

Most workers who experience role underload will either leave their jobs in search of more satisfying work or resign themselves to their situations by emotionally detaching from their work roles while seeking more intense stimulation in roles and activities outside their organizations.

10.10 Role Safety Hazards

ROLE SAFETY HAZARDS *reflect perceived threats to one's physical and psychological safety during the performance of one's professional role.*

Safety concerns are underscored by the number of workers who die (more than 10,000) or are permanently disabled (more than 100,000) each year in industrial accidents. Safety concerns also involve the threat of industrial diseases produced by exposure to radiation, chemicals, fumes, and other toxic materials. While the literature on occupational safety hazards focuses primarily on industrial and manufacturing settings, safety concerns are shared by a large number of occupational groups. Fears for our personal safety have increased, in part, due to the overall rise in interpersonal violence in our culture. In my work with organizations across the United States, I have been surprised at the pervasiveness of the fear of physical violence in the workplace and how that fear has grown over the past two decades. But role safety transcends industrial accidents and interpersonal violence. Role safety issues can be of concern to a wide range of workers, from the professional athlete who fears a debilitating and career-ending injury to the receptionist who must traverse ice-covered sidewalks on the way into the workplace.

It is also important to note that role safety hazards, as stressors, emerge from our *perception* of vulnerability regardless of whether such fear is grounded in reality. According to all available data, for example, there is very little risk of health care workers contracting AIDS through the care of an AIDS patient as long as the workers use universal precautions. This objective reality is countered by the exaggerated and irrational fears many health care workers experience when they encounter their first patient with AIDS.

Threats to psychological safety also can be a major stressor to workers. Threats to psychological safety can affect the worker in constant fear of verbal abuse from a punitive supervisor, the human service worker in danger of being overwhelmed by the pain and trauma in the lives of his or her clients, or the worker whose decisions have a profound impact on the health and safety of others (surgeons, air traffic controllers, or hostage negotiators, for example).

10.11 Role Insecurity

ROLE INSECURITY *is the degree of uncertainty experienced in relation to one's future role in an organization.*

Role insecurity is a stressor that often emerges out of turbulence in the exosystem and macrosystem. Major changes in economic and political policy reverberate down to affect the job security of individual workers. This is an area in which such macrosystem issues as foreign competition, interest rates, national foreign policy, and federal and state funding trends can lose their abstractness and directly affect a worker's assurance that he or she will have a job tomorrow. As macrosystem turbulence ripples downward in the form of business closings, downsizing through layoffs and forced early retirement, reductions in hours worked, and erosion of benefits, workers experience increased apprehension about their future economic security.

The fear and apprehension about future job loss can be more distressing to some people than the actual loss itself. In systems in which rumors of layoff continue for months and the system of selecting workers for layoff is irrational and unpredictable, role insecurity will take its toll on all workers. Even following the layoff, those workers remaining will continue to feel vulnerable, and where "bumping systems" exist, many workers may experience survivor guilt.

Role insecurity can also be produced by internal organizational issues. New organizational leadership, reorganizations, and acquisitions always create varying degrees of worker apprehension about role security depending on how well such changes are managed.

10.12 Role-Connectedness Problems

ROLE-CONNECTEDNESS PROBLEMS *refer to one's degree of isolation from or overconnectedness to other members of an organization.*

High demands for adaptation occur both when a worker is overconnected to other organizational members and when a worker is excessively isolated from other organizational members. Earlier chapters explored how the overattachment among organizational members can break down the boundary between a worker's personal and professional lives, increasing stressors and cutting off sources of outside support and replenishment. Overattachment is reflected in an excessive degree of dependence in a relationship between co-workers, or in a style of supervision in which the supervisor's omnipresence and intrusiveness communicate to the worker the supervisor's lack of confidence in the worker's knowledge, skills, and capacity for independent judgment. In my studies of professional distress, there was also a high casualty rate among workers whose roles left them extremely detached and isolated from other organizational members. In human service agencies, for example, a high level of stress can be found among workers assigned to outreach roles and those who work alone in satellite offices isolated from the main organization. Such workers experience the same or a higher number of stressors as other workers, but have fewer supports by virtue of their isolation. Such isolated roles can be found in most organizations.

10.13 Role Deprivation

ROLE DEPRIVATION *is the sudden or gradual removal of all significant responsibilities from a worker.*

Role deprivation retires the worker on the job. That such a move would create a loss in status, a crisis in self-esteem, and increased isolation from other workers is obvious. Workers forcibly retired on the job may resign themselves to that status or, more frequently, begin exaggerated and futile efforts to maintain their visibility and personhood. The worker's defensive response is construed as further evidence of his or her inability to handle responsible job assignments. The character in Ralph Ellison's *The Invisible Man* could have been speaking for the role-deprived worker when he said:

> I can hear you say, 'What a horrible, irresponsible bastard'? And you're right. I leap to agree with you. I am one of the most irresponsible beings that ever lived. Irresponsibility is a part of my invisibility; and anyway you face it, it is a denial. But to whom can I be responsible, and why should I be, when you refuse to see *me*?

Role deprivation grows out of a number of conditions in the work environment. It may reflect a personality conflict between a supervisor and worker. It may reflect problems of role-person mismatch that the organization has failed to correct. It may also reflect the growing number of chronically distressed workers who have been moved to positions of diminishing responsibility.

John was hired to direct planning and research activities for a city of 50,000. While his research skills were quite strong, John found himself lacking a broad spectrum of the skills needed to adequately direct the city's planning operations. When this became clear to nearly everyone around him, John was "promoted" to the position "Research Consultant" and another individual was hired as "Director of Planning." In his new position, John was moved to an isolated office, assigned no significant responsibilities, and excluded from all (significant and insignificant) city meetings. John was rendered invisible—retired on the job.

Marsela had worked for three very productive years as a computer programmer when a new supervisor took over her department. The chemistry between Marsela and the new supervisor was, from the beginning, like oil and water (some co-workers suggested "gasoline and fire" as an apt metaphor). When the supervisor's efforts to fire Marsela failed, Marsela was given no meaningful work assignments, was excluded from all team meetings, and was ignored both professionally and socially in the work unit—retired on the job.

Most of us have read about sensory-deprivation experiments in which individuals are placed in a soundproof, pitch-black room that deprives them of nearly all external stimulation. Under such sensory deprivation, individuals become extremely anxious and disoriented. Role deprivation in the workplace is a form of professional sensory deprivation that exacts its toll on the physical and psychological health of workers.

10.14 Role-Termination Problems

ROLE-TERMINATION PROBLEMS *involve the failure to provide permissions, procedures, and processes to allow employees guilt-free exit from an organization.*

Role termination refers to the process by which organizations bring to a close an individual's responsibilities in a particular role, or bring to a close an individual's organizational membership. We have already noted, in the chapter on professional closure, the inability of workers to get out of closed organizational families with their self-esteem intact. At the other end of the continuum, in porous organizational systems, the exit of members from the organization could be more aptly described as staff fallout rather than staff burnout. Their exit is no more acknowledged than their presence was, for they have been rendered "invisible" for some time before their exit.

A major component of organizational health is the ability of the organization to allow members a guilt-free exit and to provide processes whereby members can leave with a sense of fulfillment and closure on their organizational family experience. It is remarkable how much time we spend on the technology of bringing people into an organization and how little time we spend figuring out better ways to let people out of the organization. Chapters 13 and 14 will explore some strategies to facilitate this process in ways that can promote the health of those leaving and the organization itself.

10.15 Role Stressors and the Organizational Family Continuum

Chapters 4 through 9 developed the contention that the level of worker stress increased at both ends of the continuum of organizational closure. It was stated that worker distress was highest in the enmeshed and disengaged organizational family types. This chapter outlined thirteen role stressors in the microsystem that increase stress-related casualties among workers. Consistent with this book's perspective on professional stress as a problem of ecological dysfunction, it is important to point out to the reader the relationship between these mesosystem and microsystem issues.

There is a direct relationship between the degree of closure in the mesosystem and role stress conditions in the microsystem. As the organizational boundary becomes too closed and nonpermeable at one end of the continuum and too open and diffused at the other, role stressors in the microsystem increase and the level of available role supports decrease.

The thirteen role stressors defined in this chapter are links to the experience of professional distress. Which of the stressors have you directly experienced during your professional career? Which are you currently experiencing? If you are a supervisor, which stressors would those who work for you report that they experience most frequently and most intensely?

≪11

Predicting and Managing Individual Vulnerability to Professional Distress

This chapter is not intended as a comprehensive primer on individual stress management. Other quite capable authors, from Hans Selye to Kenneth Pelletier, have already completed this task. This chapter and the next are, however, intended to provide a systems perspective on the management of professional distress. While we have placed great emphasis in the first nine chapters on the role organizational environment plays in creating professional distress, the next two chapters will emphasize both what the individual contributes to his or her vulnerability to distress and what actions we can take as individuals to lower that vulnerability.

11.1 Factors Influencing Individual Vulnerability
The following discussion will explore eight factors that can increase or decrease one's vulnerability to professional distress. These factors are illustrated in figure 11-A.

Developing strategies to decrease worker vulnerability to professional distress hinges on our ability to identify and influence the major factors that contribute to such vulnerability.

11.2 Your Body (Genetic and Developmental History)
The human body has incredible capacities for adaptation, but the intensity and duration of the adaptations may take their toll on our bodies' intricate machinery. This toll, however, is not exacted same on all people. Individuals vary greatly in their physical capacities to respond to sudden or sustained distress.

Each of us is provided, through the roulette of human genetics, a body that, except in the case of identical twins, is unique in both its

Figure 11-A
Factors Influencing Individual Vulnerability to Professional Distress

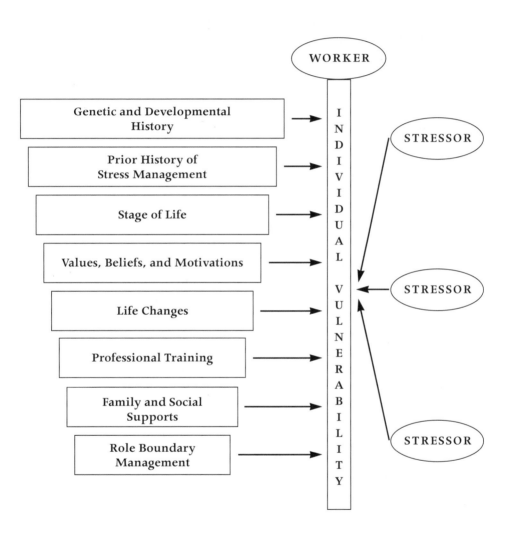

physiological capacity for stress and its physiological responses to stress. While there are generalized responses to stress that most humans share—what Hans Selye has called the general adaptation syndrome—the degree to which the body responds to stress through such mechanisms as altering blood supply and pressure, sharpening sensory acuity, and altering adrenaline production differs from individual to individual. Such genetically predetermined differences influence our tolerance to distress and our unique areas of physical vulnerability to prolonged distress. Prolonged distress reveals the weakest link in the body's system of physiological defenses.

Understanding these weakest links requires a knowledge of our unique physiology and the genetic and developmental influences that shape it. The cardinal rule of stress management—know thyself!—begins with this type of knowledge of one's own body. Some clues to our unique vulnerabilities can be gleaned by reviewing our family histories.

The issue is not just what vulnerabilities we may have inherited that make us vulnerable to high-stress environments. The issue, put simply, is given my family tree, what are the worst lifestyle choices I could make? It is tragically ironic that the worst choices we could make are often the very choices we do make. In a family tree loaded with alcoholism, it may be high risk for us to drink at all, but even higher risk for us to regularly use alcohol to self-medicate the effects of personal and professional stress. Smoking is a dangerous risk for any of us, but for those of us sitting on a family tree loaded with cancer, respiratory disorders, and cardiovascular disease, smoking—and smoking excessively in response to distress—could prove to be a most lethal choice.

In the early 1900s, temperance lecturers used to place a brain-damaged alcoholic in front of the lectern while they spoke. The alcoholic served as a living example of the horrors of demon rum. I have often had the impulse to copy this technique in my stress seminars. Imagine poor Joe fidgeting impatiently in front of the lectern, clearly overweight and underexercised, glossy-eyed from an infinity of sixty-hour workweeks and no vacations, washing down double cheeseburgers and fried potatoes with a beer, chain-smoking cigarettes between bites—all while sitting under a diagram of his family tree that shows four generations of deaths from cancer and heart disease.

The emerging field of holistic medicine has forged a definition of health as a state of harmony between body and mind and one's physical and psychosocial environment. The recognition that the majority of debilitating illnesses in this country are preventable, when that harmony exists, has sparked a revolution in our thinking about health and illness. People are reclaiming ownership of their bodies through a growing health consciousness movement that is increasing our knowledge about how to reduce vulnerability to the stress-related illnesses of modern civilization. The following pages will briefly catalog how one can decrease his or her physical vulnerability to professional stress.

Body Maintenance. There are three broad strategies for decreasing one's physical vulnerability to professional distress. These strategies are (1) establishing habits and rituals that provide regular repair and maintenance of our physical equipment so as to support rather than undermine the body's natural capacity for responding to distress, (2) learning techniques that alter and improve the body's physiological response to distress, and (3) developing an assertive role in advocating our health needs in the work environment.

The first strategy is designed to reduce the wear and tear on the body and to enhance the body's own capacity for day-to-day repair of body tissue. The most important components of this strategy are nutrition and exercise.

DIET. Diet is an essential component of effective body maintenance. By consciously controlling the type and quantity of foods we consume, we can enhance the body's efficiency and longevity. Many people under excessive stress lose touch with the needs of their bodies and fall victim to undereating or overeating. Undereating deprives the body of fuel to perform its complex functions, and deprives the body of essential ingredients for self-repair. Overeating, particularly chronic overeating that results in obesity, places an excessive strain on one's physical equipment. Over time, this can result in such conditions as diabetes and kidney and heart diseases.

Diet can have a profound influence on the availability of adaptational energy. When the body is working efficiently, energy is freed to interact with our physical and social environments and to meet other human needs. Poor diet reduces the availability of such energy and influences our emotional state. To feel well, one must eat well.

Seeking quick-fix gimmicks to correct diet problems is more a symptom of distress than an antidote to distress. Gimmicks range from grossly oversimplified claims of how various famous people lost twenty to fifty pounds, to diets that claim a particular food (for example, grapefruit) is weight-loss specific, to diets that claim you can lose weight without changing what you eat, to diets that focus on particular food groups (for example, proteins), to diets that claim you can lose weight by buying more eggs, cheese, beef, bacon, sausage, and mayonnaise while buying less fruit. These quick fixes are often dangerously combined with sudden demands for excessive exercise or drugs (for example, amphetamines) that have no proven utility in long-term weight reduction. The inevitable failure of such gimmicks marks one more excessive behavior in our lives that held out promise for relief and then let us down. Those of us who need to decrease our vulnerability to distress by altering our weight and long-range pattern of food consumption must pass up the temptation of quick fixes and seek out assistance that can help us achieve more enduring solutions to our dietary problems.

EXERCISE. Exercise can reduce our physiological vulnerability to high-stress work environments. The body's total physiological response to distress is designed to prepare us for a high level of assertion through a fight-or-flight response. Since neither fight nor flight is a viable option for most workers, distress provokes a level of physiological arousal that has no outlet. The physiological chemistry that prepares the body to respond to distress becomes toxic in the face of inaction, and over time produces a host of physical and emotional problems that Hans Selye christened "diseases of adaptation." Exercise serves as one of the most efficient vehicles to discharge excess arousal and enable the body to return to a more normal state. In addition to this direct link with the stress response, exercise also improves the overall health and efficiency of the body and expands one's tolerance and capacity for distress.

Nutrition and exercise need to be integrated into an overall health-promoting lifestyle that serves as a counterbalance to the high-stress work environment. Elements of such a lifestyle include utilizing physicians, dentists, and other health care providers for regular preventive health maintenance checkups, eliminating toxic habits (smoking, excessive consumption of caffeine, alcohol, and prescription and over-the-counter medications), and developing and sustaining relationships that allow one to be emotionally and physically nurtured.

The second strategy for averting the physical destructiveness of professional distress involves learning techniques that can alter the body's responses to such distress.

STRESS-MANAGEMENT TECHNIQUES. Stress-management techniques are becoming an essential part of modern medicine. These techniques, ranging from biofeedback to various meditation techniques, can actually save lives by altering the body's normal physiology. Figure 11-B catalogs a number of the more popular techniques. The techniques are highly recommended for people who are already experiencing stress-related physical problems or who are at high risk of developing such problems. A word of caution about the promoters of such techniques is, however, in order. Some will assure you of everything from complete freedom from anxiety to entrance into the promised land. Carefully sift through the sales pitches and decide which techniques can be of benefit to you.

Figure 11-B:
Techniques and Rituals
that Alter the Body's Physiological Response to Stress

Aerobic Exercise Training. Aerobic exercise is a systematic program developed by Dr. Kenneth H. Cooper designed to improve overall health through the strengthening of the cardiovascular system. Aerobic exercise can serve as a preventive health maintenance activity and can be used strategically as a means of discharging pent-up distress. Aerobic activities include jogging, walking, cycling, and swimming (Cooper 1977).

Autogenic Training. Autogenic training is a technique popularized by Johannes Schultz that combines self-hypnosis and a series of physical exercises to produce deep relaxation (Schultz 1959).

Benson's Technique. Benson's technique is a simple breathing and meditation exercise developed by Herbert Benson of the Harvard Medical School. Detailed instructions on the use of the technique can be found in *The Relaxation Response* (Benson 1975).

Biofeedback. Biofeedback utilizes one or more instruments to provide immediate information on what is happening inside our bodies, as well as techniques through which various physical processes can be modified. The instruments and the techniques target such areas as breathing, pulse rate, blood pressure, body temperature, muscle tension, and brain-wave levels. Advocates of biofeedback recommend it in the prevention and treatment of a wide variety of stress-related disorders (Brown 1977).

Clinically Standardized Meditation (CSM). CSM, developed by Dr. Patricia Carrington, involves an easily learned technique of meditative relaxation. Detailed instructions on the use of the technique can be found in *Freedom in Meditation* (Carrington 1978).

Progressive Relaxation (PR). PR is a technique developed by Dr. Edmund Jacobson. As the name implies, PR involves progressive muscular relaxation to prevent and treat stress and anxiety. The technique is easily learned and is described in *Progressive Relaxation* and *Modern Treatment of Tense Patients* (Jacobson 1929, 1970).

Tension-Reduction Exercises. There are a number of tension-reducing exercises, such as tai chi chuan and yoga, that can be used to reduce muscle tension and stress.

Transcendental Meditation (TM). There are a wide range of meditative techniques that have been used to alleviate excessive stress. TM was introduced in the United States in the 1950s by Marharishi Mehesh Yogi and has since grown to substantial popularity. Proponents recommend this meditation technique in the treatment of stress-related illnesses, drug abuse, ulcers, high blood pressure, and cardiac conditions (Hemingway 1975).

The third strategy for reducing physiological vulnerability to professional distress involves advocating for your own health needs in the work environment. Such advocacy requires skills in asserting your needs, and a style of negotiating for those needs that will succeed in your work environment. Working conditions that threaten your physical comfort and/or safety must be confronted. Conditions, ranging from overcrowding to exposure to toxic substances, from unsafe equipment to exposure to extreme temperatures, must be assertively challenged rather than passively accepted. When it comes to conditions that threaten physical comfort and safety, we must become activists—or pay the physical price for our silence.

11.3 Your Stress-Management History

Each of us brings to the work environment a unique history and style of managing stress and distress. Viewed as a whole, these personalized styles reflect enduring personality characteristics, a constellation of preferred defense mechanisms we use to maintain our self-esteem, and our unique areas of personal vulnerability.

There are several dimensions to the preferred defense structure that can work to increase our vulnerability to stress. Some of us may have difficulty revealing personal weaknesses or verbalizing strong emotions. Our thinking or our actions may become increasingly rigid. We may have difficulty accepting support from others and may, when distressed, push away the very assistance we need. Some of us may also have physical or emotional conditions that seem to quickly blossom when we are distressed. This is all a way of underscoring just how predictable most of us are. The best way of predicting how we will respond to distress in the future is to examine the often very consistent ways we have responded to distress in the past. It is that consistency that restricts our freedom of action in the high-stress work environment.

If we are to decrease our personal vulnerability to work-related stress, we must develop ways to increase the strength and flexibility of our preferred defense structure. The following are some suggestions in this area.

Personal Defense Structure–Organizational Match. It is essential that we recognize what types of work environments will be most conducive to our emotional comfort and health. Choosing an organization is not unlike the process of establishing and maintaining an intimate relationship. When the chemistry is right, the rewards to both the worker and the organization can be immense. When the chemistry is bad, the pain and turmoil in the relationship can disrupt the health of the organization and undermine the health of the worker.

The person-organization match begins by examining the congruity between one's personal style of managing stress and distress, and the explicit and implicit directives on how those conditions are to be managed in the work environment. For example, an individual with a very good history of stress management can enter an organization that won't permit him or her to use those previously successful methods and that fails to provide alternative methods of managing work-related stress. The worker could become a stress-related casualty in spite of his or her history. Conversely, a worker with a poor style of stress management may do very well in an organization that discourages his or her old styles and provides alternative methods of stress management.

When the economy and job availability provide choices, you should select an organization as carefully as you would select an intimate partner. The consequences of your job choice on your health and happiness may be as important as those of your choice of partners. The ability to make this match assumes that we have taken the time to examine our personal stress-management style and our areas of personal vulnerability.

Knowing Your Early-Warning Signs. Each of us has a unique early-warning system that indicates when our personal defense structure is approaching overload. It takes a conscious effort, however, for most of us to learn what our early-warning signs are and to sensitize ourselves to recognize when we are reaching overload. Scan figure 1-B in chapter 1 and see if you can identify the indicators you are most likely to exhibit when distressed. See how specifically you can identify the earliest indicators of excessive stress. What we often call our "early" warning signs actually signal an advanced level of arousal to distress. To discover what some of your true early-warning signs are, you can ask family members, friends, or co-workers for feedback on your style of managing excessive stress. Ask them what they first see that tells them you are having a bad day. Their answers may provide you with a number of subtle (and surprising) indicators of personal distress.

The importance of recognizing these early symptoms can't be overemphasized. All the stress-management techniques in the world are useless if we don't recognize when we need to use them. Early distress signals represent an internal feedback system that tells us when we are reaching the limits of our physical and emotional defenses. To ignore these signals is to invite serious physical and emotional illnesses. Such signals may also reflect areas of needed skill development, a need for time-out periods (vacations, for example), a need to take the next step in our professional development (school, job change), personal needs outside the work setting that are being neglected, or a need to reestablish a more equitable balance between work life and personal life.

Expressing Emotion. The ability to express emotion decreases our vulnerability to distress and strengthens our personal defense structure. Those of us who grew up in families in which the healthy expression of emotion was not the norm must acquire this skill.

Verbalizing emotion discharges the feelings and high level of physiological and psychological arousal that accompany stressful situations. When strong feelings cannot be verbalized or are discharged in an uncontrolled manner (for example, rage reactions), our personal defense system breaks down in a way that further erodes our personal and interpersonal health.

The ability to manage emotion is particularly important to people in service occupations who may encounter clients in great physical and emotional pain. The primitive emotions stirred by working with the abused, the diseased, the dying, and the deprived must have an outlet. Workers who are incapable of discharging this emotion, rather than helping others, are at risk of becoming victims themselves.

So how do we begin to improve our capacity for emotional expression? Perhaps we begin by identifying when, where, and with whom we can safely ventilate feelings elicited by our work experiences. Then we must take the risk of sharing. Expressing deep emotion, like other areas of communication, becomes easier with practice. Those for whom this is a difficult area may need to seek out specialized training that can enhance their communication skills.

Utilizing Counseling Services. One of the problematic aspects of professional distress is the difficulty of identifying whether our emotional turmoil is due primarily to distress in the work setting, to our unresolved emotional issues, or to problems stemming from our outside-of-work intimate and social relationships. There is a broad spectrum of counseling services that can help identify and resolve the sources of our discomfort.

Professional counseling can be of great assistance in examining and strengthening our own defense structure. As we come to understand our defense structure, we are able to achieve a much higher degree of self-acceptance and personal fulfillment. The patience and tolerance that can come from such self-examination make us much easier to be around, which, in and of itself, begins to reduce some of the self-provoked stressors in our lives.

Pace Setting. Our physiology and personal defense structure combine to provide each of us an optimum pace at which to conduct our day-to-day activities. A major part of managing excessive stress is controlling and shaping events around us in order to operate at that optimum pace. Trying to operate at someone else's optimum pace can be disastrous. Maintaining a pace consistent with our biological nature reduces the physical wear and tear of distress. One must recognize whether he or she is a turtle or a racehorse and act accordingly. While each has value, to ask the turtle to model the racehorse (and vice versa) would be absurd. When selecting professional organizations and professional roles, we need to match both to our biological nature. How would you compare your natural pace to that of your current workplace?

Limit Setting. A major contributor to vulnerability to professional distress is an inability to set limits. Professional advice to distressed workers often includes the following: Recognize the limits of your knowledge and expertise. Learn to say, "I don't know." Recognize the limits of your physical energy and how these limits change. Learn to say, "No, I can't" to additional role responsibilities during periods of low physical energy. Recognize the limits of those situations you cannot emotionally handle alone. Learn to say, "I need help." Recognize the limits of your emotional endurance. Learn to say, "I need time for myself." Clarify the priorities between your responsibilities to work and your responsibilities to those you love outside work. Decide under what conditions you must clearly say, "My needs come first."

Limit setting is a behavior that requires a belief in the legitimacy of our own needs and the skills to assert those needs in our interactions with the outside world. Assertiveness skills do not come naturally to many of us, particularly those of us who have been programmed for most of our lives to respond to the needs of others. For us, assertiveness training may be an important stress-management technique to acquire.

Using Time-Out Periods. Time-out periods are rituals that allow us to step out of stressful role demands and replenish ourselves. We can enhance our use of time-out periods by taking regular breaks during the day to replenish ourselves, and by taking vacation days and other days off to physically and emotionally replenish ourselves.

Laughing Your Way to Health. Laughter is one of the most important signs of both individual and organizational health. To laugh is to recognize our need to play, to stop taking ourselves so seriously, and to celebrate life and our affection for one another. Laughter demands that we slow down enough to observe and appreciate the lighter side of our day-to-day interactions. How might you be able to bring more laughter into your life?

11.4 Your Stage of Life

Daniel Levinson, in his classic study *The Seasons of a Man's Life*, and Gail Sheehy, in her best-seller *Passages*, outlined the problems, concerns, and needs that characterize the stages of adult development. Their studies have brought terms such as "mid-life crisis" into common use in our culture.

Their studies are important because they show how our individual vulnerability to personal and professional distress can change during different stages of our lives. Whether it is the young adult just entering his or her profession, the middle-aged manager, or the worker looking to retire in two years, each person's response to professional distress is partially shaped by his or her stage of life. What would you consider to be the most important developmental task of your current stage of life?

Knowledge of Human Developmental Issues. Knowledge of human development can be an important tool in understanding our changing vulnerability to professional distress. Ideally, one shapes a professional career with a beginning, a middle, and an end. Ideally, that career evolves in tandem with our personal and family development outside the workplace. Understanding and anticipating developmental changes along the way can smooth the process and increase the strength and flexibility of our defenses as we undergo developmental transformations.

11.5 Your Values, Beliefs, and Motivations

Values and beliefs can play important roles in determining our vulnerability to professional distress. In a survey I helped conduct some years ago of hospice nurses working with terminally ill patients, the majority of the nurses indicated that their personal and religious beliefs provided an important resource for managing stress in the care of the dying. The doctor, police officer, business entrepreneur, politician, union steward, and social worker all must draw on their personal values to make sense out of their professional experiences. We must each draw on or develop a set of values and beliefs that reconcile us to the realities we confront in our professional lives.

Seek Spiritual Replenishment. Professional "sense making" is enhanced when we seek out opportunities with co-workers to discuss values and beliefs and their relationship to our work. The effort can be enhanced by establishing sharing rituals with our professional colleagues that allow us to reinforce these values and beliefs. Whether religious or nonreligious, these value systems help reduce our vulnerability to professional distress. During times of rapid change and excessive demands for adaptation, rituals of sharing can help keep us grounded. It is under such turbulent conditions that it will be most important to be able to say, "This is who I am, and this is what I believe."

Sort Out Professional Motivations. It is not unusual for many of us to discover we are in a job or profession that we did not choose. In some cases, the profession may have been chosen for us by our family. In other cases, we may have simply fallen into the profession by accident or financial necessity. Sometimes these accidents work out and we are very satisfied in the type of work we are doing. More commonly, however, we experience added distress because of the mismatch between our professional role and our personal needs and aspirations. In interviews with extremely distressed workers, I have heard the following phrase repeatedly: "I didn't want to be a teacher [or nurse, or police officer, or minister, etc.] anyway!" Career counseling can assist us in determining whether we should seek a change in role or career and how to effect such a change.

Examine Our Personal Motivations and Expected Rewards. Professional distress is sometimes linked to the motivation that brought us to a particular field or role. Many people have been drawn by glamorized portrayals to particular occupations only to experience sustained reality shock when they actually get into such a role. The comment, "It wasn't anything like what I expected" typifies the reality shock inherent in transitions into the military, the ministry, and a wide variety of other technical and service occupations. Even when there is no such reality shock, our motivations can change as we age, necessitating a reevaluation of the fit between a particular field or role and ourselves. How are your motivations for working in your field different today than they were when you began working in the field?

11.6 Your Professional Training

Education and training can increase or decrease our vulnerability to professional distress depending on whether such training provided the knowledge and skills we needed to perform our expected role responsibilities, provided adequate preparation for the emotional demands of the profession, provided information about the nature of the organizations in which we would be working, and provided us methods of problem solving that were adaptable to changing conditions in the work environment.

The most basic element of professional stress remediation is to bridge the gap between the knowledge and skills that we bring to our roles and the knowledge and skills required to perform our roles.

Change is occurring so rapidly in most professions that nearly all workers experience some distress related to knowledge and skill deficiency.

There are a number of strategies that can reduce our vulnerability in this area. These include self-study through reading journals and texts that keep us abreast of new technology in our field, the return to a formal program of academic study, attendance at workshops, seminars, and other continuing education opportunities, and cultivating professional mentors both inside and outside one's work environment.

It is also helpful to try to match professional development activities as closely as possible to those stress-provoking areas of knowledge and skill deficiency you experience in your professional role. Self-examination and the use of supervisors, colleagues, and mentors to help identify and correct skill deficiencies are crucial aspects of reducing one's vulnerability to professional distress. It is also helpful to read the broader professional environment outside our organization and, by reading the directions in which that environment is evolving, identify those skills we are most likely to need in the future.

In the health and human services field, there is another deficiency often not addressed in preparatory training and education, and that is how to manage the emotional pain often inherent in such work.

A number of experiences can help prepare health and human services workers who are likely to face such emotional crises in their work. These include

- Peer support groups
- Therapy or analysis to explore one's areas of emotional vulnerability
- Supervision to clarify and work through biases, personal agendas, and issues that can increase our vulnerability in helping relationships
- Critical-incident training in which more experienced clinicians provide structured opportunities for us to emotionally debrief critical situations in the counselor-client relationship

11.7 Your Level of Life Changes

Another factor that influences our individual vulnerability to professional stress is the overall pace of change we are experiencing in our lives. Much of our knowledge in this area is based on the early research of Richard Rahe and Thomas Holmes, who studied the relationship between the pace of life changes and the onset of major illness. Using an instrument called the Social Readjustment Rating Scale, they numerically scored major life changes, such as deaths, separations, marital and legal difficulties, and changes in day-to-day lifestyle, to come up with a total score of life-change units. They found that the probability of onset of major illness rose significantly as one's life-change units increased (Holmes and Rahe 1967).

If we look at stress as the demand for adaptational change, it is clear that the pace of such demands could accelerate to the point where it surpassed our capacity for adaptation and resulted in the onset of stress-related physical and emotional problems. A big component in any strategy of stress management thus becomes how to control the pace of change in our lives. Examining our demand for adaptation and our level of supports to absorb such change can allow us to alter the pace of change. Figure 11-C illustrates four possible combinations in level of stressors and level of supports, and the implication of each combination for our vulnerability to stress-related problems.

Our ability to cope with stress can be improved by managing the pace of change in our lives and by working to enrich our level of social supports. If, for example, we find ourselves in a position of high stressors and reduced supports, we can reduce our vulnerability by cutting back nonessential obligations, setting limits on taking on added demands, and using our energy to rebuild sources of support.

11.8 Your Family and Social Supports

The major sources of support to ameliorate the effects of professional distress need to be built into the same work environment in which the distress is generated. That doesn't change the fact that many organizations fail to provide such supports, and that one's family and social network often are the only buffer between work-generated distress and the physical and emotional consequences of that distress. Lacking such supports in the work environment, many of us must develop a network of replenishing relationships and activities outside the work setting to ameliorate the effects of professional distress.

In health and human services, it is crucial that workers leave the work setting each day and emotionally replenish themselves through nurturing relationships and activities. When such replenishment occurs, workers can continue to enter the work setting and give emotionally of

Figure 11-C
Planning Change Matrix

High Stressors	High Supports	Your life is delicately balanced. Unexpected change could provoke serious distress-related problems. Work diligently to balance stressors with nurturing people and activities. Set limits and listen to your early-warning signs.
Low Supports	Low Stressors	You are understimulated. First, develop new relationships, then increase positive stimulation. Good time to take on challenges and responsibilities as long as support system is developed first.
You are in a position of high vulnerability. Reduce demands on your time and energy, and invest time in building new relationships. Use caution in making major life decisions. Stress-management techniques may be essential to avoid illness.	You are in a position of low vulnerability. You have adaptational energy available to increase change and stimulation in your life. It is a good time to take on new challenges.	

themselves to those in need. When workers fail to get such replenishment, they continue to give and give until they are empty—an emotionally numb and spent victim of professional distress. For workers in highly demanding roles, the development of a replenishment network is an important, if not essential, aspect of reducing one's vulnerability to professional distress.

Assess your own replenishment network by completing the diagram in figure 11-D using the following of instructions.

The Replenishment Network Diagram consists of six circles in which you will be asked to list the names of people or activities.

Figure 11-D
Replenishment Network Diagram

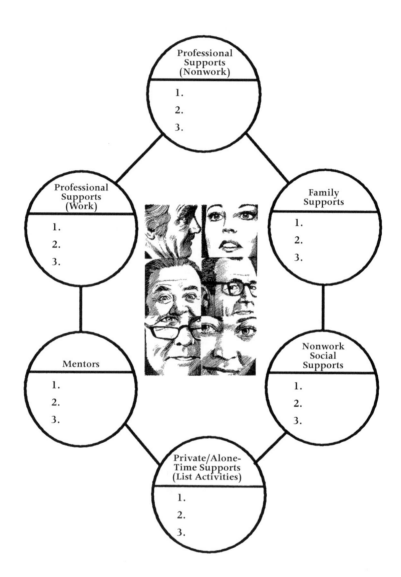

1. Beginning with the top circle, list the names of three people you
    consider to be professional peers, with whom you share ideas
    about work, and from whom you receive emotional support
    while discussing work-related issues. The catch is that none of
    these people can be employed by the organization for which
    you work.
2. Dropping down to the first circle on the right, marked "Family
    Supports," list the names of three people from either your nu-
    clear family (partner, son, daughter, etc.) or your family of ori-
    gin (mother, father, brother, sister, etc.) from whom you receive
    the most emotional support and personal affirmation when you
    return home from a particularly distressful day at work.
3. In the lower circle on the right, list the names of three people
    with whom you regularly socialize and from whom you receive
    positive affirmation about yourself in nonwork roles. Do not list
    people who have any affiliation with your organization or with
    whom you spend the majority of your time together talking
    about work-related issues.
4. In the bottom circle, list three leisure-time activities that are
    self-nurturing. The activities listed must be things you do
    alone—by yourself, for yourself.
5. In the lower circle on the left, list the names of two people (men-
    tors) you look up to, people in whose footsteps you see yourself
    following, and who provide you guidance in your professional
    development. These people may be from either inside or outside
    your current workplace.
6. In the upper-left-hand circle, list the names of three people who
    provide you with the most personal and technical support in-
    side your current organization.

Professionals from all over the country have filled out the Replenishment
Network Diagram as an exercise in my training seminars. Based on this
experience, I would like to share some observations about each component of the diagram. Organizational concepts from earlier chapters will
also be integrated into this discussion. What you should focus on are
those areas of the diagram that were most difficult for you to complete.

Professional Supports (Nonwork). Workers who have difficulty filling
in this circle often come from professionally closed or geographically

isolated organizations. When all of our professional supports and our professional identity are tied to one organization, our vulnerability to professional stress increases dramatically. Imagine the trauma of being the scapegoat in such a situation, and *all* of your professional relationships being with co-workers inside that organization.

We can decrease our vulnerability by developing professional peer relationships that transcend our organizational boundary. We can consciously expand this network by building relationships with professionals in allied agencies, by attending seminars and workshops, or by participating in local, state, and national professional associations. The key here is to have a network of people who affirm our professional competence and value even when that value may be undermined in our own organization.

Family Supports. This circle is fairly easy for most workers to complete. It can become difficult, however, for people who are single or divorced, people geographically or emotionally isolated from their family of origin, or whose family relationships have become more a source of distress than a source of support.

We can decrease our vulnerability to professional distress by creating a surrogate family, if none exists, nurturing our family relationships to ensure that they continue to be reciprocally supportive, and intensifying our energy in rehabilitating a toxic intimate relationship or terminating the relationship.

Nonwork Social Supports. For individuals without substantial family support, this circle becomes critical in reducing vulnerability to professional distress. It is through this circle that we create a small network of intimate relationships that can function as a surrogate family.

Workers may have difficulty in completing this circle if they lack skills in initiating and maintaining social relationships, or if they have recently moved to a new geographical area. Difficulty in filling in this circle can also reflect organizational dynamics. Workers in organizations that have gone through a process of social closure, or who are experiencing role overload, may have difficulty sustaining nonwork social relationships. Such social isolation is also typical of workers whose roles involve extensive travel.

Workers under excessive levels of stress, who have family supports but minimal nonwork social supports, may place undue strain on their families. One of the reasons there is such a high marriage casualty rate among workers in professionally and socially closed systems is that the family becomes the sole blotter to absorb work-related distress. Workers in such systems spill work-related distress into their families while bringing insatiable needs for support into their marital and family relationships—needs that no family by itself can be realistically expected to meet.

Nonwork social relationships allow us to affirm our value and broaden our identity beyond the work role. Such relationships provide a clear time-out period from work-related issues and a cushion of acknowledgment and support as a buffer from work-related stress. A work-dominated social network can be seductively pleasurable when things are good at work. But if things get bad, a worker may suddenly find himself or herself isolated, alone and vulnerable.

We can decrease our vulnerability to professional distress by avoiding a work-dominated social network and by cultivating nurturing relationships and roles totally unrelated to our profession and our work environment.

Private/Alone-Time Supports. Alone-time supports consist of activities or rituals that allow us to step out of our professional roles and interactions and center ourselves by experiencing who we are outside of these roles and relationships.

When our work life becomes frantic and spills over into an equally frantic personal life, we may find ourselves experiencing something just short of terror if we finally confront ourselves in isolation. Developing pleasurable and self-nurturing activities, enjoyed alone, allows us to catch up with ourselves and decide whether we like what we see and, above all, respond to our own needs and desires rather than others' needs.

Mentors. A mentor can be a powerful source of affirmation and support. With the possible exception of people very early in their careers, this is often a difficult circle for workers to complete. It seems many of us outgrow our mentors or discover they have clay feet. When we move beyond the early stages of our careers, it takes work to find and cultivate these special mentor relationships. As important as such relationships are, they cannot be measured in terms of frequency of contact. A mentor may be seen only a couple of times a year, but each visit can fire one's enthusiasm for learning for months.

Organizational dynamics can also influence our choice of and access to mentors. In closed systems, most workers will list a mentor from inside the organization (usually the high priest/priestess). The lack of boundary permeability in such systems restricts access to outside professionals who could become mentors.

Professional Supports (Work). This is probably the easiest circle for most workers to complete. Workers seem to develop supportive alliances even in those organizations that combine the highest level of aggregate stress and the lowest level of built-in supports. Exceptions can be found among workers who experience role underload or role deprivation, and among those who have been victims of scapegoating.

Looking at the Whole Replenishment Network. Having spent several decades studying high-stress work environments and the people who work in them, I feel very strongly that a network of nurturing relationships can serve as an antidote to many of the dire consequences of professional distress. The replenishment network, represented by the filled-in circles in figure 11-D, constitutes a protective shield.

The detachment from toxic relationships, the development of a nurturing network of professional, social, and family relationships, and the cultivation of self-nurturing activities serve as powerful antagonists to professional distress.

11.9 Your Role-Boundary Management

A major portion of this book addressed how professional distress spills into and corrupts the quality of our personal lives. While such spillover is often given momentum by forces in our work organizations, it can also reflect a worker's inability to establish and enforce a boundary between work life and personal life.

We have already discussed some recommendations related to boundary management, such as the development of multiple and varied life roles and the avoidance of a work-dominated social network. One of the most important additional boundary-management strategies is the development of decompression routines.

Decompression routines are rituals that signal to ourselves and others that one part of our life is ending and another part is beginning. These routines represent a "rite of passage" from our work life to our personal life. Our rituals often unfold in three stages: (1) rituals performed during the last thirty minutes of one's workday (for example, reviewing the day, organizing the first tasks for the following morning, cleaning one's desk), (2) rituals performed during the transition between work and home (listening to music in the car, reading the newspaper on public transportation, or stopping to work out), and (3) rituals performed in the first thirty to sixty minutes one is home (changing clothes, going for a walk, or planning the evening). Decompression rituals collectively allow us to diffuse the emotional energy from work and enter our personal lives with a minimum of spillover. In the absence of such rituals pent-up energy and feelings may be discharged on our family and friends in ways that undermine these relationships. How would you describe your own decompression (exit, transition, and entry) rituals?

11.10 Controlling Your Relationship with an Organization

I have tried to present in this chapter an overview of strategies and techniques that can reduce one's vulnerability to professional distress. A major theme that emerges from this review is that we can each take responsibility and control to shape our relationship with an organization. By taking care of ourselves, we can give our best to an organization. At the same time, we can demand an organization's respect for the physical and emotional needs we experience while in the work environment. When an organization is insensitive to those needs, and all efforts to negotiate more humane responses fail, then it is time to leave the relationship. Reduced vulnerability comes from our ability to assertively negotiate mutual needs as an active partner in our relationship with an organization, and, ultimately, from our power and freedom to terminate that relationship. In the next chapter, we will expand on this theme by exploring how one can respond to particularly toxic roles and organizational cultures.

⫸ 12

Surviving Toxic Systems

In the last chapter, we focused on how to assess and reduce your personal vulnerability to professional distress. In this chapter, we will explore what to do when that distress reaches an extreme state. Whereas the last chapter focused on preventing distress and enhancing our resilience in high-stress work environments, this chapter will focus more on strategies to directly respond to distressing environments.

12.1 Going Crazy: Is It Me or Is It This Place?

Toxic work environments make us question our very sanity. When we are caught up in such systems, we often can't figure out if it's us who's crazy or the situation we're in. It's hard to solve a distressing problem when we don't even know if the problem is inside or outside of us.

The question, "Is it me or is it this place?" is a legitimate one that requires serious analysis. There is always the danger of projecting our own periodic emotional turmoil onto an organization. We may wonder if our worsening view of the organization is the result of worsening work conditions or a change in our own emotional state. Organizations, like intimate partnerships, can serve as blotters for such projections.

The problem in closed systems is that we lose access to the kinds of feedback that can help us answer the "Is it me or this place?" question. When we are caught up in the soap opera of the closed system and our own increasing anguish in such a system, there are three things we must examine. First, we must ask ourselves two questions: What part of this current difficulty did I bring to the situation? What have I done if anything that has made the problem worse? These first two questions explore whether our current dilemma is part of some long-term pattern that we brought to the job or whether we may have inadvertently done something that contributed to our problem. These questions help us identify potential defects of character that may have contributed to our involvement in this particular type of organization, role, or situation.

The second area of inquiry requires a cold and unfiltered examination of the organization. Here we ask the following two questions: What conditions in the organizational environment have created or contributed to my distress? What actions or inactions of organizational leaders have created or worsened this distress? These questions help us diagnose environmental stressors as objectively as possible and to discover if our distress is unique or shared by other workers.

The third area of inquiry is the relationship between the individual and the organization. This inquiry explores the potential of restructuring this relationship for mutual benefit. It places blame not within yourself or the organization but with the space in between the two: *the relationship*.

Based on what we have discovered in our exploration of these three areas, we can begin to formulate our response to the most important question: What do I need to do? But before detailing potential responses to that question, let's explore our preliminary questions in a bit more depth.

How Did I Get in This Situation? It is only natural for someone in a miserable work situation to blame themselves for their decision to come to work with the particular organization. There are the inevitable questions: Why couldn't I have seen what was going to happen here? Why couldn't I have waited for a better situation? But unless such decisions are part of a chronic pattern, a subject we will return to shortly, there are many reasons why we can find ourselves in unbearable professional situations.

Some of us may have been in a situation in which our financial needs left us no choice but to accept the position we did. Even if we had other choices, it is important to understand how easy it is to misread the nature of toxic systems. As we noted earlier, some of the most toxic systems seem wonderful from the outside looking in. It is also probably true that we all share some attraction to such systems. Closed systems are attractive because they dramatically simplify the process of day-to-day living. We plug ourselves into the closed system, and it initially acts like a backup generator. The more of its power we use, the less we need to use our own power. Our autonomy and strength weaken through such reliance, as our personal comfort and harmony in the group increases. High priests/priestesses and the milieus of closed systems can be quite seductive. The structure, the isolation, the warmth and camaraderie, the powerful and benevolent leader, the exclusivity and elitism—all of these provide a powerful pull. The pull is particularly intense for those who have been wounded. Closed systems offer solace to the victimized even as they replicate the conditions for further victimization. The wounded have little suspicion that the promise they made to cast off their spoiled identities and be reborn was their first step toward revictimization.

It's easy to end up in a system that is harmful. Some are drawn to closed systems because they are in search of just such a system. Others drift in by mistake. Others enter healthy organizations that become toxic during their tenure. And still others are recruited by closed organizations because they have something that the organization greatly needs. In response to the question of how we got into such a situation, most of us need to tell ourselves simply, "Hey, it could happen to anyone." The exception is when our current situation is part of what appears to be a pattern. People can develop a long series of unhealthy relationships with organizations in the same way they can develop a series of such relationships with intimate partners.

Recognizing Enduring Patterns of Self-Sabotage. When we are trying to identify the source of our discomfort in the workplace, we tend to blame ourselves or project blame onto the organization and its key representatives. The truth may lean toward one end or the other but is often found in the middle. We may be left with a situation that calls for personal change, environmental change, or a change in our relationship with the organization.

Recognizing developmental experiences that lead us to seek out distressing situations doesn't take anything away from the organization's responsibility for what it does to, or fails to do for, its employees. Such recognition doesn't project blame for system dysfunction onto those who were drawn to and harmed by the organization, but it does help us take responsibility for our own propensity to be drawn to such systems.

12.2 Trapped in a Toxic Role or System: Assessing Options

In earlier chapters, we described potentially harmful organizational conditions. A toxic role is one a worker cannot perform over time without experiencing distress. A toxic role can evolve in an otherwise healthy organization. A toxic organization is one a worker cannot exist in, regardless of role, without experiencing a deterioration of physical or psychological health. Toxic organizations generate and sustain toxic roles for the bulk of their members. Every day there are workers in America realizing that they are in such roles or in such organizations.

It is important that the distressed worker explore our earlier questions to determine whether he or she is in a toxic role in an otherwise healthy organization, or if he or she is in a toxic organization. As healthy organizations evolve in response to internal and external needs, conditions arise in which toxic roles can inadvertently emerge. What makes these organizations healthy is their rapid recognition of the toxic elements in such roles and their willingness to change them. Distress in healthy organizations is usually transient. Toxic systems, in contrast, tend to perpetuate harmful conditions over long periods of time. While there may be some ebb and flow to the intensity of such conditions, over the long haul the conditions progressively worsen until the system self-destructs or goes through a radical reconstruction of its character. Workers in toxic systems need to find pathways of escape. They must recognize that any on-the-job resolution of their discomfort will be transient and that their continued affiliation with the organization will poison their health and happiness. On the other hand, workers in basically healthy organizations that are going through difficult developmental stages may benefit from sticking with their organizations and investing resources in helping to restore system health. The best of organizations go through such periods of transition and find ways to re-center themselves and restore their health and vitality. Such organizations reward those employees who provide loyalty and leadership through periods of crisis and transition. So the first thing workers must do is define as objectively as possible the circumstances in which they work.

Assessing the potential of an organization for change is risky. All systems resist change, but the degree of that resistance varies widely across organizations. Closed systems are by definition particularly resistant to change. They react, often extremely, to anyone who even implies there may be a need for change. In porous systems, internal change agents are simply ignored; in closed systems, internal change agents are scapegoated and extruded. This suggests that testing the limits of change should be done by design and with some forethought about one's safety in the organization.

To identify the most toxic organizations, look for extremes of organizational character that never seem to be tempered. Look for dictatorial leadership or invisible, ineffectual leadership. Look for organizations that have rigid, almost cultlike values, or that have no articulated values or values defined on any given day by the highest bidder. It's at the poles where systems do their most damage.

There are three basic strategy options you can use when confronted with growing strain in your relationship with a distressed or toxic organization. You can take an activist stance to change the organization or the nature of your relationship to it. You can take on a self-containment strategy, which allows you to disengage from some of the more negative aspects of the relationship. Or, you can leave. We will spend the rest of this chapter exploring these three strategies.

12.3 Professional Activism in an Organization

To consider the activist role, we have to look at what an organization needs—in other words, its developmental stage, and we have to look at what we need, where we are in our own personal/professional development. Where the needs of an organization and what we have to offer match, the activist stance is a viable choice. There are times, however, when we simply will not have the ability to pursue this path, and when nonactivism is an equally legitimate choice. Even the most dedicated professional will (and should) have a career marked by periods of engagement and disengagement. We must, as the folk adage goes, choose our struggles carefully.

Assessing One's Own Potential as a Change Agent. Exploring the option of activism in an organization must begin with a look at ourselves. We must determine whether we are characterologically suited to the activist role, whether we have the temperament and skills to assume the role, and whether we currently have the emotional resources and time to assume the a role. This is not a matter of judging ourselves good or bad if we answer yes or no to these questions; it is just a recognition of what is. If we are unsure of the answers to these questions, talking with a confidant who knows us well and who is not part of the organization may help us determine whether activism is a viable personal option.

Assessing an Organization's Potential for Change. Once we have looked at ourselves and judged activism to be a potential option, it is time to look at the organization. Perhaps the best way to assess an organization's potential for change is to look at its history. The best predictor of what an organization will do tomorrow is what it did yesterday. In spite of all the current management rhetoric about embracing revolutionary change, most organizations, like the individuals who populate them, are creatures of habit. You may not like where an organization is at today, but if its history demonstrates a capacity for self-evaluation and self-correction, it is usually worth sticking around and being part of the solution to its current difficulties. Where no such pattern exists, only those temperamentally suited to martyrdom are advised to pursue the activist role.

When Staying Can Do Harm. There are circumstances in which continuing to contribute to the sustenance of toxic organizations can perpetuate harm beyond our own growing distress, and yet many of us remain in such circumstances because of our loyalty to the organization's mission and aspirational values. Loyalty to an organization is a worthwhile value as long as the organization's mission and methods are characterized by viability and integrity. Viability means that the mission can be pursued and achieved in the current organization. Integrity means that the mission and the methods used to pursue that mission are worthy of emulation.

Organizational missions and methods can become outmoded and counterproductive. Aberrations in leadership, structure, and group process can create organizational systems that harm everything they touch. Expending energy to rescue such systems only postpones their demise and sustains for another day their power to do harm. Even where an organization's mission is noble and achievable, its history and character may preclude its attainment. In such cases, it is better that the organization die and its mission be assumed by another body more capable of bringing the original vision to fruition. By using their energy and skills to postpone such deaths and rebirths, well-meaning people can inadvertently increase the harm done by toxic organizations and see their own health deteriorate as well. It is a situation in which the best in us gets manipulated into serving the worst in a toxic organizational system. It is helpful to separate our commitment to a mission from our commitment to an organization that purports to pursue that mission. Whereas commitment to the mission may be unswerving, commitment to an organization is best left on a more probationary basis. Activism is a viable choice only when the potential for renewal is real. Consider the following scenario.

Walter proudly worked in a human services agency that had earned a reputation for service commitment and excellence. However, under new leadership the agency slowly drifted away from its historical focus on client and community service. Walter became increasingly concerned about what he perceived to be a misuse of agency resources (particularly the concentration of wealth at the top of the agency). Though disturbed by what he saw as a lost sense of mission and a growing movement into gray areas of ethical and legal conduct, Walter remained at the agency because of his commitment to its clients and his hope that he could be a positive force for change and renewal in the agency. His commitment continued in spite of what became a progressive escalation in the number and intensity of internal problems that compromised the quality of services to clients. One day a professional colleague from another agency shared with Walter the rumors that were circulating about Walter's agency and the fact that people were doubting that the rumors could be true because of their faith in Walter's and other long-term staff members' integrity. It was in this conversation that Walter recognized that his agency had crossed a line, and that its capacity for doing harm had surpassed its capacity to do good. He further recognized that his continued presence and that of other good members enabled the institution and its leaders to perpetuate what had become a toxic institution. As a result, Walter left the agency after a final failed attempt to use his influence to get the agency refocused.

Activism is a choice when an institution's capacity for good has not been irretrievably corrupted. To those who see themselves as activists and who see that their organizations possess viability of mission and integrity of methods, the following may be of help.

Developing an Activist Psychology. There are two things one must do to embrace the activist role in an organization. The first is to change the very image of what an activist is. The activist is willing to commit his or her energy and skills beyond the scope of his or her role responsibilities to enhance the health of an organization and the achievement of its mission. An activist is not the person who complains the loudest, files the most grievances, or is the first to call for action against an organization. Activism need not be visible or virulent, but it must reflect an appreciation of one's personal power.

Second, most of us have to change our view of ourselves in relationship to the organization. Workers often say that they have no ability to
make changes until they get to be a leader. While there are some things
one clearly can't affect from the bottom of an organizational hierarchy,
this view of staff impotence is fundamentally flawed except in the most
toxic of systems. It is flawed because it defines influence in terms of hierarchy. It may be more helpful for those considering an activist role to
look at the organization not as a vertical hierarchy—a pyramid—but as a
network of overlapping circles. It then becomes possible to define, intensify, and then extend our sphere of influence. Change is ultimately
brought about by injecting new or renewed values, technology, and relationships. By bringing in new or refined technology, new ideas and
values, or something the organization needs, one's sphere of influence
can be extended.

Studying the Organization. As an activist, you must become a student of
your organization. You must step back from your day-to-day enmeshment in the organization and truly study the system with fresh eyes. You
begin by analyzing its political and market environment, its structure,
its leaders, its rituals of communication, its responses to threats and opportunities. You use models to help identify the organization's strengths
and weaknesses. You study its internal and external boundary transactions. You identify each unit's role stressors and role supports. What will
begin to appear from such analysis is a deep sense of the organization's
needs. Then it's time to look for vacuums.

Finding and Filling Vacuums. A vacuum is a blind spot—something that
the organization needs to address but that no one has seen or that no one
has mobilized resources to address. Filling vacuums is the fastest way to
affect change in an organization because the vacuum is unclaimed turf.
Moving into a vacuum provokes much less resistance than changing an
already existing structure or process. Also, look for mechanisms of influence that have potential but are currently ineffective. This approach involves strategically using one's skills and energies to renew such things
as a quality improvement committee, a planning process, an ad hoc task
force, or something as routine as a staff meeting.

Injecting Missing Ingredients. I have learned as an organizational consultant and as an organizational activist that the most significant thing I

can do to positively affect an organization is to bring it an essential ingredient that is weak or missing. Organizations, like individuals, are prone to excesses of character—certain traits are extolled and exaggerated at the expense of other traits. You can formulate this strategy of filling vacuums by studying an organization and the needs of its service constituents, and then asking three questions. First, if this organization were a person, what would be its dominant personality traits? Second, what traits or experiences are missing and needed? And third, how could I act out these needed elements through my role and relationships in the organization?

There are three categories of things the activist can bring to the organization: new ideas/technologies, emotions, and values. All are delivered through relationships.

Seeding Ideas/Technologies. Most organizations operate in very turbulent and rapidly changing ecosystems and do so based on ideas and technologies often designed for a world that no longer exists. Ideas are the medium that allows an organization to close the gap between itself and its environment. That's not to say that organizations welcome new ideas. It is the rarest of occasions when an idea is embraced immediately because it so clearly galvanizes a needed shift by the organization. More often, a new idea will be viewed as an infectious agent and organizational antibodies will be released to fight it. Such resistance should be expected. Those of you who wish to seed your organizational cultures with ideas must view your ideas as time-release capsules. Many ideas will be resisted and lie dormant before they are activated and implemented. That's the nature of change. Organizations can utilize new ideas only when they are developmentally ready to receive them. By modeling a love for ideas and an openness for creativity and innovation, you can enhance the readiness of your organization to receive new ideas.

Seeding Emotions. The process of seeding an organizational culture with emotion is somewhat similar. Sometimes organizational cultures are almost emotionless. Such cultures have sacrificed emotional experience for analytical thinking and highly formalized relationships. What such systems need is a healthier balance between cognitive and emotional experience. To get that balance, missing ingredients must be brought in that define and model the professionally appropriate expression of emotion. The ability of a single employee to openly express emotion that everyone is feeling but not disclosing can have an enormously positive effect on organizational culture. It helps such cultures evolve rituals of dealing with powerful emotions in a healthy manner. Lacking channels of expression, emotions often get discharged indirectly and destructively.

There's an interesting story that illustrates this process. An organization had called me in to assess problems of employee morale, but scheduling problems resulted in a lag of about six months before I actually arrived on site and began individual and group interviews. What struck me was the dramatic difference between the problem as presented to me in the consultation request and the relatively good morale I found during my consultation visit. When I asked about this change, many workers referred directly or indirectly to the effect of a recently hired employee. As I listened to their descriptions, it suddenly became clear to me what had occurred. A vibrant and effusive new employee brought to a formal and overly serious organization that which it desperately needed in its culture. The new employee had brought *laughter* to the organization.

Seeding Values. I believe that all organizations are by their very nature conscienceless and essentially predatory. An organization is healthy only to the extent that individuals continue to infuse positive values into it, values that can guide its internal and external relationships. Once well-meaning individuals breathe life into an organization, it takes on an independent existence and operates to protect and perpetuate itself. Some organizations develop an almost viral appetite for growth, and feed on anything that enhances their size and image. Such organizational monsters can turn the most democratic of leaders into controlling autocrats. Many years ago the political scientist Robert Michels described this process as the "iron law of oligarchy." What tempers the organizational monster is a daily infusion of values from organizational leaders and members. Continual reminders of aspirational values help prevent aberrations that turn healthy organizations toxic. A single employee can have an enormous impact on sustaining or restoring such positive values.

This is the essential point: As an activist, you must bring to an organization what is weak or missing. To a decaying system, whose life force is ebbing, you must bring energy. To the frenetic organization, you must bring calmness. To the grieving organization, you must bring hope and

joy for life. To the shallow and frivolous organization, you must bring
seriousness. To the organization fixated on control, you must bring creativity. To the creative organization, you must bring a capacity to facilitate consensus. You must become an instrument of that which is needed.

This strategy raises an obvious question: What happens when what
the organization needs is something you don't have? Facing such a
dilemma, you can either work to cultivate that needed dimension, or
you can decide that the activist role is inappropriate given this circumstance. Choosing a strategy of activism or self-containment or disengagement is not just a personal question. One must be aware of the
potential fit between what one has to offer and what an organization
needs.

The Power of Questions. One of the most important weapons of the organizational activist is the power to ask the right question at the right
time. There are activists who make statements critical of an organization
and who propose specific policies or actions, but such strategies often
provoke resistance. Confronting an organization often comes out of our
own ego needs and usually excites an equally ego-centered response
from those who feel responsible for what we are confronting. Another
strategy is to ask questions rather than make statements. There are, of
course, questions that are in fact statements. Socrates was sentenced to
die for posing such indicting questions. An alternative style is illustrated in comic caricature by Peter Falk's old television character, Lt.
Columbo. Columbo operates in a style that might be called "passive confrontation": the timing and presentation of a question that bypasses the
listener's normal defense structure.

There are some simple keys to the effective use of questions as an activist. The first is to pose the question at a time when key individuals
can hear and absorb its import. What you are waiting and looking for is
a developmental window of opportunity in which the question can be
posed so as to elicit its greatest impact. Second, learn to suppress your
ego in posing the question, so as not to invite defensiveness or retaliation. Columbo, the apparently befuddled detective, demonstrates the
technique wonderfully. Third, imbue the question with true wonder
rather than have it stand as a rhetorical confrontation. To be effective,
the question must truly be a question, not an implied statement. For example, asking the question, "Why aren't we releasing the board minutes
or a summary of board activities to employees?" to a CEO is guaranteed

to trigger defensiveness because of its implied indictment. In contrast, the question, "Would there be any advantages to providing staff with board minutes or a summary of board activity?" is much more likely to elicit a nondefensive, positive response. "Why" questions nearly always prompt defensiveness, whereas "what if" questions often stimulate a reasoned discussion of alternative strategies. Learning how to frame such questions in your organization and perfecting the timing and tone of their presentation are essential activist skills.

The job of the activist is to make sure the right questions are being raised. It is not the question we cannot answer that poses the greatest threat to our organizations. It is the question no one sees. It is the question in everyone's mind that no one dares ask. Those are the questions that can kill an organization! The well-timed, well-framed, and genuine question can be a powerful intervention.

Building Activist Subcultures. My reference to Socrates suggests that there are risks inherent in the activist role. The most dangerous position in an organization is the isolated activist. If you are going to assume this role and survive over time, it is crucial that you build systems of support both inside and outside the organization. What you want to build inside the organization is an activist subculture—a group of individuals who are open to the potential for change and will support change even in an indirect role. Those individuals may not themselves be activists, but they are willing to be part of the activist subculture.

You begin building an activist subculture by seeking out others who share your key values and who respect your ideas. Informal networks nurture the most resilient activist subcultures, but there may also be formal structures that one can positively infiltrate. There may be key standing committees or ad hoc task forces in the organization through which one can pursue an activist agenda. One of the most overlooked sources of positive change in the workplace is labor unions. Many unions have become as hierarchical and abusive as the companies that spawned their births, but there are renewal movements underway in many unions that constitute very positive forces for employees and their work environments.

Whistle-Blowing. Whistle-blowing occurs when an employee, believing that the interests of the public outweigh the interests of his or her company, discloses to some outside party the company's involvement in illegal or unethical activity. Whistle-blowing often involves calling attention to actions that are either illegal or that could involve harm to innocent parties.

Because whistle-blowers are rarely protected from retribution by the company, whistle-blowing is one of the purest and highest-risk forms of activism. Those organizations most hurt by whistle-blowers are those that provide no alternative to whistle-blowing to resolve concerns over potentially illegal or unethical actions. When all other doors of redress are shut, a company invites whistle-blowing. There are circumstances under which there are no alternatives to whistle-blowing to prevent serious harm, but it's important to consider the personal costs of whistle-blowing. The choice should be considered with your eyes open and with a clear awareness of the potential consequences that may be involved. That an act of whistle-blowing is morally and ethically justified does not serve as a protection from organizational retribution.

Activism and Self-Repair. Activists must periodically isolate themselves from the stage of activism and wrap themselves in a cocoon for either self-repair or metamorphosis. Those who don't, end up self-destructing, sometimes in ways that do great harm to the very causes they sought to advance. When you look at an organization as a whole, there is ideally a balanced cycle of people moving in and out of activist roles. I've often seen change fail due to a breakdown of synchrony between such cycles. The very existence of a change effort—in fact, the very existence of an organization—can be threatened by the simultaneous disengagement of those who have invested the most passion and energy into bringing effort to fruition. Ideally, what occurs is a movement of some activists into a period of disengagement at the same time others are moving into renewed activism. Healthy organizations develop remarkable instincts about how to balance such cycles.

The Time Perspective: Pace Yourself. Social activism in closed systems must be balanced with efforts at self-protection. Earlier we discussed the power of closed systems to coerce, scapegoat, and extrude. Martyrdom is rarely an effective strategy of organizational change. The martyr's very existence can be erased from the system's history, or that history can be rewritten to portray the martyr as fool, lunatic, or traitor.

There is a very real danger of getting overwhelmed while pursuing the activist path. Taking on the whole system—particularly a complex and entrenched system—almost guarantees a process of confrontation, failure, bitterness, and cynical disengagement. People who want to take on such systems must enlarge their sphere of influence—in short, must begin to organize a social movement inside the organization or on the boundary between the organization and its environment. This strategy not only requires allies, it requires a unique time perspective. Everyone who takes on such a mission should post this slogan on their wall to look at every day: "PACE YOURSELF—IT'S A MARATHON!" There are many activists who become burned-out cynics because they mistakenly perceived the process of organizational change as a hundred-meter dash.

There are also alternatives to taking on a whole system. I think one of the best is to define a sphere of influence within which one can make a difference. This involves focusing your energies on a defined arena and a restricted range of activities. This strategy breaks the process of social change up into manageable bites and plots a strategy between that of activism and our second strategy option: self-containment.

12.4 Self-Containment and Self-Protection

An alternative to activism for the worker in a toxic system is a strategy of self-containment and self-protection. There are times when activism within a profession or an organization is not a viable option. There is a stance of self-contained dignity and productivity that is an option. With this stance, the individual defines his or her sphere of influence and works within this micro-world to make a contribution while staying disengaged from the broader organizational turmoil. Both the activist and nonactivist may require cocooning.

The Cocoon Analogy. The cocoon is a striking and mysterious metaphor. We know the unsightly caterpillar weaves a web around itself only to emerge as the butterfly of uncommon grace and beauty. But the mystery remains regarding what occurs in the cocoon that affects such a transformation.

I have found remarkable tales of strength in people whose life circumstances forced such a period of disengagement. For some, distress-related disengagement from social intercourse was reflected in a loss of speech. Maya Angelou, following a physical and psychological trauma, rarely spoke during her childhood and was only drawn out through poetry. She went on to develop remarkable speaking and writing voices. The actor James Earl Jones went through a similar period of silence due to a severe stuttering problem. Out of his silence was born one of the most powerful dramatic voices of all time. R. Buckminster Fuller, in a near suicidal state, decided he was not going to speak until he had something to say; he went on to legendary achievement in a variety of fields. Eric Hoffer, the waterfront philosopher, was blind from ages seven to fifteen and feared he would never read or write. When his sight returned, his appetite for both reading and writing were unquenchable and remained so throughout his life. There are personal and organizational messages in these stories. There are periods of detachment that can be transformative. People and organizations require periodic rituals of self-reflection, self-repair, self-focusing, and recommitment.

Creating Pockets of Hope. Focusing on a defined sphere of influence does not necessarily mean that one gives up on the organization as a whole. It involves creating pockets of hope that exemplify in real life what the organization needs to move toward. It is a way to seed the larger organizational culture by infusing a unit or project with principles and processes needed by the parent system. These pockets of hope can be thought of as unfunded, personally initiated demonstration projects. Gandhi once said, "We must become the world we wish to see." That's how pockets of hope work. Rather than getting embittered by the state of the larger system, we draw a circle of influence in which we have some degree of control—no matter how small—and create a model for the whole system within that circle.

Maintaining Personal Standards. Creating pockets of hope isn't easy when the milieu surrounding such activities is dripping with negativity and cynicism. Some of us absorb such negativity by osmosis and simply become part of the process of decay. This is the defense mechanism known as introjection. An alternative is to develop personal and professional standards that are not tied to the workplace. If your work environment is characterized by insensitivity and vulgarity, then you have to find a way to maintain some sense of honor and decency in that environment or you have to leave. Even the most benign bureaucracy tends to numb our sensitivities through sheer repetition and routine. The challenge is to transcend this bureaucratic Novocain by finding ways to periodically resensitize ourselves. One way to do that is through the use of external mentors.

Relying on External Mentors. External mentors are individuals outside our organizations who inspire us to rise above the negativity we sometimes face in our work life. When supports diminish inside the organization, one must either leave or develop a network of external personal and professional supports. You must go shopping for people who can enrich neglected dimensions of your own experience. You must assemble a network of special colleagues, teachers, coaches, and personal consultants. Shop for such people through your social network, through professional associations, and through colleges, universities, and training institutes. The key is to assemble a network of people who help you sustain your professionalism and integrity in spite of organizational conditions that challenge both.

Trapped: The Option of Passive Resistance. Now let us consider the kind of worst-case scenario in which many workers find themselves. Let's say you are in a very toxic organization, where conditions are nearly intolerable and where there is minimal potential for either activism or positive self-containment. Personal circumstances, however, preclude your imminent exit from the organization. What choices are available when you are trapped in this way?

First, it's important to acknowledge the suffocating feeling that being trapped in such a situation evokes. My general recommendation is for a person in such circumstances to focus all of his or her energy on gaining as rapid an exit as is possible. Where timely exit is not possible, I recommend that the individual quietly initiate a form of personal/professional strike by doing two things. First, doing only what work is assigned, and do it only at an acceptable level of performance while volunteering nothing, particularly one's enthusiasm and ideas. This is what unions refer to as "working to rule." The goal is to withdraw one's most valued resources—one's commitment and one's mind—from the organization. Ayn Rand illustrated this theme in her novel *Atlas Shrugged*, the story of how a cadre of leading minds chose to strike in protest of the values that had come to dominate American society.

Second, refuse to participate directly in activities that do harm. This is a strategy of passive resistance. In the literature on professional ethics, this is called "conscientious refusal." It reduces one's ethical culpability while one is part of an organization that may be committing illegal or unethical acts. Such a stance is reminiscent of Aleksandr

Solzhenitsyn's observation that the most precious thing in life is to not participate in injustice. By leaving toxic systems or refusing to participate in the injustices perpetrated by such systems, we withdraw the fruits of our labor. We go on strike. We refuse to allow our energy and our skills to be used to give credibility and sustenance to a toxic organization. There are risks of extrusion, of course, when one seeks to withdraw one's energy and skills at the same time one seeks to reap the continued benefits of organizational membership. The withdrawal of one's energy and ideas is best considered a transition to activism or exit rather than an enduring strategy.

12.5 The Process of Leaving

Choosing to leave a professional situation that is causing us distress can be a difficult decision, one that is sometimes as difficult as actually leaving. The answer to the question "Is it time to leave?" varies according to our life circumstances and what we want out of the relationship with the organization. We have to periodically reassess and attempt to make adjustments in our relationship with the organization. We can stay in the relationship as long as there is reciprocity, as long as our needs and those of the organization are being satisfied. It's time to consider leaving when our needs are not being met, when new, discomforting elements have been brought into the relationship, and when all efforts to correct the loss of reciprocity have failed. In short, it's time to leave when the price we're paying is greater than what the organization is paying, and I'm not referring exclusively to money here.

People who achieve the most successful exits from toxic organizations generally use two interrelated strategies. First, they begin to build a network of social and professional supports outside the organization in which they are working. The network provides them encouragement and links to other employment opportunities, and helps them with reality testing during the termination process. Second, they begin to rebuild their professional identity and self-esteem. The key here is that they develop a sense of professional identity that is not tied to the current work site. Seeking training on one's own to prepare for the next professional move and joining and participating in professional organizations are examples of actions that can help rebuild professional identity and self-esteem. In the most closed of organizations, some workers have also engaged a professional counselor to support them through the separation process.

Why Leaving Is So Difficult. There are several factors that make it difficult to physically and emotionally leave a closed organization. By closing off our contact with professional relationships outside the organization, closed systems deplete the very networks we could utilize to find new opportunities. The first difficulty separating stems from this isolation. Perhaps more insidious is that closed systems tend to cultivate our dependency on them. It's as if a nurturing patriarch says, "Stay here, we will take care of all your needs; it's not safe out there." There are no guilt-free pathways out of a closed organization. Exiting for any reason is viewed as a betrayal. Disgruntled workers are often emotionally or financially manipulated to remain in their organizations. The self-esteem of workers in closed systems becomes tied to their identification with their organizations. It's as if they have no identity and no value separate from the organization. Understanding this erosion of self-esteem is critical to understanding the failure to separate. When morale deteriorates inside the system, we talk constantly about finding other jobs, but it is only a remarkably small number of us who actually take the initiative to separate. The reason is that we feel we have little to offer outside our present system. In our isolation, we have developed a fear of the outside world and don't feel adequate to move into direct competition for new professional positions in that world.

Through the progression of closure, there is a fusion between the individual and organizational identity. Identification with the organization is such a central part of one's identity that the prospects of exiting provoke a high degree of anxiety. It is as if one has no identity and value separate and distinct from the organization. One's greatest fear is banishment from the group. Even organizational members who leave may find such separation so disorienting that they return to the fold of the organization.

Working within a closed organization over time encourages a form of emotional regression and this regression must be reversed as one prepares to leave. Because of the emotional symbiosis that has developed, leaving the closed organization becomes much more than just changing jobs. It is also important to understand what happens to people socially when they leave a closed system. The person exiting is rendered a nonperson, a pariah, and continued contact with the exiting person is often openly prohibited or viewed as a sign of organizational betrayal. To leave a job is to sever ties with an entire professional and social network. This can be particularly difficult where one's work relationships and personal relationships have become synonymous.

Nothing underscores the difficulty of leaving a closed organization more than observing how even the staff who have suffered abuses of power within the organization have great difficulty reaching the decision to leave. Marc Galanter has written about what Anna Freud called "identification with the aggressor." What he points out with great insight is that the abuse of an employee by a high priest/priestess takes place in the context of a historical relationship in which crucial needs of the employee were met (Galanter 1989). In this context, employee capitulation and outright compliance are more likely than is overt resistance or flight. The abuse of power is all the more unforgivable because it occurred in the safety of a historically nurturing and dependent relationship. What can one do when one is isolated, and when the source of one's pain is also the source of one's emotional sustenance? The double bind is an enormous one. Many readers will have already made the comparison between this description of people leaving closed organizational systems and the difficult, disorienting process of leaving an abusive relationship or leaving a cult. The first act of self-forgiveness once outside such a system is to let go of the self-blame for not leaving earlier.

How Not to Get Out. When organizations become toxic to the physical and emotional health of those inside and when all efforts to alter those conditions fail, there is no alternative but to escape. One must be careful of second-guessing the manner in which workers extricate themselves from such quagmires. Where there is room to maneuver and plot one's path of exit, there are important considerations. I often tell workers in such situations to structure a process of leaving that they can feel good about—to do everything they can to exit in a manner that reflects the highest levels of dignity and professionalism. The emotional intensity of feeling trapped in an incestuous organization creates a sense of desperation that can result in flight—a form of adult runaway behavior—or explosive aggression. The key is to leave in a way that will help you gain some emotional closure on the experience.

There are times when circumstances preclude exit, such as when a worker is tied to a particular geographical location with no employment alternatives or is locked into financial needs that don't allow a reduction in salary. Under such constraints, one can experience the suffocating feeling of being trapped—that one's soul has been bought and that one has lost all control over one's destiny. There are three primary coping strategies to use here. The first two we have referred to already: building internal and external supports to get one through an intolerable situation, and developing the self-containment/pocket-of-hope approach to self-protection. The third is to stay value-focused with a particular emphasis on values and experiences that transcend the work environment. Examples of how one can stay value-focused, include volunteering, cultivating mentor relationships reflecting one's core values, or pursuing academic or other personal-development activities. The more we can satisfy our emotional needs and express our values outside the workplace, the less vulnerable we are to the influence of an unhealthy work environment.

Disorientation Following Exit. The experience of leaving a closed organization varies with the individual and with the length of time one was in the system. But there are some things that can be anticipated. There is usually a mix of newfound freedom and anxious disorientation. It is important that one acknowledges the ambivalence and the disorientation he or she feels after leaving. Emotionally, some just leave and never look back, particularly when they have a more positive situation to throw themselves into. Others, particularly those most wounded by an organization, will find themselves facing a flood of emotion after they leave. All of the things they weren't free to feel inside the organization are magnified when they get outside. There is clearly a needed period of emotional decompression.

Predictable Stages of Healing. When people leave closed systems, they often experience a mix of confusion, anxiety, relief, a sense of violation, fantasies of revenge and retaliation, an incredible feeling of vulnerability, and senses of lost identity and lost integrity. Decompression from closed systems is about the rediscovery of self. Decompression involves relearning how to physically and emotionally listen to oneself. Decompression is about recognizing the legitimacy of one's own needs. It's about feeding the individual soul.

There are critical times, particularly after trauma or events of high emotional intensity, when the umbilical cord to the outside world must be severed and one must journey within. What one finds there can be surprisingly intense and scary. Anger is one of the most dominant emotions of people leaving toxic organizations. It is particularly strong when an employee feels betrayed and victimized by an organization or its key representatives. In light of this, the surprise is not that we have episodes of ex-employees returning to commit acts of sabotage or violence against an organization and its representatives, but that such acts happen so infrequently.

Most people can experience some degree of emotional closure simply with the experience of verbally expressing the anger to others in the form of storytelling. For most, the anger dissipates simply with the passage of time and the accumulation of new experiences. But when individuals perceive themselves as having been betrayed and humiliated, when the monetary loss is accompanied by a symbolic loss of identity, and when replacement experiences are not available, the anger can grow rather than dissipate. This is when we can get an ex-employee who begins to stalk a former supervisor six months *after* he or she was fired.

The lessons of anger are clear: (1) anger is normal when one has left an organizational relationship that has gone from positive to poisonous; (2) we need to find healthy ways to express anger to keep it from injuring ourselves or others; (3) when our anger doesn't naturally dissipate, we need to seek professional assistance to help us get emotional closure on this chapter of our life.

Reconnecting with the Outside Professional World. Moving on to new relationships and new activities is an essential step in rebuilding one's life outside a closed organization. The problem lies in how one is handicapped in building those new relationships and finding those new activities as one exits a closed system. If you have existed inside a self-contained professional and social world, your skills to communicate with the mainstream have deteriorated. Your language and daily rituals have been shaped inside this enmeshed organizational culture. If you then leave that culture, you are suddenly thrown into another world in which people think, act, and talk differently. It is not an overstatement to say that many people leaving closed organizations must relearn how to talk. Language inside closed systems is rarely transferrable to the outside world.

You could achieve this resocialization by slowly moving yourself (or throwing yourself, depending on your personal style) into new social and professional relationships.

Rewiring Your Brain. Leaving a closed organization after many years is like leaving your own culture or country or neighborhood and then returning many years later. It's almost as if your brain has to get rewired when you leave the toxic system. There probably is an actual neurological foundation for what we often describe as getting over a bad work experience. The needed rewiring may be minimal if our experience in a toxic system was a relatively short one, but more extensive rewiring may be necessary if we leave, or are suddenly thrust out of, an organization in which we've been enmeshed for ten years.

We've explored in detail how identities get transformed inside closed systems. What has to happen when one leaves such a system is a reconstruction of one's identity. We do that primarily through story construction and storytelling.

When people leave toxic systems, their state of disorientation includes a host of questions. Why did I ever go to work there? Why did I stay so long? Was the problem me or them? For those who were quickly scapegoated and extruded, there is the most basic question: What happened? Story construction is a way we frame an answer to those questions. The story also evolves through the healing process. In the days following an exit from such an organization, an individual may place total blame on himself or herself, or may project all the blame for what happened on the organization or a particular supervisor. In the weeks and months that follow, a more balanced picture of the organization and the former employee will be reflected in the story of what happened.

People leaving closed organizations are often angry for letting themselves be used by the system. They can't understand how they could have been so naive or stupid. One perspective that is very helpful in understanding experiences in toxic systems is that one's vulnerability to closed systems may spring from the best in him or her. Closed systems demand passionate commitment. The person least vulnerable for sustained involvement in a closed system is the person who simply doesn't care. A capacity to care deeply about ideas and people are the very things that can make us vulnerable to being drawn into and wounded by such organizations.

Getting a few key ideas or metaphors to help organize a story of what happened can be very helpful as well. The story we construct to explain the events needs to be metaphorically true in the sense that it rings with emotional truth. Whether it is factually true is less important. There is a very primitive metaphor that survivors of toxic systems have used in describing their experiences. They commonly describe feeling as if their organizations took possession of them—that their lives and selves had been consumed by the organization. To extend this metaphor, survivors need rituals that exorcise the organization from their lives and their senses of who they are. Rituals that sever connections with organizations, such as story construction (sense-making) and storytelling, can serve as rites of exorcism for survivors of toxic systems. Part of healing is letting go of the experience and reclaiming one's life—one's self. Now I don't believe that organizations actually possess people in the way we usually think of that term, but the metaphor of being possessed strikes an emotional truth to many people who have escaped these closed, cult-like systems.

What you have to hang onto in leaving a well-meaning but toxic organization is your memory of it when it was closest to achieving its aspirational values. You can hang onto the values rather than the memory of its later corruption. What you don't want is for your anger to obliterate your ability to see the best in the history of the organization and the positives that came from your participation in it. That's what you want to take away as a legacy, not the pain.

Scapegoating: Getting Isolated and Extruded. The person who has been scapegoated and extruded from a closed organization faces unique problems achieving emotional closure on the experience. First, the extrusion can occur very rapidly and completely (being led out of one's workplace by a security guard). Many people victimized in this manner spend years looking back trying to make sense of their experience. In the worst cases, former employees talk about their organizations years later with an emotional intensity that belies the passage of time. There may be temporal distance but there is not yet sufficient healing to produce emotional distance.

Some scapegoats have found it helpful to discover the processes that unfolded after they left or were extruded from their toxic organizations. Seeing the continued pattern of scapegoating that followed their exit helped many scapegoats depersonalize what happened to them. Scapegoats can also take solace in knowing that those people most differentiated from the enmeshed organization are most likely to be scapegoated. It is from this perspective that family therapists suggest that a family scapegoat is often the healthiest member of a enmeshed family.

The Pull to Go Back. What may be most surprising to some readers is that people who fight to leave a closed organization may later go back to work at the same place, sometimes repeating this process two or three times. Closed systems can become so all-consuming, so socially isolating, so identity-defining that one is emotionally overwhelmed when one exits such a system. The often predictable response is a return to the fold. This phenomenon is common in cults. Each time an individual leaves and returns, the price of readmission is a greater piece of the individual's self. At the extreme, the individual self finally disappears, leaving only a collective self.

My interviews have revealed a predictable pattern among people who have left and then returned to closed organizations, sometimes many times. After describing horrible experiences in their organizations, they are finally speechless in their efforts to explain their decisions to return. A typical remark goes something like this: "I know, given everything I've said, the decision to go back sounds crazy. I can't explain it." What they can't explain is their erosion of selfhood, their social isolation, and the powerful call to return to the closed system at times of emotional vulnerability.

It is so hard to get emotional closure after leaving a closed system that some people are pulled back in an effort to get some closure on the experience. It is like the family. If we don't leave home well, we have to keep going back and trying it all over again. Trying to leave closed organizations is very similar to trying to leave closed families: There are no healthy, guilt-free pathways for exit. We go back to closed systems for the same reasons we go back to toxic intimate relationships—to understand, to play out a fantasy that it can be different this time, to get a degree of emotional closure that allows us finally to move forward with our lives.

If we don't have emotional closure, we can even be emotionally involved in a system after we leave. People who have left the same closed system are intensely drawn to one another. I have heard story after story of survivors banding together for some process of collective decompression. Former employees (survivors) of one particularly toxic system continued to meet regularly for lunch for years after they left. It became a well-organized network that helped decompress each new generation of workers being extruded from the system. Their descriptions of their weekly lunches sounded remarkably similar to group methods that have been utilized to emotionally debrief prisoners of war.

As paradoxical as it might sound, some such groups can take on some of the same qualities as the system the members left. Groups of cult survivors banding together are themselves at high risk of taking on a cultlike quality. There is danger in creating what might be called an "ex-cult cult." Without their awareness, survivors can replicate major elements of the cult in their interactions.

The same thing occurs when one leaves a toxic organization but keeps the organization as the psychological center of one's life. Contact with former members of a closed system can be very helpful in the early stages of exit. Such contact helps one escape feelings of craziness and appropriately label toxic elements in the system. The danger is that in sustaining such relationships and such repetitive rituals of storytelling, one is actually sustaining one's emotional ties to the closed system. This can prevent severing the umbilical cord to the closed system and developing a new identity not tied to the system. By staying within the physical and social orbit of the closed system, one is also at risk of returning to it. Until the physical and emotional ties to the closed system are finally severed, one is like a stretched rubber band, always vulnerable to snapping back into the system.

From the Frying Pan to the Fire: Escape to Another Closed System. It is also common to hear of people who leave one distressing work environment only to be surprised and a little self-disgusted when they later find themselves in a very similar situation in another organization. How do we explain this? There are a number of possible explanations. The first is that such occurrences are a reflection of the growing number of unhealthy organizations in our culture. A second possibility for this frying-pan-to-the-fire syndrome is that unfinished business in one environment leads us to seek out a similar environment. People who leave closed systems often migrate to other closed systems. Painful and unresolved conflict with one high priest/priestess leaves us vulnerable to seeking out another high priest/priestess through whom we can resolve the original conflict. A similar phenomenon suggests a third explanation. One could ask the question, What is it about my personality and my needs that draw me to these types of organizations and these types of relationships? It is my experience that people coming out of closed family systems are inevitably drawn to closed organizational systems.

The same issue of compulsively recapitulating organizational dramas is equally apt for the fallen high priest/priestess in closed organizations. High priests/priestesses tend to move from one self-destructing system to another. It is a remarkable phenomenon. When Clutterbuck and Kernaghan tracked the careers of executives who had presided over the disintegration and complete collapse of companies, they found that the majority learned nothing from their mistakes. Most projected blame onto external circumstances and went on to replicate their mistakes in the next organization. The failure to recognize, acknowledge, and learn from failure is a major Achilles' heel of American organizations and their leaders (Clutterbuck and Kernaghan 1990).

Correcting this propensity to recapitulate failure at the top of American companies requires, as Tom Peters and others have suggested, a complete overhaul of our attitude toward failure. We need to celebrate "fast failure" as a discovery of valuable information rather than hide or rationalize failure. We need to individually and collectively come to terms with the phenomenon of failure. We all fail! We need to create rituals in which we identify and extract meaning from failure. We need to look at failure as feedback rather that as a sign of our individual or collective shame. If we acknowledge and learn from each small failure, we may be able to break the cycles of recurring failure that can threaten the health of individuals and organizations (Peters 1988).

The good news is that there are people every day doing just that—learning from their experiences in distressed environments. There are people every day achieving emotional closure on their experiences in toxic organizations. They heal, they learn, and they go on. There is life after a toxic organization.

12.6 Self-Care Strategies

There are lessons that people who have survived working in very toxic systems have to teach us about managing professional distress. The people who best recover from working in these systems developed a capacity for self-containment; went through cycles of engagement and disengagement in the organization by carefully choosing the issues and projects in which they were willing to invest energy; and developed elaborate networks of replenishing relationships and activities outside the workplace. They also became students of their organizations. Their ability to study and intellectually label what was occurring in the organization gave them an increased degree of personal protection and control. The experiences of workers who have survived extended periods of distress in very unhealthy work environments reveal four essential strategies of self-care.

The first involves the use of centering rituals—activities that allow us to stay focused on our own sense of what is important in our personal

and professional lives. These can be everything from prayer and meditation to reading value-centering literature. The key to this activity is that
we do it alone—it is a way for us to maintain some sense of personal
identity apart from all the social roles we perform.

The second strategy involves mirroring rituals—activities that bring
us into relationship with people who share our values and aspirations.
These can include both collegial and mentor relationships as well as our
intimate and family relationships, which are often neglected by personal
change agents and social activists. A participant in one of my workshops
once shared a very apt saying from his family: "There is danger in bringing light to the community that our own house is left in darkness." This
beautifully sums up the activist's tendency to give of himself or herself
to everyone except those closest. Mirroring rituals require relationships
that help us keep the faith—that reinforce the best in us.

The third strategy involves acts of self-care, which include everything from eliminating toxic habits from our lives to building in daily
activities that physically, intellectually, emotionally, and spiritually replenish us. Given the nature of the work performed by the professionals
I most often work with, I try to recommend activities in this category
that involve play and laughter.

The last strategy involves acts of service. I recommend that all people
involved professionally in personal and social change participate in volunteer service. This strategy reflects a unique paradox of professional
service. People who are drawn to service work over time begin to shrink
their commitment to service more and more into the professional arena.
Service ceases being service and becomes a job. As a result, people lose
touch with the sensitivities and desire for service that initially drew
them to such professions. The numbing effects of human services bureaucracies and prolonged exposure to intractable personal and social
problems inevitably blunt one's sensitivities. Many of us need to recapture our passion for service. Volunteer service reconnects us to the value
of personal and social change unrelated to our professional advancement
and financial rewards. I'm aware that this is an unusual recommendation. There were times in the late 1980s when I was sure someone was
going to throw a net over me and haul me off for codependency treatment for making such a recommendation. But the recommendation
stands.

⫷13

Systems Interventions: Boundary Management

From the opening pages of this text, we have explored the idea that preventing and managing workers' professional distress are contingent on creating and sustaining healthy organizational milieus. We further described how worker distress escalates as organizations get stuck at the closed or porous ends of the organizational family continuum. This chapter will describe how effective boundary management can promote organizational health. We will focus on how to prevent sustained organizational closure and how to intervene to open closed systems. The chapter will conclude with a brief discussion of interventions to help porous organizations.

Responding to professional distress can increase worker health and productivity, improve the reciprocity and mutuality in the relationship between workers and an organization, and enhance the overall ability of an organization to achieve its mission and goals. Failure to confront this issue can be measured in lowered productivity and morale, the continual drain of technical knowledge and skills from the organization, increased interpersonal conflict, and the escalation of distress-related health care costs. In spite of the risks of not addressing work-related distress, few organizations have made a systematic analysis and sustained response to the issue. The next two chapters will outline how such a response might be planned, implemented, and evaluated.

13.1 Avoiding Initial Pitfalls

What plagues closed and porous organizations seeking to reduce worker distress and improve organizational health is their own institutional history of problem solving. Closed and porous systems alike are prone to self-defeating styles of problem identification and problem solving. The closed system tends to deny problems or project blame for problems on infidel insiders or outside enemies. In porous organizations, there can be genuine confusion as to the nature and source of the problem. Even when porous systems clearly diagnose their more critical problems, there is often an inability to follow through with solutions. The employees of such systems may be numb from the relentless, year-after-year onslaught of consultants, task forces, climate surveys, change seminars, focus groups, team-functioning surveys, and leadership evaluations. What people don't see in porous systems is the ability of any of these highly visible interventions to enhance overall system effectiveness or to positively alter the worker's day-to-day experience. In short, interventions in closed and porous systems are often inherently flawed and doomed not just to failure, but to producing unintended harm.

Two analogies from medicine can underscore the dangers of poorly planned and executed organizational interventions. First, imagine that every time you encounter the slightest infection, your doctor places you on antibiotics and that in each episode of infection you take the prescribed antibiotics only until you begin to feel better—littering your medicine cabinet with half-filled bottles of medicine. Over time you discover three things: you seem to be getting infections more frequently, the symptoms in each episode seem to be getting more severe, and the antibiotics seem progressively less effective. This pattern of intervention produces unintended side effects that may be worse for long-term health than if no intervention had been applied and the body had been left to mount its own defense against the infections. Weak interventions into organizations are analogous to the overuse and misuse of antibiotics. They may temporarily suppress symptoms, but they often generate more virulent problems that are more resistant to future interventions.

Second, imagine that you go to a doctor with a number of troubling and painful symptoms that are in actuality a rapidly spreading cancer. Let's further imagine that the doctor fails to diagnose the cancer but instead gives you medicine that suppresses your discomforting symptoms, leaving you with the impression that all is well. By the time the symptoms resurface in even more stark and painful forms, it is too late to intervene and save your life either through surgery or other therapies. The doctor you praised for alleviating your pain in the short run in reality contributed to your premature demise. A similar process can occur in the relationship between an organization and a new leader or an outside consultant brought in to help address organizational problems. Organizational interventionists entering closed and porous systems tend to, using our medical analogy, cosmetically alter situations that desperately require surgery. By prematurely and superficially suppressing an organization's pain, the new leader or consultant contributes to its long-term demise.

I am not suggesting that new leaders and consultants consciously seek to harm organizations by misrepresenting their evaluations of the nature or severity of the problems they see. But there is a confluence of interests that can lead to this outcome. No new director or consultant wants to deliver a diagnosis of malignancy. Organizational boards and leaders resist severe problem diagnosis because of obvious feelings of responsibility. Under such circumstances, consultants and organizational leaders alike can misrepresent reality by creating the illusion that everything will work out for an organization with a few minor adjustments. In a period of making superficial changes, an organization may pass by the one window of opportunity it had to save itself. The problem is that what makes us feel good in the short run may work against our long-term health. The superficial response is the first pitfall to overcome in addressing professional and organizational distress.

The second pitfall to overcome is overcorrection, which involves creating new and unforeseen problems as a result of actions taken to fix other problems. When problem solving is approached in a highly reactive manner, such outcomes are almost guaranteed. I'll illustrate this pitfall with two stories. In the first, a small company responds to the discovery that one of its laptop computers has disappeared by implementing an elaborate system of control for all property. The system requires an enormous amount of paperwork and staff time and engenders growing conflict between technical staff members and those who come to be known as the "property police." Four months after the new system is implemented, the missing laptop is discovered in the drawer of an unused office. In this case, the solution to the misdiagnosed problem of computer theft created significant costs (in staff time) and ill will. The "overkill" solution created greater injury to the organizational culture than would have been incurred by the actual loss of the computer.

In the second story, a porous organization on the brink of disaster hires a charismatic leader who rescues the organization in a flurry of brilliant moves that within two years places the organization near the top of its industry. But within another two years, significant problems begin to develop in the organization, and by year six of our resurrected organization, we are entering all the stages of professional, social, and sexual closure described earlier. Overcorrection suggests that the seeds of tomorrow's problems are often buried in today's solutions. In the case described, the same high priest/priestess who saved the floundering organization in year one (the year of rebirth) went on to nearly destroy the organization in year six.

As we explore strategies to reduce personal and organizational distress and enhance personal and organizational health we must keep our eyes open to the risks of intervening superficially or too aggressively.

13.2 Creating a Comprehensive Strategy

Efforts to address professional and organizational distress are most often plagued by a lack of comprehensiveness, continuity, and follow-through over time. Many organizations feel they have responded to distress if they have an employee-assistance program or host an occasional stress-management workshop. In other organizations, responses to distress may be fragmented and uncoordinated among departments. In others, work-related stress is a fad topic that one year generates a wide variety of activities only to give way the next year to the next fad issue.

A systematic response to work-related distress requires a comprehensive plan developed with the participation of workers at all levels of the organization, and implemented with the full support of organizational leadership.

One model of strategy development combines the use of outside consultants with an internal task force. The task force is made up of organizational members who represent various departments, disciplines, and levels of authority. In unionized settings the task force is most successful as a joint management-labor venture. The task force is mandated to identify the nature, extent, and consequences of work-related distress, and to formulate both short- and long-range strategies to address the problem. Consultants are hired to help the task force to collect data, convert ideas into a cohesive written plan, identify strategies and programs used by other organizations, and implement an approved plan.

A comprehensive plan to address work-related distress should encompass, through needs analysis and strategy development, all the levels of the work ecosystem discussed in chapter 3. Examples of the issues to be addressed by the task force include the following.

The Individual. One function of the task force is to assess the personal vulnerabilities and costs of work-related distress in an organization. Looking at workers in the aggregate, what can one conclude about the collective vulnerability of the work force? The task force may examine the following:

- Are there medical problems that workers in the organization are particularly prone to contracting?
- Are there unique work stresses inherent to the professional disciplines that make up the organization?
- Do workers seem prone to a particular type of distress response (for example, self-medication, suicide)?
- Does the age composition of the employees make them vulnerable to particular types of professional distress?
- Given the nature of the organization and work roles, are there characteristics that would make a worker particularly vulnerable to stress?
- Given the answers to these questions, are there programs the organization could implement to reduce the individual vulnerability of workers?

Examining the above questions can help tailor a strategy that fits the unique needs and vulnerabilities of an organization's employees. A police department that collected data on the above questions concluded that it needed to have employee-assistance programs that focused on education and intervention in the areas of alcoholism, marital problems, and suicide. Another organization, composed mostly of men thirty-five years of age and older, looked at its casualty data and concluded it needed to do something to reduce employee risk of cardiovascular disease. Its overall strategy included components to reduce individual vulnerability through dieting, exercising, smoking cessation, and training in stress-management techniques.

The Microsystem. A major focus of the task force is to identify the sources of the distress workers experience in their work units. This data can be collected through surveys, one-to-one or small-group interviews, or larger employee forums. The goal is, first, to identify the intensity of stressors in the physical environment, in the organization of work roles, and in worker relationships, and then to identify the supports available to workers in these same arenas. The next chapter will catalog a number of strategies aimed at managing microsystem stressors and supports.

The Mesosystem. At this level of analysis, the task force examines professional distress in the context of the total organization by seeking answers to such questions as the following:

- What costs to the company are attributable to stress-related problems? (Employee benefit-utilization data such as health care costs, sick-time utilization, and worker-compensation claims can provide startling data when carefully analyzed.)
- Are there stressors caused by lack of clarity of organizational goals and objectives?
- Are there stressors caused by conflict between units of the organization?
- Is there sufficient organizational closure to give employees a sense of mission, purpose, and direction?
- Is there sufficient organizational openness to allow members to easily meet professional and social needs outside the organization?
- Is the pace of change in the organization congruent with workers' capacities for adaptation?
- Are there mechanisms built into the work environment to respond to distress casualties and help such workers back to health and productivity?

The Exosystem and Macrosystem. In the final level of analysis, the task force looks at how conditions and events outside the organization affect the level of distress experienced inside the system. This analysis is designed to help anticipate, identify, and plan for organizational change. The process requires organizational members to scan the environment and evaluate the organization. The goal is to create a shared big picture that can help workers understand and even anticipate changes unfolding in the organization and its environment. Whether one anticipates dramatic growth or decline as a result of changes in the organizational ecosystem, a plan needs to be developed to control the pace of that change and to support staff members through each stage of the process.

The combined mandate of organizational leaders, the task force, and the outside consultants is to capture on paper and implement a comprehensive plan to address worker distress. The plan should be capable of addressing distress at multiple levels; its strategies should be consistent with the evolving organizational philosophy and goals. The costs of implementing the plan should be based on an understanding of the organization's fiscal and human resources constraints.

13.3 Creating a Continuum of Support

I have frequently been asked, "If you could begin to intervene at one place in the organizational hierarchy to impact distress-related problems, where would you start?" After more than two decades experimenting with such interventions, my answer today without hesitation is that the most critical focus of attention should be on organizational leaders, managers, and supervisors. While there may be components of a comprehensive plan that are amenable to quick resolution (such as the elimination of some environmental stressors), the success of most plans hinges on the understanding, commitment, and skills of organizational managers and supervisors.

The reason for this focus is twofold. First, managers bear major responsibility for implementing organizational strategies of stress remediation. The ability of managers and supervisors to control boundary transactions makes them essential to the success of mesosystem strategies. Their ability to control the level of stressors and supports at the work-unit level makes them equally important to microsystem strategies. Second, the implementation of these strategies hinges on the ability of supervisors to use sources of emotional and social support to manage their own work-related distress. The point is not only that managers need to serve as role models regarding stress management and problem solving; it is also that managers who handle their own distress poorly have neither the desire nor the energy to implement strategies to reduce worker distress.

In a health and human services organization, for example, there ideally exists a continuum of support in the service environment. Clients and their families get service and support from direct-care workers, who get technical and emotional support from supervisors, who in turn get support from department managers and organizational administrators. Stress-related problems at the top of this continuum ripple down the hierarchy, resulting in increased distress-related problems among direct-care staff members and decreased quantity and quality of services to clients.

A key component of strategies to reduce professional distress thus is the training and supervision of supervisors and managers. Training begins with an analysis of a manager's own response to personal and professional distress, and then builds knowledge and skills to manage distress. At a minimum, such training should include personal and organizational indicators of excessive stress, opportunities for a manager to assess his or her own style of stress management, personal strategies and techniques to improve the manager's capacity for adaptation, supervisory strategies to identify and reduce role stressors, supervisory strategies to increase role supports, and supervisory strategies to respond to victims of excessive stress.

Supervision of supervisors and managers focuses not just on budget management and production goals, but also on the "process" being utilized to lead and manage individual and team performance. Such direction and consultation help a supervisor shape the long-term health of his or her unit and anticipate and resolve problems that threaten the unit's health or that of its members.

13.4 Gatekeeping and the Art of Boundary Management

While there is a whole range of organizational strategies for reducing stress-related casualties, the remainder of this chapter will focus on one of them. When we examined the relationship between excessive stress and the permeability of organizational boundaries, we saw that distress-related casualties were high both in closed organizations, with their rigid, impermeable boundaries, and in porous organizations, with their diffuse, almost nonexistent boundaries. The self-regulated organizational family was described as the ideal model of health due to its flexibility to move toward either greater openness or greater closure depending on the changing needs of members and changing conditions outside the system.

Managers are the primary gatekeepers in any organization. Their decisions determine the ease with which ideas and people from outside a system cross the boundary and enter an organization. Their decisions also determine who, when, and under what conditions organizational members will cross an organizational boundary to make professional transactions with the outside world. Much of the gatekeeping function is done by instinct with little conscious thought or design. It is clear from the concepts outlined in earlier chapters that boundary management has a profound impact on the level and intensity of professional distress experienced by an organization's members.

By regulating boundary transactions, a manager can increase or decrease the pace of organizational change and the level of professional stimulation, tighten or loosen intimacy bonds among organizational members, increase or decrease demands for adaptation, and inhibit or promote access to outside sources of replenishment. A manager has the capability of moving the work unit back and forth along the continuum from closure to openness based on assessments of the needs of the organization, the team, and the workers.

Clearly, there are times when both individual and institutional needs dictate that a manager reduce boundary transactions and increase organizational closure. The newly created organization must have a level of closure to finish building its own infrastructure and allow workers time to define themselves as a group. The recently reorganized agency, or the agency directed by new leadership, needs a period of closure to redefine itself and clarify its future directions. The organization facing external threats needs to rally itself into self-protective closure. The organization quaking from rapid change needs closure to restabilize itself and allow members a reprieve from the overstimulation of change. The work unit in which members have been overextended due to vacation schedules, sickness, or unfilled positions may need closure to reduce demands on workers and allow the unit to catch up to its production expectations. These all are conditions that a manager can analyze and respond to by regulating boundary transactions. As such situations stabilize and institutional and worker needs change, a manager can then alter the gatekeeping function.

Likewise, there are events in the lives of organizations that require managers to open systems through increased boundary transactions. Decreased sales of products or use of services, combined with increased competition, may demand opening a system to achieve heightened visibility. The growing community agency may have to increase boundary transactions if it is to successfully launch a capital fund drive. The organization needing to redefine its service program due to dramatic changes in the needs of its consumers may have to increase boundary transactions in its search for new ideas and new technology. Organizations seeking to grow must increase contact with their outside environments. The organization trapped in a process of professional, social, and sexual closure needs to increase boundary transactions if it is to avoid the disastrous consequences of prolonged closure described in earlier chapters.

A manager's gatekeeping functions include regulating both external and internal boundary transactions. In more complex organizations, for example, a major part of a manager's role may involve shaping the nature, intensity, and frequency of interactions between his or her work unit and other work units in the organization. Regulating such internal boundary transactions can be as important for controlling the level of worker distress as regulating external boundaries.

13.5 Preventing Dysfunctional Closure: An Overview

Chapters 4 through 8 described in detail the repercussions of chronic closure on the health of an organization as a whole and on the physical and emotional health of organizational members. The next few sections of this chapter will outline strategies designed to prevent such closure.

Strategies aimed at preventing the professional, social, and sexual closure of an organizational system must fit the unique characteristics of that organization and its work force. Strategies developed for a manufacturing firm will differ significantly from those developed for a police department or an insurance company. Through most of this book, I have covered a variety of organizational settings, but in this section, I will narrow the focus to strategies I first used in my consultation work with health and human services agencies. Though these approaches have been adapted for use in manufacturing companies, financial institutions, schools, police departments, prisons, sales organizations, and a variety of governmental agencies, the problems generated by organizational closure, and the abuses of power associated with such closure, present unique problems in health and human services because of the particular vulnerability of service consumers in that setting.

There are general principles common to all strategies used to prevent sustained organizational closure. Such strategies seek to

- ensure the mutual boundary transactions of ideas and people between an organization and its outside ecosystem
- influence the level of cohesion and intimacy among organizational members
- enhance the access of organizational members to outside sources of professional and social replenishment
- control and limit forces in the work environment (for example,

role overload) that break down the boundary between workers' professional and personal lives
- build into the work environment mechanisms that facilitate change while controlling the pace at which it occurs

13.6 Preventing Professional Closure

Professional closure begins with the assumption that all of the professional needs of an organization's members can be met inside that organization. This assumption is enforced through gatekeeping functions that inhibit staff members from developing and sustaining professional relationships outside the organization. The following strategies are designed to change that assumption and reverse those gatekeeping activities.

Avoiding the High Priest/Priestess Role. High priests/priestesses create or enforce dogma, cultivate the dependence of their followers, and build walls within which the rituals of leader worship can occur. While some organizational leaders may consistently seek out high priest/priestess roles based on their personality needs, many such roles evolve over time, based on the collective needs of and chemistry in an organizational family. Many managers dislike themselves in such roles but are unsure of both how they got into the role in the first place and how to get out of it once there. While there are times in the life of any organization when powerful, charismatic leadership may be needed, the creation of an enduring high priest/priestess role is a major contributor to an organization's progressive closure.

To organizational leaders wishing to avoid or get out of a high priest/priestess role, the following recommendations may be of help.

A. Recognize that organizational family members may need a high priest/priestess, especially under conditions of high distress and low supports. Under conditions of low self-esteem, emotional depletion, and escalating demands for adaptation, workers will trade their freedom and autonomy for the safety and security provided by a high priest/priestess. Decreasing stressors and increasing supports reduces the collective need for someone to fill that role. The microsystem strategies outlined in the next chapter can be beneficial in reducing the need for charismatic leadership.

B. Decentralize power and decision making in the organization.

Authoritarian styles of leadership are congruent with the high priest/priestess role. Moving to a more participatory style of management and decentralizing power and decision making decrease the dependence of workers on a centralized leader. Increasing the power of workers diminishes the awesome power that can accumulate in the role of the high priest/priestess.

C. Model boundary transactions. Cultivate outside sources of professional support and development for your leaders, managers, and workers. The high priest/priestess is reinforced when affirmations from the leader come only after shows of loyalty and devotion by his or her subordinates. The manager who visibly uses outside consultants, seeks new ideas from outside his or her organization, and develops an outside network of professional support tends to have staff members who are willing to do the same. Such activities work to humanize the role of the leader and avoid the image of omniscience that characterizes a high priest/priestess.

D. Identify ways to facilitate or acknowledge decisions rather than make them. The overinvolvement of the high priest/priestess in organizational decision making reinforces low self-esteem among workers and prevents their professional maturation. The effective manager delegates and rewards appropriate levels of decision making throughout his or her organization. By helping others think through their decisions rather than making decisions for them, the effective manager decreases worker dependency and increases the capabilities and self-esteem of subordinates. By discovering those situations in which being a consultant is more appropriate than being a decision maker, the effective manager resists the seductive power of the high priest/priestess role.

E. Learn to say "I don't know." The high priest/priestess is all-knowing, never makes mistakes, refuses to reveal his or her human frailties, and generally enforces expectations of perfection in a punitive fashion. To avoid playing such a role, learn to model such phrases as the following:
    • "I don't know. Let's find out."
    • "I don't know much about that. I'd like for you to research that question and let me know what you discover."

- "I made a mistake in that decision. Next time we face that situation, I think I'll have a much better idea of how to handle it."

Such communications model honest self-disclosure; give workers permission to make, talk about, and learn from mistakes; reinforce learning rather than perfection as an organizational value; and counter the omniscience of the high priest/priestess role.

Adding New Members to the Organizational Family. Perhaps the most significant boundary transaction a manager controls is the selection of people to become members of his or her organizational family. The management of recruitment and selection of new members can significantly influence the level of professional closure in an organization. As was noted in chapter 5, the homogenization of a staff is a critical early stage of professional closure.

While the primary selection criterion for new members should be their ability to provide needed knowledge and skills, there is room within this standard to make selections that broaden the outlook of an organizational family. Cultivating diversity among a staff not only improves the quality of client services, but it also provides a rich kaleidoscope of perspectives and ideas that will enhance creativity and inhibit professional closure.

Early attempts by a manager to diversify the composition of his or her organizational family must be done with an awareness of the following two points.

- Under conditions of high stress, groups tend to isolate, scapegoat, and extrude those members who are most different from the majority.
- New members from backgrounds different from that of the organizational family may need increased supports to ensure their professional and social inclusion.

The Code of Professional Practice. Establishing a code of professional practice can help in preventing organizational closure and professional distress. I will outline the overall function of such codes as there will be numerous references to it later.

If an organization is to assemble a heterogeneous staff and then open up an inward flow of new ideas, there needs to be some mechanism that establishes the standards of professional and ethical practice to which all members will be held accountable. I strongly recommend that all service-oriented organizations establish such a code of professional practice. A code serves multiple purposes, including defining organizational values, protecting the health and well being of consumers of an organization's services, enhancing public safety, and protecting the health, integrity, and reputations of staff members and an institution as a whole.

A code of professional practice establishes standards of behavior related to personal conduct, professional conduct, conduct in client relationships, conduct in staff relationships, conduct in professional peer/ agency relationships, and conduct related to public safety.

A code of professional practice may include traditional ethical rules (such as prohibitions against conflicts of interest), the collective folk wisdom of organizational members related to key issues, procedural directives (for issues too idiosyncratic or complex to be standardized), and an articulation of organizational etiquette.

Such standards should be developed methodically with full worker participation, reviewed with all new employees, presented in periodic refresher training, and periodically reviewed and refined.

Now, with this background, how does a code of professional practice work to prevent professional closure in an organization? A code defines expectations for the frequency and nature of boundary transactions by organizational members. For example, a health and human services agency code could state the following:

A. The agency does not have the resources to meet all of the professional development needs of its employees. Staff members are therefore strongly encouraged to seek outside opportunities for continued knowledge and skill development.

B. Professional development activities, to include activities outside the organization, are not an optional benefit but a nonnegotiable expectation of all employees.

C. Given that the organization does not have the resources to meet all of the critical needs of its clients, staff members shall be expected to utilize, through referral and collaboration, the full network of health and human services to aid clients.

D. Staff relationships with other professionals and agencies are strongly encouraged and should be marked by openness, respect, and an appreciation for workers with other areas of expertise and interest.

Such statements in a code of professional practice, reinforced consistently by managerial communications and behavior, not only legitimize but also mandate professional boundary transactions by staff members. They can break down the isolation, myopia, and us-against-the-world stance of closed incestuous systems.

Exclusive versus Inclusive Organizational Philosophies. A key element of the closure process—exclusivity—can be illustrated by looking at a human services system organized around a rigid, unchallengeable service philosophy. Rigid philosophies are attractive to organizations whose staff members lack knowledge and skill or suffer from excessive levels of stress. The rigid belief systems generate fixed, mechanical responses to clients that reduce the amount of thought and decision making required of the staff. Rigid client admission criteria are used to screen out potentially undesirable clients. Admitted clients receive treatment by recipe. Success is measured more by whether the client accepts the belief system than by whether the services are of benefit to the client. When clients get better in such a system, it is due to the truth of the organizational belief system. When clients don't get better, it's the fault of the client. This scenario unfolds almost anytime a closed organization attempts to fit a heterogeneous client population into a narrow, exclusive treatment philosophy.

A major strategy in the prevention of professional closure in a human services agency is the development of inclusive treatment and program philosophies. Such philosophies can be summed up by the adage "different strokes for different folks." More technically, these philosophies suggest that human problems spring from diverse and multiple causes, and that treatment approaches may vary depending on the characteristics and needs of the client. While they may create more humane and effective responses to clients, these philosophies require greater knowledge and skill and greater levels of adaptational energy on the part of a staff.

Every organization needs a philosophy to integrate and make sense of the activities of organizational members, but there are key elements in the development of a philosophy that are essential to the prevention of professional closure.

1. A philosophy must be broad enough to encompass the diverse needs and problems of an organization's current and potential customers.
2. A philosophy must be flexible enough to allow exceptions to prescribed policies and procedures, when such exceptions are in the best interest of a customer.
3. There must be mechanisms of feedback and self-examination in a system to allow a philosophy to evolve over time in response to the changing needs of customers and the development of new knowledge and technology.
4. Inclusive philosophies require higher levels of day-to-day support if workers are to sacrifice rules and rote behavior for the more difficult task of individualized assessment and service planning.

Planning Change. Closed systems are known for their resistance to change. Strategies to avoid closure entail building into organizations mechanisms that facilitate needed change, allow member participation in the planning of change, and control the pace of change.

Cataloging the array of planning technologies that can assist in this process is beyond the scope of this book. It is worth mentioning, however, some of the aspects of the planning process that can be helpful in preventing professional closure. Many organizations advance to the point of building employee participation into the planning process, but some neglect the need to increase professional boundary transactions. Closure is offset by using multiple mechanisms of feedback in the planning process. These mechanisms can include outside technical experts, literature surveys, and customer surveys.

The key elements of the planning process that relate to professional closure are (1) the belief that change has positive value if it enhances the mission and goals of an organization; (2) the increase of feedback into the system through boundary transactions; and (3) the identification of the supports and pace of change required to sustain quality of service and protect the health of workers through the change process.

Tearing Down Walls/Building Bridges. In chapter 8, I noted how xenophobia, the fear of outsiders, can become a strong component of organizational culture and drive a system into professional and social closure.

At other times, closure occurs because of ego battles, turf issues, competition, and conflict between community agencies. This process not only is a disservice to the clients allegedly being served, but also is destructive to all of the agencies and workers involved. Strategies to reduce professional closure will encompass any plan that promotes interagency collaboration and increases the ease with which professionals can cross the boundaries of their respective organizations and interact with one another. Plans that create joint planning, service, and case-coordination councils; shared training activities; and staff exchanges all serve to decrease professional closure.

Acknowledging Boundary Transactions. In closed systems, organizational rewards recognize commitment, allegiance to the high priest/priestess and one's social affiliations more than competence and performance. Professional and social closure can be prevented by the clear message that money, status, and other rewards will be distributed based on one's performance. This strategy works best when workers are told that their performance evaluation will focus, in part, on their initiative in seeking professional development activities and in establishing positive relationships with outside organizations and professionals.

Implementing a Comprehensive Human Resource Development Strategy. The most important way to prevent professional closure is unquestionably to design and implement a comprehensive human resource development (HRD) strategy. Historically, training and professional development have been viewed as luxuries and, as a result, have been the first areas to be sacrificed during budget cutbacks and reorganizations.

While comprehensive HRD strategies do require a significant financial investment, some HRD components, such as training, can be significantly expanded with a minimal financial investment and a lot of creativity. Consider the following example: A hospital department with twenty-four employees experienced a cut in the training budget to a level that represented an embarrassingly low investment in the staff's knowledge and skill enhancement. Having little to invest in training for each staff member forced creative options: Staff members agreed to implement a cost-sharing policy in which part of each training was paid for by the hospital and part was paid for by the staff member attending so that more people could attend outside training. Unit managers negotiated with state conference organizers to trade conference presentations by some staff members for free admission of additional staff members. The unit began to conduct workshops for a fee for other organizations and used the income to supplement the training budget. Each staff member who attended an outside training conducted an in-service workshop for other staff members on the material upon his or her return. A training-of-trainers course was provided to all staff members to increase their skills in making such presentations. The unit traded in-service training presentations with other agencies without cost to either. The unit used site visits to other programs as a professional development activity that required only mileage costs.

These options illustrate the point that training activities are possible even in the worst of financial conditions if there is a strong organizational and staff commitment to pursue the goal.

Comprehensive HRD strategies can have a potent effect on reducing professional closure by providing opportunities for staff members to meet professional needs and develop professional identities outside the organizational family. Such HRD strategies include career planning, the development of career ladders and career paths, support for academic education, assistance with professional certification, provision of technical consultation, support for affiliation with professional associations, and provision of in-service and off-site training programs.

That HRD strategies, such as training, increase the knowledge and skills of staff members and improve performance are important but not exclusive benefits. As a manager, I often sent staff members to outside training events in which learning was not the primary goal. Training events and other HRD activities can provide benefits that go beyond knowledge and skill acquisition. HRD strategies can provide staff members nourishing time-out periods from a high-stress work environment, facilitate staff members' development of outside networks of professional peer relationships, give staff members access to outside professionals who can serve as mentors, provide staff members sources of personal and professional acknowledgment from outside the organization, break down the myopia of a closed organizational system, and reinforce the use of outside resources for upgrading and problem solving in the system.

HRD strategies are potent forces in the prevention of incestuous organizational closure.

Termination: The Art of Letting People Go. I noted earlier that a shared characteristic of closed organizational families is the inability of members to leave a family guilt-free. The forces that bind members to closed organizations are so powerful that individuals must often leave in the way adolescents separate from closed family systems—they act out and are extruded or they run away. An important strategy in the prevention of professional closure is the development of permissions, procedures, and processes to allow members healthy and guilt-free pathways out of an organization.

Preventing organizational closure requires building mechanisms into the work environment that allow members to exit with a sense of fulfillment and a sense of completion, and with their self-esteem intact. Such mechanisms help protect the health of the exiting member and that of the organizational family through the termination process. Healthy termination strategies include the three components mentioned earlier: permissions, procedures, and processes.

A. PERMISSIONS. Workers can be told, as part of their initial orientation and their ongoing professional development, that they are not expected to remain with the agency for their entire career, that when the time comes to leave, the organization can assist them in making this professional transition, and that their exit can be planned so as to enhance their feelings about their job experience and to minimally disrupt the flow of services to clients. Managers can help employees wishing to leave by providing them feedback on the types of work they think employees would do well in, serving as professional references, granting time off for interviews, and using professional contacts to help employees identify job leads. This position recognizes that there are highly legitimate needs, such as money, broadening one's professional experience, and career mobility, that may make leaving an organization not only desirable but necessary. The alternative is the prolonged presence in an organization of a worker who is poorly motivated and probably providing client services with minimal enthusiasm, and whose negativity may be contagious to other staff members. By providing open pathways of exit from an organization, we can also avoid the disruptive effects of staffers job hunting via the "secret mission" approach, which is rarely ever secret. What a manager can ask

in return for such clear permission and assistance in exiting
an organization is that the worker continue to provide high-
quality services right up to the day he or she leaves.

B. PROCEDURES. Health and humans service organizations need
procedures that allow for a phased termination process between
an exiting staff member and his or her clients. These procedures
should build into the termination process a progressive decrease
in responsibilities, a smooth transfer of responsibilities to other
staff members or the exiting staffer's replacement, and a close
supervision of termination with clients.

The development of step-by-step termination procedures
meets the organization's needs to maintain efficient completion
of work tasks through the transition period. It also provides
daily evidence that the staffer is in fact leaving, which works to
counter denial of the impending separation and the tendency
to act as if the person isn't really leaving, right up to the point
he or she walks out the door.

C. PROCESSES. The termination of relationships in an organizational
family, like any significant loss, can trigger primitive group
emotions. Such responses capture the whole range of ambivalent feelings that surround the exit of a significant member from
an organization. The range and power of the emotions, when
not appropriately expressed or channeled, can prove extremely
disruptive to the health of the organizational family. Providing
members guilt-free exit from an organization requires that rituals be built into the termination period that facilitate the reciprocal emotional detachment between the worker and the
organization.

The group response to terminations can be described as a grief and
mourning process, with stages similar to those of any response to the
loss of a significant person. One can see during these stages denial that
the employee is leaving, a desire to leave with the exiting employee,
anger at the exiting employee, avoidance of the exiting employee, sadness that the employee is leaving, and acceptance that the employee is
leaving.

This grief and mourning process occurs at three levels in health and
human services organizations. The worker leaving the organization is
going through these stages in response to the losses of the agency, staff,

and clients. The staff is experiencing the loss of one of its members. And the exiting staff member's clients are experiencing their own sense of loss. When rituals of emotional separation are not provided, workers and clients get stuck at various stages of the mourning process with potentially destructive consequences to all concerned.

Termination rituals that help promote the health of an organizational family and the exiting member can include such supervisory actions as the following:

- Make repeated verbal references to the impending exit of the member from the organization.
- Identify the short- and long-range implications of the loss by answering each remaining staff person's self-query, "How is this going to affect me?"
- If the exiting member is a manager, quickly identify interim authority and the process and time line to reestablish more permanent leadership.
- When a supervisor announces his or her resignation, address the safety and security needs of subordinates by immediately increasing their access to the next higher level of organizational authority.
- Phase down the exiting member's activities and responsibilities. Decreased responsibilities will speed the transition among workers and the exiting member from professional role relationships to social relationships.
- Establish the transfer of support in the exiting member's key relationships. Consider moving to co-therapy to ease the clients' loss of their old counselor and to enhance relationship building with the new one. Identify the workers to whom the exiting member provided the most emotional and technical supports. These workers may need increased supervisory contact to help manage their loss.
- Allow the expression of anger by members (for example, "I feel like Jerry is abandoning us"; "It's such a bad time for Marsha to leave"), but protect the exiting worker. Help the worker process this aspect of termination. Try to prevent the worker from personalizing the anger by explaining that such feelings are a normal part of the process of ending significant role relationships.
- Build in time for individual good-byes. Make sure the exiting

worker is available to other organizational members. At all costs, avoid letting the worker resign and immediately leave the work environment; or resign, immediately take a two-week vacation, and leave without contact with other organizational members.

- Provide some form of ceremony that marks the final step in the termination process. Such ceremonies clearly, visibly communicate that the person is no longer a member of the organizational family. (These rituals are as much for the benefit of the ongoing health of the organizational family as they are for the benefit of the exiting member.)
- Build into final ceremonies other nurturing activities that meet members' needs (eating, drinking, playing, laughing).
- Provide some group-oriented activity immediately after the termination to allow the organizational family to redefine itself without the former member.

This section focused on how to prevent professional closure by shaping how new members come into an organization, how professional boundary transactions are maintained and increased, and how to allow members guilt-free exit from an organization.

13.7 Preventing Social and Sexual Closure

The social and sexual closure of organizational systems often grows out of the reduced boundary transactions, increased stressors, and decreased supports common to professional closure. The strategies outlined to prevent professional closure are thus an integral part of the overall approach to preventing social and sexual closure. Additional factors that influence social and sexual relationships among organizational family members include the following:

Role Modeling of Managers. Supervisory staff members provide, through their behavior and interactions, the model for interpersonal relationships in an organizational family. Given that health and human services work generally takes place in the context of interdisciplinary team relationships, this managerial function has profound implications for the health of the organizational family and the quality of client services. Important elements of the role-modeling function include the following:

A. LIFE-SPACE BOUNDARY MANAGEMENT. Do the managers have clear
    boundaries between their work and personal lives? Do they
    model through their lifestyles the need for personal and social
    replenishment outside the work setting? Managers who don't
    possess and model such boundaries are much less likely to
    either reinforce or respect them in their subordinates.
B. LIMITS OF SELF-DISCLOSURE. Do managers set limits on their level
    of self-disclosure to other organizational family members and
    thereby communicate that there are areas of their lives both out-
    side the reach of other members and inappropriate to bring into
    the organizational family? Managers, as well as clinicians, can
    use the self-disclosure in the human services setting more for
    their own self-growth and emotional healing than to respond to
    the needs of clients. Do managers respect intimacy barriers of
    other organizational members by refraining from overinvolve-
    ment in members' personal problems? Or do they create emo-
    tional dependence in subordinates by being overly intrusive or
    serving more as therapists than as supervisors?
C. LIMIT ON SOCIALIZING. Do managers refrain from developing
    work-dominated social networks? Do they inadvertently create
    competition and conflict based on their inclusion or exclusion
    of staff members in social relationships? Have they helped cre-
    ate an "in" group and an "out" group in the organizational fam-
    ily based on their patterns of socializing with co-workers
    outside the work setting?
D. MANAGEMENT OF ONE'S OWN SEXUALITY. Have managers re-
    frained from involvement in seductive behavior and sexual rela-
    tionships with other staff members? Supervisors who have been
    involved in sexual relationships with other staffers are power-
    less to confront problems arising from such relationships among
    other organizational family members. Have they modeled non-
    exploitive interactions with clients? Are managers comfortable
    enough with their own sexuality to talk to their staffs about
    sexuality and make it an issue in clinical supervision?

Orienting Staff Members to Problems of Social and Sexual Intimacy. Another aspect of preventing social and sexual closure in an organization is
to orient all new and current to the potential problems of social and sexual intimacy with other members. New members can be familiarized with

the issues as part of their orientation by a supervisor. Heightening the awareness of current members can be done in in-service discussions or workshop formats.

Such information probably does little to prevent problematic social and sexual relationships among co-workers, because the relationships spring from primitive needs that are likely to be only minimally modified by cognitive processes. The goals of providing the information, then, are

- granting permission to talk about intimacy issues as they relate to worker-worker and worker-client relationships
- providing words and labels to help a staff understand what is happening when problems in such relationships occur
- providing clear communication that social and sexual relationships among organizational members will be confronted as supervisory issues anytime they spill into the work environment and impair individual performance, team relationships, or service relationships

The Code of Professional Practice Revisited. Some organizations address social and sexual closure by setting guidelines, in personnel policies or codes of professional practice, that prohibit sexual relationships among members and the hiring of employees' spouses or relatives. Such guidelines may differ significantly from agency to agency. In general, a code of professional practice can reduce social and sexual closure in health and human services organizations by explicitly defining

- the responsibility of workers to sustain their physical, emotional, and social replenishment both for their own benefit and for that of their clients
- the values and standards that should guide peer and client relationships

Changing Role Conditions that Violate Personal Life Space. Any conditions in a work environment that break down the barriers between workers' professional and personal lives will promote the social and sexual closure of that organization. A key preventive strategy is to identify and alter those conditions. Conditions frequently mentioned as disruptive to workers' private lives include role demands that require overtime and taking work home, extended periods of on-call/

emergency responsibilities, excessive travel demands causing limited time with family and friends, shift work that creates social isolation, extensive demands for nonwork-time meetings and activities, and the inability to accrue or take compensatory time.

Structuring the Social Needs of the Organizational Family. Dynamics of interpersonal relationships can occur within organizations by design or the lack of it. Organizations that have decreased the most blatant and destructive aspects of social closure attempt to structure the relationships, identity, and process of the work group. Such organizations define roles, maintain task-oriented directives on a day-to-day basis, establish professional competence and performance as the criteria for achieving status, and provide managerial models for worker-worker relationships. In addition, these organizations recognize and manage the needs of workers as social beings.

It is important to realize that people working closely together will develop close friendships and alliances with their group as a unit, and that people need occasions in which they can celebrate their existence as a group and their affection for one another. Celebration rituals can include an organizational family and its extended family (spouses, children, and patrons). These rituals often take the form of parties for organizational anniversaries, birthdays or significant member achievements, reaching organizational goals, or saying good-bye to exiting employees. One agency I studied noted, after some very destructive social and sexual relationships among staff members, that many of its difficulties had started when the staff, due to program difficulties, had stopped meeting as a group in a structured setting. It appeared to the staff members that those meetings provided a healthy model for what staff relationships should look like outside the work setting. Without such ritual contact, the contact between group members continued but in a much more destructive manner.

The goal is to utilize social relationships to enhance the quality of life in an organization without having staff social needs supersede the achievement of organizational objectives. The group process of health and human services agencies can be monitored by supervisors to make sure the group's energy has not moved from the provision of services to clients to a focus on the social interactions of staff members. This monitoring process involves looking at the amount of time staff members spend with clients compared with the amount of time they spend with one another and the tenor of meetings in which the organization and, in particular, clients are discussed.

Shaping the Sexual Culture of the Organization. I noted in chapter 7 that every organization has a sexual culture reflected in the language, artifacts, ethics, values, attitudes, and relationships present in its environment. Sexual cultures differ significantly from organization to organization, as well they should. The sexual culture of every organization needs to be congruent with the system's mission. The sexual culture of a clinic specializing in the treatment of sexual dysfunction or that of a counseling center for rape survivors obviously needs to be different from the sexual culture of a job-placement center. In the former examples, the sexual culture of the organization is itself an integral part of the helping process. To illustrate how aspects of sexual culture can be shaped to inhibit sexual closure, the section below outlines the sexual culture of an organization whose services may include helping clients with issues related to sexuality. Review these as illustrative examples, and remember the admonition that sexual cultures must be shaped to reflect the unique needs and clientele of an organization. The following were components of the sexual culture of organizations such as mental health centers, youth services agencies, family counseling programs, women's shelters, and chemical dependency programs. The purpose of these strategies was to promote healthy, nonexploitive relationships among workers and among workers and clients.

A. PERMISSION TO ADDRESS SEXUALITY. There are clear permissions in the environment, reinforced by staff training, for staff members and clients alike to address problems and concerns related to sexuality. There are clearly stated values and expectations that staff members will address issues of sexuality in highly professional, direct, and nonjudgmental ways.

B. THE LANGUAGE OF SEXUALITY. A shared language has been developed to discuss issues of sexuality. The language contains carefully selected words that facilitate communication and are nonderogatory, nonexploitive, and inoffensive to clients and staff members.

C. FEELINGS VERSUS BEHAVIOR. The culture acknowledges that sexual attractions will sometimes occur between co-workers and between workers and clients, and provides a structure (clinical supervision) in which such feelings can be expressed. There are, at the same time, warnings about sexual relationships between staff members and strong prohibitions against worker-client sexual relationships.

D. WORKER-CLIENT BOUNDARY ISSUES. The organization's code of professional practice explicitly states guidelines and standards for worker-client boundary issues.

E. SEXUALITY AND SUPERVISION. Clinical supervision of counseling activities is designed to assist counselors in managing sexuality issues in helping relationships to the benefit of clients. Supervisors can also confront the progressive violation of intimacy barriers in helping relationships by noting warning signs that often precede worker-client sexual contact.

An organization can also use the supervision process to confront internal problems created by outside social or sexual relationships among staff members.

F. SEXUAL HARASSMENT. There is a strong prohibition in the sexual culture against any form of sexual harassment. Repetition of unwanted sexual advances, demeaning sexual humor, and the use of language that is debasing or disrespectful is consistently defined and confronted as inappropriate behavior.

G. GOSSIP. Gossip about the outside social and sexual activities of staff members is confronted as a professionally inappropriate act of personal and organizational sabotage.

When to Confront Outside Social and Sexual Relationships. The question of when to confront problems caused by staff members' outside social and sexual relationships is a difficult one for many managers. After numerous mistakes in judgment, the considerable graying of my hair, and the accumulation of at least some hard-earned wisdom, I recommend the following position. The role of the manager in this area involves three discrete functions:

1. A manager must confront any behavior of staff members that violates the letter or intent of the agency's code of professional practice.

2. A manager must confront problems directly related to the role performance of individual employees.

3. A manager must confront problems that disrupt team relationships and productivity, whether the source of the disruptions
is inside or outside the work setting.

Social and sexual behavior of staff members that does not impinge on
any of these areas is none of the manager's business, and to confront
such behavior would be a violation of the privacy of an employee.

13.8 Opening Closed Systems: Guidelines and Cautions

How does one begin to reopen an organizational system that has gone
through, and is still in the stages of, extreme closure as described in
this book? This is the question that often confronts the manager who
knows something is seriously wrong with his or her organization but is
unsure what to do about it. The question may also confront the new director who inherits a closed organizational family, or the organizational
consultant who has been called in to help with one of the crisis
episodes in the life of an incestuous organization. While many of the
strategies to prevent closure outlined in this chapter can also be used as
corrective measures, there are problems unique to the process of revers-
ing organizational closure.

Good-Intentioned Strategies That Create Casualties. When I first was
asked to come into closed systems as a consultant, I entered them with
a belief shaped by my clinical training as a group and family therapist
that most problems in complex systems were at their core ones of communication. I believed that if we got everybody locked up in a room for
several hours with a good facilitator, there were no problems that were
not solvable. Now, consider what I was doing: I was bringing together
people who as a group had layer upon layer of hidden agendas and mas-
sive levels of pent-up aggression, and who individually had personal
defense structures that were as fragile as they were brittle. What those
people needed was not the emotional stimulation of a process-oriented
group (which, unlike a task-oriented group, exists primarily for the expression of strong emotion and the enhancement of intimacy among
group members) but rather just the opposite: safety and structure and
replenishment!

At the point a consultant is brought in to work with a closed organizational family, most organizational members are physically and emotionally depleted. They usually are in a state of extreme vulnerability.

Staff members who have been hanging on by their fingernails may snap under the emotional intensity of process-oriented group meetings. What staff members need is a reprieve from the emotional stimulation of the closed system, not an intensification of that stimulation via group therapy. Process-oriented groups break down intimacy barriers and increase bonding among group members—the exact conditions members of closed organizational families do not need.

An important principle in planning interventions into closed organizations is that there are high risks of emotional casualties with any strategy that increases intimacy among members, increases emotional stimulation, or increases new demands for adaptation by opening the system too quickly. Whereas process-oriented groups may be ideal for porous systems, such groups may be counterproductive for closed systems, producing, at worst, more emotional casualties than problem resolution.

What to Do with the High Priest/Priestess. When opening closed systems, an important question is whether closure can be reversed without a change in leadership. The answer depends on the degree of closure that has been reached. Many leaders recognize fairly early in the closure process that there is a need to address internal problems before they seriously undermine the mission of the organization and the health of organizational members. These leaders may even suspect that there are aspects of their own role that are contributing to these problems. Under such circumstances, a system may be able to open up under its current leadership. Once the late stages of closure have been reached, however, it is doubtful that closure can be reversed without new leadership.

Many managers, including me, at some time in their careers have reached the decision after much soul-searching that organizational problems were unresolvable under their leadership, and that the best thing they could do for the organization was to leave. Unfortunately, management science has not found a way to reward such honesty by providing these managers a way out of their organizations with their self-esteem intact. Organizational leaders who neither perceive the need nor feel the desire to remove themselves from the high priest/priestess position continue to escalate the closure process to the point where no outside intervention is possible until a major crisis occurs. Such a crisis is usually precipitated by a gross deterioration in the health and performance of the high priest/priestess—deterioration that can include psychiatric illness, addiction, sexual exploitation of clients, misuse of agency funds, or other breeches in ethical and legal conduct. Outside intervention is then possible through a board of directors or a new organizational leader.

With increased sophistication in our knowledge of organizational life, it may be possible to avoid much of the above pain and turmoil. It may be possible to define predictable developmental stages in the life of an organization—each of which may require different leadership styles, personalities, and skills. Some managers may have the flexibility to adapt and effectively see an organization through all of these developmental stages; others may become specialists who will be brought in to provide leadership during one developmental stage and then leave as the next developmental stage emerges. Some managers may be selected to create, others to maintain. A career specialty is slowly evolving in which managers do nothing but start new organizations or come in to restructure organizations in crisis. Rather than chastising them for their inability to stay with one organization for the long haul, we are beginning to see these individuals as highly competent and valued management specialists. Such a perspective could help us understand the need for a change in leadership or a change in a leader's role and function as an organization's needs dictate movement from closure to greater openness or from openness to closure.

Bringing Replenishment to a Depleted System. The most important initial role of any consultant (or new director) working with a closed organizational family is to provide a source of needed replenishment for its members. Recommendations for the consultant or new director include the following:

A. Listen. Begin by assessing the individual and collective health of the organizational family. In organizations experiencing high levels of emotional pain and conflict, this can best be done through one-to-one interviews with the staff. (One-to-one meetings also weaken the group cohesion in closed systems.) In systems experiencing less conflict (and closure), use a combination of one-to-one and small-group interviews. The purpose of these interviews is to collect data and to build a supportive, nurturing relationship with each organizational member. In these interviews, a manager can give each staff member an opportunity to

- share information about his or her personal background (implying I am interested in you as a person)
- share his or her history in the organization and how he or she has experienced that history (I need your help to understand our history)
- identify the strengths and weaknesses of the agency (I need your help to plan our future)
- identify stressors and areas of insufficient support (I want to enhance your health and your enjoyment of what you do)
- provide recommendations on resolving problems and suggest future program directions (I will listen to and respect your ideas)

The interviews can provide an important vehicle for emotional catharsis and support for organizational family members. The process can also break the pattern of secret meetings with unstated agendas that usually plagues closed systems. A consultant or director can announce to all staff members the purpose of the interviews, distribute written copies of the major issues or questions to be addressed, and stick to the prescribed structure.

    B. PROVIDE AFFIRMATIONS. Through the interviews and interactions with staff members, a manager's or consultant's major goal is to replenish the self-esteem of organizational members. This is done through personal contact, listening, and providing verbal praise to individual members, organizational units, and the organizational group as a whole. All early interactions and activities should seek to reduce emotional demands and increase emotional rewards.

    C. OUTSIDE REPLENISHMENT. Boundary transactions can slowly be increased to provide an additional source of personal and professional strokes from outside the system. The increased presence in the organization of outside professional resources and increasing member access to outside sources of support can be instrumental in rebuilding the self-esteem of the organizational family.

Making Sense of the Pain and Chaos. One of the most disturbing aspects of the late stages of organizational closure is the inability of members to comprehend what has happened to them and the group. Member confusion is internalized as personal "craziness" or externalized as anger toward other organizational members. The humanistic passions and values that fueled the creation of an organization can go stale and leave members emotionally untouched. Meaningful professional and personal relationships can be ruptured, leaving nothing but remnants of unresolved conflict and resentment. Mutual support and loyalty can be turned to fear and paranoia. Collective guilt can flourish over an organizational impasse and the past scapegoating and extrusion of members from a group. The incongruence between group ideals and a soap-opera atmosphere can eat away at family pride and replace it with shame and self-indictment. Such primitive emotions scream for an answer to the question, What happened? The second function of the outside consultant who intervenes in a closed system is to help provide members an answer to that question.

It is the task of a leader or consultant to help organizational members find words and labels to describe and understand the changes that have occurred in themselves and in their organizational family. One of the most fulfilling aspects of my organizational studies has been watching the healing that occurs when I describe to workshop participants the stages of organizational closure and its consequences on individual staff members. The concepts, descriptions, and labels help bring order out of chaotic emotional experiences. By providing a cognitive handle on those experiences, a consultant is able to relieve some of the pent-up emotional energy and initiate the first stages of healing in an organizational family.

This healing is made possible by providing a cognitive model that reduces individual guilt, relieves members' fears about their sanity, decreases the need for blaming and other forms of projection, and affirms the value and integrity of individual staff members and the organizational family as a unit. Messages implicit in this cognitive model include the following:

- You are not alone! Many organizations have gone through the closure process with only minor variations. It is the rare service organization that doesn't go through the process at some point in its history.
- You are not insane! The emotional turmoil you all are experiencing springs from aberrations in the structure and process of the group, not from individual psychopathology. You are bright, sensitive people who inadvertently got caught up in a process that undermined your individual and collective health.

- No single person is to blame! There are no villains; there are only victims. The turmoil in your organizational family grew out of a slow and subtle progression of closure that no one recognized or consciously controlled. Most closure occurs because there is a period when it meets our needs. We all participated in the process without an awareness of its eventual consequences.
- The process is reversible! We may not be able to go back to where we were, but we can move forward and regain our individual health and restore respect and harmony in our relationships with one another.

Providing Structure and Safety. At an early stage in the intervention process a consultant will have collected a tremendous amount of data from organizational members and have begun the process of emotionally replenishing members. Some conditions in the environment will already have begun to improve. Some improvement usually occurs when there is an open acknowledgment of a problem and an announcement that an outside consultant will be brought in to provide assistance. Many workers already will have become more positive in their approach to their work, and there will usually be increased expressions of hopefulness about the future of the organization. The history of closure in the organization, however, will have most members continuing to fear what is going to happen. The task of a consultant or director at this stage is to provide both structure and safety.

Providing structure and safety usually involves creating a plan and process aimed at resolving organizational family problems, decreasing immediate stressors, and bringing a halt to any scapegoating.

A. THE LONG-RANGE INTERVENTION PLAN. At an early stage of intervention, organizational members will have begun to make sense of the closure process and have come to some understanding of how problems developed in the organizational family. The goals at early stages are to give members a clear sense of future directions and ensure their involvement in the problem-solving process. Based on the data gathered in staff interviews and on consultant and managerial recommendations, a plan is prepared and presented to the organizational family. The plan and its verbal presentation should openly acknowledge the major problems confronting the agency. The first goal is to break the no-talk rules governing communications about agency problems. A written outline of problems and strategies should be presented at the time of the verbal presentation. There is something about capturing such issues on paper that increases our control over them. The goal is to make hidden agendas explicit. The new message is: Agency problems will be brought out into the open, confronted directly, and resolved. The plan should clearly articulate the future of the organization. It should say where the organization needs to be with its problem six months from now and a year from now. It should include both the programmatic and the service issues that must be resolved to meet those time goals. The plan should outline in broad terms the process by which each problem will be addressed. This area is generally less well-defined and is open to refinement and input from the staff. The basic message is: Directly confronting and resolving problems is not negotiable; how we approach solving problems is negotiable. Organizational leaders should get organizational family members to participate in the problem-solving and healing processes.

B. DECREASING IMMEDIATE STRESSORS. By decreasing immediate stressors, organizational leaders demonstrate that the process started will result in concrete, observable changes in the work environment. These actions demonstrate good faith on the part of leaders and instill hope in the change process. Actions that can decrease stressors include the postponement of nonessential projects, the renegotiation of production time lines to free up emotional energy for the change process, and the establishment of interim communication procedures that enhance role clarity and increase performance-related feedback.

C. ABORTING THE PROCESS OF SCAPEGOATING. One of the most dramatic steps that leaders can take to decrease fear and increase feelings of security and safety is to bring to a halt the continued scapegoating of any organizational members. Such action decreases feelings of vulnerability not only for the scapegoats, but for all members. The new director of a closed system often inherits a situation in which a scapegoat is on the verge of extrusion. He or she can check continued scapegoating by modeling appropriate respect for and inclusion of the scapegoated member, assigning the former scapegoat visible responsibilities and supporting his or her performance, and eliciting help from other system leaders to restore the former scapegoat to full membership in the group. By preventing extrusion and restoring the functioning of the scapegoat through increased supports, the new leader sends a powerful message about how staff will and will not be treated in the organizational family.

Letting People Out: Bringing in New Blood. A new director or consultant working in a closed system will inevitably confront a backlog of individuals who, for whatever reasons, needed to leave the organization but didn't because of their emotional and financial bonds to the system and their deteriorating self-esteem.

Given the above, it is not a goal of the new director to keep all current staff members in the organizational system. In fact, the success of a new leader is measured in part by his or her ability to assist members in getting out if their needs can no longer be met in the system. In these cases, the director's job is to

- enhance the self-esteem of these workers so they feel they have something of value to offer and are marketable (or can become marketable) outside the organizational family
- enhance these members' boundary transactions to increase the chances that they will find a position that meets their current professional development needs
- decrease the emotional bonds between these individuals and the organization
- help these members get out of the organizational family with a sense of completion, fulfillment, and emotional closure
- demonstrate to other organizational members both the permission to leave and the preferred process for doing it

The old values of the closed system must be changed through a perspective that views the exit of a member as a potentially healthy and desirable event. It is important to recognize that there are employees who developmentally are in a role parallel to that of a teenager in a nuclear family system. For the health of the individual and the system, constructive ways must be found to facilitate his or her departure.

If there is a failure to let such individuals out of the system, they can prove disruptive to the processes of healing and redefining the organizational family. It is, quite honestly, too much to ask of them to emotionally reinvest in and recommit to a system from which they need to separate. When they are allowed to move out of the organizational family, new members with new ideas and perspectives can be brought in to further open the system.

Untangling Current Relationship Agendas. Perhaps one of the most difficult and painful jobs of a new director or consultant working to open a closed organizational family is untangling the relationship problems caused by the professional, social, and sexual closure of the system—problems that impair the ability of the team to function effectively. Suggested guidelines in this area include the following:

- Old relationship wounds between organizational family members that don't impair work performance should not be reopened by the supervisor except at the request of the individuals involved. Given the emotional depletion of closed organizational family members, raising old agendas may increase rather than decrease conflict.
- Where relationships have deteriorated through social and sexual closure, separate those individuals to the greatest extent possible in the organizational structure and, particularly, avoid placing them in power-oriented relationships with each other (for example, supervisor-supervisee). The goal is to prevent old and current nonprofessional emotional agendas from spilling into the process of client treatment and team functioning.
- Recognize that emotional conflict in some relationships can be so painful and so primitive as to be unresolvable in the short run. It may be necessary to assist members with emotion- and conflict-ridden relationships to separate from the organization both for their own needs and for the long-term health of the organizational family.
- Generally, any relationship problems that impair worker performance will be confronted and either resolved by participants or, at a minimum, suppressed so as not to interfere with job functioning.
- The goal in interventions into closed systems is to clean up old emotional agendas and move problems into the present tense by bringing them into the supervisory process as they occur.

Burying Old Ghosts. Individuals who have been extruded by, who have run away from, or who have left an organization under conditions of extreme emotional conflict often become ghosts that haunt the organizational family. Members continue to feel their presence or the emotions surrounding their terminations. These ghosts are created by the lack of permissions, procedures, and processes essential for the effective separation of members from their organizational families. A key factor in opening closed systems is the ability of a director or consultant to bury these old ghosts. Burial requires that organizational family members bring to emotional closure their feelings about lost members and the events surrounding their exits from the organization.

Renegotiating Values and Beliefs. Another critical step in opening an organizational family is renegotiating family norms, values, and beliefs. This involves not only moving away from the inflexibility and dogma of the closed system, but also building in a process by which values and beliefs can be refined based on changes in the outside environment, changes in the needs of organizational family members, and changes in the needs of clients.

The involvement of members in rethinking their professional philosophy and approaches and in developing an agency code of professional practice can be key components of this reformulation of who and what the organizational family is. Such reformulations often result in a broadened treatment philosophy, allowing more individualized approaches to client needs; a clear articulation of ethical and client boundary issues; and a professional stance that increases professional interactions and relationships outside the system.

The Ongoing Process of Opening the System. At early stages of intervention, most of the strategies for the prevention of professional, social, and sexual closure can also be used to promote movement toward the middle of the organizational closure continuum. The only caution is, again, that the pace of opening the extremely closed system should be carefully monitored. If the pace is too rapid, it will be stressful to organizational family members, who may once again seek refuge in the closed system.

The most common mistake of new organizational leaders and consultants is attempting to open closed systems too quickly. When this occurs, the leader or consultant is vulnerable to scapegoating and extrusion (as the history of Mikhail Gorbachev, among others, attests). The stimulation of increased boundary transactions must be offset by a commensurate level of emotional and personal supports from within the organization.

Every intervention into a closed organizational family is unique. I hope, however, that the guidelines set forth in this section will help other organizational leaders and consultants conceptualize and plan such interventions.

Intervening in Porous Organizational Families. I would be remiss if in this chapter on boundary management I neglected to make at least brief comments on interventions into porous organizational systems.

Chapter 4 described a continuum of three organizational types based on their degree of closure as measured by boundary transactions. The types included the closed (enmeshed) organizational family, the self-regulated organizational family, and the porous organizational family. The self-regulated type was described as the healthy model due to its ability to move back and forth on the closure continuum in response to changing needs. It is obvious from this model that interventions in porous systems would be remarkably different from interventions in enmeshed systems. The goal of interventions in porous systems is, in fact, to create a greater degree of organizational closure. A detailed discussion of such strategies is beyond the scope of this book, but some general ideas that have been used in interventions in complex, bureaucratic porous systems include the following:

- Developing a clear and cohesive statement of mission and purpose
- Articulating core values, strategic goals, and standards of professional and ethical conduct
- Increasing the visibility and physical presence of organizational leaders in their organizational family
- Increasing large-group activities to reinforce agency identity
- Establishing more charismatic, less formalized leadership
- Loosening the intimacy bonds in an organization's microsystems
- Increasing boundary transactions among microsystems
- Developing an organizational culture (history, philosophy, symbols, rituals, heroes, and heroines)

- Tightening gatekeeping functions periodically to reduce boundary transactions and increase internal cohesion and identity

I hope that this brief list will give the reader pause the next time he or she picks up a management recipe book that assumes organizations are homogenous entities controllable by a set of fixed interventions. When it comes to management strategies that affect boundary transactions, it should be clear that a highly successful intervention in a closed organization could prove disastrous in a porous organization.

⫸ 14

Promoting Health in the Microsystem

The purpose of this chapter is to move away from broad organizational strategies related to boundary management and to catalog distress-reducing interventions at the microsystem. This chapter will address the following four questions:

- What strategies are available to managers to reduce those stressors that are most frequently experienced by workers and that produce the severest distress-related deterioration in performance?
- What strategies can be used by managers and supervisors to increase the level of personal and professional supports in the work environment?
- What organizational strategies can be used to promote the overall health of workers and reduce their individual vulnerability to professional distress?
- What approaches can managers use to respond to employees who are experiencing distress-related deteriorations in performance and personal health?

14.1 The Goal of Role Balance

A model for the microsystem analysis of professional distress was outlined in chapter 10. This model examined the levels and intensities of role stressors and supports and how they were filtered through the personal defense structure of each worker. The implicit goal of this model was to help managers organize the work environment in such a manner that each worker could achieve and sustain role balance. Role balance was described as a condition in which a worker could successfully perform his or her role responsibilities without experiencing distress-related disruptions of his or her health and interpersonal relationships. The model identified three points of analysis and intervention for stress-related problems. When managers or supervisors suspect workplace problems that stem from professional distress, they can

- identify the role stressors in the work unit and manipulate the environment to reduce those over which they have control
- identify the role supports in the work unit and manipulate the environment to increase them
- recognize problems in workers' personal defense structures and intervene individually and collectively to enhance the strength and flexibility of those structures

14.2 Strategies to Assess Role Stress Conditions

Many managers and supervisors are instinctively aware of distress-related problems in the work environment, though they often under-estimate the impact of such problems on individual workers and the work unit. The initial step in addressing such problems in the work environment is the systematic collection of data to identify the nature and intensity of role stressors. This analysis can be conducted as part of the broad organizational strategy recommended in the last chapter, or it can be initiated by a departmental manager or unit supervisor.

Many organizations already have available data that can reveal the impact of professional distress on their employees. It can be extremely useful for an organization to look at the following categories by work-site location, work unit, and job title or category: health care costs, worker-compensation claims, absenteeism and tardiness, employee turnover, accidents, grievances, requests for unit transfers, lost materials due to breakage or theft, consumer complaints regarding services or products, and exit interview data from employees leaving the organization.

Additional sources of data can come from formal employee surveys, ongoing feedback mechanisms ranging from suggestion boxes to employee forums with top managers, employee health screenings, and the use of special outside consultants to conduct formal assessments of distress-related problems. The goals of this initial step are to identify the extent and nature of role stressors in the organization, assess the impact of those stressors on the organization, and establish areas of baseline data by which future intervention strategies can be evaluated.

14.3 A Schema for Strategy Implementation

I recommend the following seven-step process for implementing microsystem strategies to reduce role-stress conditions:

1. Identify and define stressors as clearly and completely as is possible.
2. Develop a strategy with employee participation to address the major stressors, and identify what data will indicate whether the strategy has been successful.
3. Implement the strategy on a small scale and on a time-limited basis.
4. Check data to evaluate the strategy.
5. Identify unanticipated repercussions of the strategy on other parts of the organization. (Did reducing stressors in one role or unit escalate stressors in another role or unit?)
6. Based on outcome, either fully implement the strategy or develop and test alternative strategies.
7. Build in a mechanism to continue to evaluate and refine the strategy.

The following sections will outline intervention strategies to address the thirteen role stressors discussed in chapter 10.

14.4 Strategies to Address Role-Person Mismatch

Role-person mismatch was defined earlier as the misplacement of a worker in an unsuitable role given his or her levels of knowledge and skills, level of stress tolerance, or style of stress management. Strategies to reduce role-person mismatch problems include the following.

The Recruitment, Screening, Selection, and Role-Placement Process. Most role-person mismatch problems occur due to flaws in the process of selecting new members to add to the organizational family. A review of the process must include a recognition of the forces that contribute to errors in employee selection and role placement. The following observations refer to this process:

- Increases in the workloads of team members that often accompany the loss of one or more team members create pressure to make speedy, but not necessarily effective, hiring decisions. An

appropriate and short-term reduction in unit workload will
decrease such pressure.

- Forces at work in the applicant, from financial need to the ego-
involved competition for a job position, contribute to role
misplacement. Relying on the judgment of an applicant about
whether he or she can perform a particular role is highly questionable under such circumstances. It is the judgment of the
manager, who knows the knowledge and skill demands and the
stress inherent in the open position, that must determine the
issue of match, not the ego-involved judgment of the applicant.

- Making assumptions about candidate qualifications and failing
to validate those assumptions, either through an employment
interview or reference checks, are two major contributors to
role-person mismatch.

- Once a manager gets an inkling during an interview that he or
she has found the person for the job, the thoroughness of the
interview tends to radically decrease. It is imperative that managers recognize this tendency and force the continued rigorous
examination of their candidates. Such "first inklings" are often
triggered more by the personality of the applicant than by the
applicant's technical knowledge and skills.

- Interviews measure presentation of self and one's ability to articulate how to perform a job. Such skills are not necessarily
synonymous with actual performance abilities. Reference
checks are essential to ensure that a candidate's performance
skills are commensurate with his or her interview skills.

- Most job applicants are inclined to list references who will assure the prospective employer that the candidate can walk on
water. Insist on supervisory references in addition to co-worker
and collegial references. Test the objectivity of references with
direct questions related to the candidate's weaknesses, areas of
needed skill development, types of roles the candidate would
find most stressful, and problems in prior roles and how they
were resolved.

- Once role misplacement has occurred, numerous forces will
work to postpone correction of the problem. New employees
are often given a "honeymoon period" of low expectations.
Supervisors often postpone raising performance issues on

the assumption that early performance problems are just the transition to a new role and will work themselves out. New priorities after the open position is filled divert the supervisor's attention and decrease close observation of the new employee. There is a tendency for new employees to overachieve during the role entry period. And any supervisor may be hesitant to confront the fact that he or she has made an error in judgment in the selection and placement process.

A systems perspective on role-person mismatch dictates a formal review and refinement of the process of recruiting, screening, selecting, placing, orienting, and monitoring persons entering new roles. Such a perspective is imperative to avoid blaming and punishing workers for what is essentially a flaw in the structure and process through which new members are added to the organization. Many areas of private industry have refined this recruitment and selection process to an extremely sophisticated science. The small health and human service agency whose limited resources preclude the use of high-priced consultants in this area, may find local volunteer resources from the private sector who can provide invaluable assistance in refining organizational procedures to reduce problems of role-person mismatch.

Honesty versus Salesmanship in Position Promotion. Objective data is crucial for managers to determine whether candidates will meet the needs of their organizations. Objective data provided to applicants on the reality of organizational life is equally crucial in their decisions about whether their needs can be met in an organization. Whereas the last section cautioned managers about the overzealous, potentially underqualified candidates who sneak into organizations, this section cautions managers not to attempt through salesmanship to seduce reluctant candidates into their organizations.

A misrepresentation of conditions in the organization and in the position an applicant is seeking can lead to serious problems of role-person mismatch. The manager/interviewer must provide an honest preview of the job role and the organization. Most managers demand a "no surprises" stance from employees who work for them. Employees joining those organizations deserve nothing less from the organizational representatives involved in their hiring. If there are fiscal problems, clearly summarize for applicants the information on this issue that is available to current organizational members at the same level. If there are serious problems of staff conflict, communicate their nature and intensity. If there are particular stressors unique to the role the applicant is seeking, communicate them clearly and completely. If a manager/interviewer has done an effective job, a new employee should enter an organization without illusions, and find exactly in the work environment both the demands and rewards he or she had been led to expect.

With some positions, it may be helpful to offer a selected candidate an opportunity to spend a half or full day at a job site before making his or her final decision to accept or decline the position. This allows a prospective employee to sense how he or she would feel in the physical and social environments and the realistic parameters of the role he or she would be assuming.

Permission for Early Exit. Even in the best of circumstances, both a manager and an applicant may overestimate the applicant's ability to manage the technical and emotional demands of a position. This shared error in judgment may be difficult to confront by both parties and, unfortunately, is usually addressed long after the traditional probation period ends. The keys to solving this dilemma are for the supervisor to rule out that performance problems are due to environmental factors over which the employee has no control and to provide training to upgrade skills and role performance. If these are done and the employee still is not a good fit, the supervisor must confront the misplacement firmly and directly and try to provide the worker with permission for an early and guilt-free exit from the role or the organization. Providing support for and supervision of a supervisor going through this situation will significantly increase his or her willingness to proceed; it is one of the most stressful situations a supervisor can face.

Avoiding Misplacement through Promotion. A type of role-person mismatch can occur not with a new employee, but with a lateral or upward movement of an existing employee in the organizational structure. In these cases, one discovers the erroneousness of the assumption that exemplary performance in one role can be used to predict successful performance in a different role. The usual scenario is that someone who has demonstrated outstanding knowledge and skills in one role is promoted to a role with different skill and adaptational demands. This type of misplacement creates a double loss. First, the organization has lost the individual in the old role in which he or she made an outstanding contribution. Second, it has lost the full benefit of the new position due to the employee's inability to transfer skills or master the new skill demands. Such misplacement first can be countered by confronting the internal dialogue of the supervisor or manager and the administrative dialogue surrounding the promotion process. Warning signals in these dialogues include the following:

- "He will be upset if he doesn't get the position."
- "We owe it to her because she didn't get an earlier position she interviewed for."
- "He has been in the department longer than anyone else."
- "We have to reward her loyalty."
- "He is going to become a management problem if he doesn't get the position."

All of the above indicate that a decision to change an employee's role in the organization is about to be made out of guilt rather than an assessment of the organization's needs and the employee's competence and adaptability.

Avoiding role misplacement through promotion hinges on two additional strategies. The first is to clearly identify knowledge, skill, and adaptation requirements for each role in the organization so that transferability of skills from one role to another can be objectively assessed. The second is to build career paths such as the following into the organization:

- Allow people through professional development activities to try on new areas of knowledge and skill for personal comfort and fit. (For example, provide people in technical roles opportunities to attend introductory workshops on supervision.)
- Prepare people internally with expanded knowledge and skills for greater role options.
- Provide career and salary ladders in technical and specialty areas. In this way, employees do not have to seek out new roles, which they might not enjoy and might struggle to perform, solely to get greater financial rewards from the organization.
- Provide outplacement counseling for advancement-discouraged employees.
- Provide paths back into specialty roles for managers and supervisors.

I prefer the term "career paths" over "career ladders" because the latter implies an expectation that one must move upward in an organization. A career path, which may move up, down, and laterally through an organization, may better meet the needs of many employees and organizations. The career path concept recognizes that the developmental needs of both the employee and the organization change over time, and it allows both to renegotiate their relationship depending on those changes.

Role-person mismatch can also reflect broader organizational problems. Closed systems encounter mismatch problems because their isolation produces a progressively depleted pool of available job applicants. Porous systems have a limitless pool of candidates, but their poor role definitions and poor gatekeeping tend to bring in many unsuitable individuals.

14.5 Strategies to Address Role Conflict

Role-conflict problems grow out of incongruous demands from simultaneously held roles.

Strategies to address role conflict must start with an acknowledgment that some degree of conflict probably is inevitable in both simple and complex organizations. Eliminating role conflict for all members of an organization is impossible. Given this, the management goal is to reduce the incidence and intensity of those role conflicts most detrimental to individual and organizational health. Such strategies include the following.

Identifying Role Conflict at an Early Stage. It is crucial that managers watch for early signs of role conflict when an organization is founded, when new units are added or deleted, and when internal roles are realigned. Signs that may indicate role conflict include worker statements indicating contradictory demands, supervisors competing for access to a worker's time and skills, worker confusion over role priorities, interpersonal conflict (that on the surface may appear to be personality clashes but may be problems in the organization of role expectations), the failure to complete key tasks because of excessive demands spawned by multiple, conflicting roles, a consistent pattern of distress exhibited by people asked to perform a particular role, and a high incidence of turnover in a role.

Defining Sources of Accountability. Where sources of accountability are undefined or vaguely defined, a worker becomes vulnerable to multiple and potentially contradictory demands in a work environment. Role conflict emerges from a failure to define key elements of power and authority in organizational relationships or from flaws in this definition process. A major worker support, which will be discussed in more detail as it relates to role ambiguity, is the clear definition of how power is distributed in an organization and how each person/role in the chain of authority can affect the worker. While a worker may experience multiple demands from an environment, it is crucial that he or she knows which demands take priority and who has the ultimate authority to judge and reward or punish his or her performance. An essential strategy in reducing role conflict is to clearly define (through organizational charts, policies and procedure manuals, and job descriptions) power and accountability in an organization.

While this premise may seem obvious and simplistic to some, it is my experience that power is a very uncomfortable issue in many organizations and particularly in health and human services organizations. Many managers and supervisors, particularly those who have risen from the ranks of helpers, fail to define power and authority due to their own discomfort with the issues. They would prefer to manage without an explicit definition of their power to control work assignments, to determine personal and monetary rewards, and to take disciplinary action, including terminating a worker. In such settings, it may be necessary to provide management training if these supervisors are to implement the strategies necessary to reduce role conflict. Managers need to not only become comfortable with the power inherent in their roles, but also learn to manage the seductiveness of that power. The intrusiveness of the ego-intoxicated manager contributes to role conflict among his or her employees, whereas the egoless manager is so uncomfortable with the mantle of authority that he or she abdicates the responsibility to resolve employees' role-conflict problems.

Reducing the Number of Sources of Accountability. Another strategy in reducing role conflict is to limit the number of sources of accountability placed on workers. A worker with two bosses will inevitably experience problems of role conflict. With rare exceptions, a worker should have one source of accountability that represents the most basic unit in his or her relationship and the organization. All expectations placed on the worker must be channeled through this relationship. This is reinforced by organizational values that prohibit bypassing the relationship to place demands on a worker. A situation, for example, in which a hospital president bypasses three levels of organizational hierarchy to place a direct demand on an employee is guaranteed to produce instant role conflict.

Addressing Role-Integrity Problems. Role-integrity problems occur when there is a conflict between one's personal values and the values of the work environment. Mechanisms to address this type of conflict include the following:

- Explicitly define organizational values so that issues of value conflict are identified in the employee recruitment and selection process, not months later as a recurring issue in role performance. (See earlier discussions on the code of professional practice.)
- Give permission to raise value conflicts in the process of supervision. There are very few professions in which ethical and value issues don't arise in the course of performing one's job. Employees who are particularly sensitive to such issues need permission and opportunities to identify and personally resolve their sources of discomfort.
- Build in opportunities for work units collectively to discuss and explore ethical and value issues concerning service delivery. Assume that your most assertive employees may be articulating issues and areas of discomfort shared by other members of the work unit.
- Where ethical or value issues between an employee and the organization become irreconcilable, either create role assignments that minimize value conflicts or allow the employee guilt-free exit from the organization.

Providing Mechanisms for Resolving Incompatible Demands. Given the inevitability of some level of role conflict, it is helpful to build in mechanisms (a person and a process) for resolving such conflict when it occurs. Take, for example, the following situation, which is common to small organizations with one secretary.

Four staff members bring in typing that each announces must be completed and mailed that day. The total amount of typing is impossible to complete in the available time. Lacking an escape valve of some kind, the secretary, experiencing a classic case of role conflict (and role over-load), must decide whose work has the highest priority.

An example of an escape valve is when such a situation arises, the secretary takes all the material to the office supervisor, who makes deci-sions on priorities, negotiates the priorities with the workers involved, or seeks additional resources to get the work completed as desired.

Building in Supports for Areas of Unresolvable Role Conflict. A basic principle of managing professional distress in a microsystem is that when a role stressor is unchangeable, additional supports must be built in to sustain worker health and performance. Consider the example of employees who by job definition must spend up to eight days a month on marketing trips out of town. Employees in such roles who have fami-lies will inevitably experience conflict between the expectations placed on them in their roles as spouses and parents and the job demands that physically remove them from their families for significant periods of time. If the travel demands are unchangeable, what support mechanisms can be built in to offset the incompatible job-role demands/family-role demands placed on these workers? Examples of increased supports could include

- flexibility in when trips are scheduled each month to minimize disruption in important family-role functions (daughter's music recital, birthdays, wedding anniversaries)
- a policy that provides a company-reimbursed "check-in" phone call home for traveling employees
- a liberal policy on allowing spouses or family to accompany workers on business trips (a reward to spouses and family members for their part in the workers' job responsibilities)
- a liberal policy on compensatory time that allows workers greater access to their families when they are not traveling

Failure to provide such supports for this type of role conflict can under-mine the health of workers and their ability to sustain personal and inti-mate relationships outside the work setting.

14.6 Strategies to Address Role Ambiguity

Role ambiguity—the lack of awareness of job responsibilities, priorities, accountability structure, and organizational rewards and punishments—is a stressful condition that reflects an organization's failure to define expectations adequately. Strategies to address role ambiguity include the following.

Defining Role Expectations. The first task in reducing role ambiguity is to clearly define the role expectations of each member of the microsystem. These definitions are communicated verbally and in writing. The written component usually includes an overall job description that clearly and thoroughly defines the activities and outcomes to which the worker will be held accountable. Wherever possible, measurable outcomes should be attached to each activity area to communicate to the worker the standard of acceptable performance by which his or her activity will be measured. A second component of this initial strategy is to communicate those general standards, for example, attendance, to which all employees are held accountable. These general standards are often defined in agency personnel policies or in an agency code of professional practice.

Defining Task Priorities. A second strategy to address role ambiguity is to define for workers a framework or a process by which priorities are set on their role responsibilities. This area communicates to the worker the different value placed on his or her various responsibilities by the organization. Such definitions, outlined in broad terms and in the day-to-day supervision process, assist the worker to make decisions when time constraints allow the worker to complete only one of numerous potential role activities.

Defining Preferred Methods of Task Completion. This area of role planning clarifies whether the worker will be held accountable for outcomes only or for both the process and outcome of role activity.

The first type of accountability says: "You are responsible for generating $75,000 in sales per quarter. How and where you generate such sales is up to you."

The second type of accountability says: "You are responsible for generating $75,000 in sales per quarter. The sales must come from only the counties listed on this sheet. Here is a pamphlet that I will go over outlining the standards we will expect you to follow in marketing our products and services."

The first example held the worker responsible for only the results of his or her activity. The second example held the worker accountable for not only what he or she was to do, but also how to do it. From the standpoint of reducing role ambiguity, either method is acceptable as long as the organization's choice is explicitly defined to the worker.

Defining the Accountability Structure. An organization should define to whom its workers are accountable. Defining each person's supervisor or manager is an integral element of reducing role conflict and role ambiguity.

Defining Organizational Rewards and Punishments. Define the rewards and punishments that will accompany successful and unsuccessful role performance. The strategies noted earlier established a framework by which rewards and punishments could be rationally organized by management and anticipated by workers. A more detailed discussion of rewards and punishments comes in the next section, which addresses problems of inadequate role feedback.

14.7 Strategies to Address Inadequate Role Feedback

This section will explore supervisory strategies to provide workers feedback on (1) adequacy of role performance, (2) methods of improving role performance, and (3) adequacy of adjustment to the work milieu.

Utilizing Basic Principles of Reinforcement. It is imperative that management systems incorporate principles from the behavioral sciences concerning the forces that shape and sustain human behavior. A few basic principles that will be used to guide later discussions are listed below.

- When a behavior is followed by a reward (reinforcement), the probability increases that the behavior will be repeated.
- The time between the desired behavior and the reward should be as short as possible for maximum reinforcing effect.
- When a behavior is followed by punishment, the probability decreases that the behavior will be repeated.
- When a behavior is followed by no response from the environment, the effect is the same as punishment—decreased probability of the behavior being repeated. (That's right—ignoring positive performance has the same effect as punishing positive performance!)

- The most powerful schedule of rewards for sustaining behavior
features intermittent rather than fixed reinforcement.

Worker Performance Standards and Consequences. The purpose of
defining performance standards is to increase the probability that a
worker will illicit a desired behavior that can be rewarded and sustained
over time. When organizationally set standards are inconsistent with the
systems of reward and punishment at the microsystem level, performance problems will decrease the ability of the organization to achieve
its mission and goals. The first task in building effective systems of feedback is thus to establish clear standards for behavioral performance and
then to ensure that the mechanisms of reinforcement (rewards) in the organization are distributed based on the effective execution of those behaviors. If the articulated organizational standard of performance is high
productivity as measured by sales, but all microsystem promotions are
based on longevity and loyalty (seniority), the system of rewards undermines the stated organizational value. The principle system of microsystem rewards is serving to undermine the stated organizational value.
The principle is a simple one: Organizations get what they reward, not
what they say they want. Bringing organizational rewards into congruence with organizational values is an essential dimension of organizational health.

A Critique of Personnel Evaluation Systems. Many organizations rely
heavily on the annual personnel evaluation as the primary mechanism of
feedback on employee performance. Let's review this practice based on
the principles of reinforcement noted above in section A. A critique of
such reliance based on those principles is illustrative. The following observations refer to the annual performance-appraisal meeting between a
worker and his or her supervisor in a health and human services setting.

   A. THE SUBJECTIVITY AND VAGUENESS OF FEEDBACK. Many organi-
       zations use annual appraisal formats that contain no objective
       performance criteria and, in fact, may contain vague categories
       of evaluation that bear little relationship to the day-to-day
       activities of a worker. About the only category that can be ob-
       jectively assessed in such systems is a worker's attendance. Con-
       sider, for example, a supervisor of a small counseling agency
       who meets with a counselor in an annual performance-appraisal

meeting and goes over a form on which he or she has evaluated the counselor on a five-point scale in the following categories: knowledge, quantity of work, quality of work, team relationships, dependability, initiative, and overall work performance. If we were to examine the annual evaluations of the six agency counselors, would we be able to identify the objective criteria by which each was scored in the team relationship category? Would a worker who scored a three in the knowledge category be aware of the body of knowledge he or she needed to acquire to move to a four rating? In general, such vaguely constructed systems provide little data that a worker can use to alter his or her performance. One way of increasing effective feedback to workers is revamping personnel evaluation systems to include measurable, behavioral-based performance objectives. Compare the nebulous value to the counselor of a three in the knowledge category with annual performance objectives that stated he or she would

- enroll in a master's level counseling program and complete at least three courses during the evaluation period
- pass the exam to become a licensed counselor
- attend two outside workshops to enhance his or her skills in family counseling

These examples are concrete, measurable, and within the counselor's control to achieve.

B. THE TIMING OF FEEDBACK. The annual performance-appraisal process, without other ongoing mechanisms of feedback, has almost no power to reinforce and sustain high levels of work performance. To assume that a one- or two-hour interview informing a worker what a great job he or she has done will sustain that worker's performance for the more than 1,700 hours he or she will be on the job before the next performance appraisal is exceptionally grandiose. The real values of an annual performance review are to summarize other ongoing mechanisms of feedback that have already provided the worker data on his or her performance and to refine the major standards and objectives that these other mechanisms will address during the coming year. The timing issue is even more critical in organizations

that have workers in key roles who have not had performance
evaluations in years.

C. THE RELIANCE ON MONEY AS A REINFORCER. Most personnel
evaluation systems rely heavily on the annual merit salary increase as the primary reward to workers and the concrete evidence of feedback on their performance. The following
observations apply to such reliance:

- In practice, annual salary increases have little to do with the
  performance of an employee. Such increases are so automatic
  in most agencies that they simply confirm that an employee
  has remained in the organization another 365 days. Since the
  increase is not tied to identifiable behavior, it has little use as
  a feedback mechanism for exemplary performance.

- In feedback-deprived systems, the distribution of financial
  rewards can become extremely competitive and conflictual.
  Lacking other sources of affirmation, a staff will use money in
  its struggle for status, personal affirmation, and recognition
  in such systems. If there are multiple sources of feedback,
  money loses this symbolic function and its power as a primary reinforcer.

- Until such time as health and human services workers have
  performance objectives and monetary incentives linked to
  the achievement of objectives that are as clear and visible as
  those in such companies as Amway and Mary Kay Cosmetics,
  more effective and sustainable mechanisms of feedback and
  reward must be built into these service systems.

Building in Mechanisms for Acknowledgment and Feedback. Feedback
consists of a regular flow of data to each worker that identifies acceptable performance, defines unacceptable performance for purposes of
self-correction, and acknowledges exemplary performance.

A. FACTORS THAT INHIBIT STROKING BEHAVIOR. Few supervisors or
managers appreciate the awesome power they command. Such
power is usually thought of in terms of control, decision making, and the more punitive authority to take disciplinary action
over others. The power referred to here is a very different kind
of power; it involves the ability of a supervisor to recognize and
acknowledge human competence, to affirm value and worth, to

express appreciation, affection, and affiliation, and to validate and bolster the esteem of each worker under his or her direction. The most neglected human needs in the workplace are those of personal appreciation and affirmation. The presence of such rewards in day-to-day role performance far outstrips money and other perks in promoting and sustaining worker health and productivity. Unfortunately, there are numerous obstacles to the effective use of this power by supervisors. Some of these inhibiting factors include the following:

- The high level of stress built into many supervisory roles leaves supervisors hopelessly overextended and emotionally depleted. Under such conditions, they have little emotional energy available for affirming others. Strategies to address supervisory distress thus become crucial to enhancing the availability of positive feedback to workers in the microsystem.

- Maintaining a high level of positive feedback in the microsystem requires the time and physical presence of a supervisor. Supervisors who experience role overload, particularly with an excess of tasks that pull them out of interaction with workers, lose both the time and access to workers to sustain such rewards.

- A supervisor, by virtue of personal style and temperament, may find providing such feedback awkward and unnatural, if not impossible. A major element in supervisory screening needs to be a search for individuals with natural skills in the identification, observation, and affirmation of competence. A desirable supervisor is the person whose own needs are met by encouraging and acknowledging success in others.

- Managerial "self-talk" can decrease one's tendency to provide positive feedback to supervisees. Self-talk is the internal dialogue that mediates external behavior. This dialogue dictates what we should and shouldn't do, can and can't do; it formulates our assumptions about the needs and motivations of those around us. Unvalidated self-talk can decrease stroking behavior; examples of such internal dialogue include the following:

  "They know they're doing a good job; they don't need me to tell them all the time."

  "Why should I acknowledge them? Nobody ever acknowledges me."

"She's so competent and confident she doesn't really need
me."

"I won't say anything, because I don't think she respects my
judgment."

Effective supervisory training reprograms such self-talk and frees
the supervisor to become more potent in his or her interactions in the
work unit.

B. Mechanisms to Provide Positive Feedback. A major goal
of supervision is to build into a work unit a large number
and variety of rewards that can be utilized to reinforce and
sustain behaviors that promote individual and organizational
health. To a creative supervisor, the list and variation of such
rewards is nearly limitless. Some of the most common forms
of supervisory stroking behavior such as verbal praise (of
individuals or work unit), letters of commendation, soliciting
ideas or technical advice, favored work assignments, and salary
bonuses.

C. Matching the Right Mechanism to the Right Worker. A
supervisor can be most effective in his or her affirming communications by starting with the premise that acknowledgment
needs to be uniquely matched to each worker's temperament,
needs, and value system. Whereas access to career-path opportunities may be a major reward for one worker, it may be a
stressor for another. The types of acknowledgment used with
a worker also need to change over time in response to his or
her changing needs.

D. Feedback and the Disciplinary Process. Feedback—the
provision of data to self-correct or affirm the behavior of a
worker—is obviously an essential component of extinguishing
undesirable behavior and enhancing worker productivity. In
fact, systems that build in high levels of appropriately communicated feedback and high levels of acknowledgment for role
mastery make little use of traditional forms of disciplinary punishment. These systems share a number of common characteristics related to their feedback processes.
  • Behaviorally defined standards of worker performance are
    established as the baseline to which feedback is directed.
  • There are consistent rewards for performance that meets
    or exceeds the defined standards.

- Worker behavior that deviates from the norm is first analyzed via a systems perspective:

  Does the worker know the standards of performance? (Provide direction.)

  Does the worker have the knowledge and skills to perform the task? (Provide training.)

  Are there environmental conditions that preclude effective performance? (Reduce role stressors, such as role overload, inadequate equipment.)

  Are additional supports needed for effective role perfor-mance? (Increase supervisory supports.)

  Are behavioral/health problems interfering with perfor-mance? (Refer to company employee-assistance program.)

  Is nonperformance being inadvertently rewarded? (Change the reward system.)

- Self-correcting feedback should be directed at behavior when it first moves beyond acceptable limits, not after it has be-come chronic or reached extreme limits.

- Performance behaviors that move back into acceptable limits are immediately reinforced.

E. PRINCIPLES OF EFFECTIVE FEEDBACK. An important skill of a supervisor is the ability to provide feedback that is honest and direct, yet protects the self-esteem of a worker. The pur-pose of feedback is to enhance collaboration, not increase worker defensiveness or create a conflict in a supervisory rela-tionship. The following statements, drawn from studies of adult learning, describe principles of effective feedback that can guide supervisory communications on observed perfor-mance problems.

- It is descriptive rather than judgmental. Useful feedback fo-cuses on behavior (what a person did); it does not focus on character (what a person is).

- It is specific rather than general. Talking to someone about his or her behavior with a particular client in a specific situa-tion is more effective than discussing the person's "attitude problem."

- It protects the self-esteem of the recipient. A nursing super-visor who says that a nurse could expand his or her patient-care skills by experimenting with more physical contact and "silent time" with patients is more effective than one who says that the nurse "talks too much" and is "too dominating."

- It is directed toward behavior that a worker can do something about.
- It is well timed. Feedback is most useful when provided as soon as possible following a behavior of concern. Timing also depends on a worker's readiness to hear and understand the feedback.
- It is checked to ensure that a worker has accurately understood the communication.
- Its accuracy can be checked with others in the work unit.
- It is best received when given out of concern, interest, and respect for the worker.

14.8 Strategies to Address Role Overload

Role overload is one of the most common role stressors reported by workers today. The following discussion highlights interventions that can reduce the role overload of workers.

Reducing the Overextension of the Organization. The overextension of workers is often a reflection of the overextension of an organization. From a systems perspective, this occurs when input (the level of fiscal, human, and material resources) is incongruent with output (the service and production goals set by the organization). The major intervention under such circumstances is not to teach workers better stress-management skills, but to clearly and realistically determine what an agency can and cannot accomplish with its existing resources. Areas of overcommitment must be honestly confronted and cut back.

Controlling the Pace of Organizational Change. Controlling the pace of organizational change to reduce the adaptational demands placed on workers has been a constant theme of this book. The strategies noted earlier to control and regulate change are particularly relevant to the problem of role overload. Role overload often occurs when unexpected and uncontrolled change escalates expectations in the quality and quantity of worker production to excessive and unrealistic levels.

Job Restructuring. In some organizations the overall scope of work may be realistic, but the distribution of that work into roles is imbalanced.

By reorganizing and redistributing task assignments, managers can reduce the stress (and conflict, resentment, and guilt) that occurs when some workers bear too much responsibility, while others bear too little responsibility.

Managing Periods of Excessive Demand. Some organizations will have predictable seasons or cycles of excessive demands, while others will encounter various milestones or crises that produce excessive demands on workers. Role overload is probably inevitable during such periods, especially when the use of additional, temporary resources is not possible. But even then, these periods can be managed to reduce wear and tear on workers. The following suggestions apply to the management of such periods:

- Openly acknowledge the excessive demands in group settings and one-to-one interactions with workers.
- Try to set a time frame on the period of excessive demands. (Most workers can manage periods of increased demands, if they know when the demands will return to normal.)
- Help workers clarify task priorities during periods of high demand.
- Present the period of excessive demands as a challenge to the team and fully utilize internal group supports.
- Provide time-out periods for the group to assess its progress and receive acknowledgment and encouragement from leaders.
- Increase the personal presence, visibility, and positive feedback of the manager.
- When the period of excessive demands ends, reduce expectations for a short time to allow workers to replenish themselves.
- Provide rewards for both individual and collective achievement through the period of high demand.

Confronting Overproduction. Some problems of role overload emerge not from the work environment, but from the personality or needs of an individual worker. Such situations may develop with workers who are chronically trying to achieve more and more in less and less time, are overcompensating for fears about the quality of their work by spending an excessive number of hours on the job, or are using the work environment as an escape from an unhappy marriage or an inability to establish outside intimate relationships and nurturing activities.

This situation poses a dilemma for a supervisor because such workers may be some of the most productive in an organization. A supervisor may, in fact, have come to rely on such individuals to pick up extra tasks or handle emergency assignments because of their dependability. What is needed by such a supervisor is a long-term perspective on overproduction. Such chronic overextension inevitably takes physical and emotional tolls on a worker. In the health and human services arena, such overproduction also denies a worker sources of outside replenishment that are essential for sustaining the quality of his or her helping relationships. A supervisor must have the perspective that overproduction may produce short-term benefits to the organization but may result in the eventual loss of a worker to stress-related disabilities.

There is a level of overproduction that must be confronted by a supervisor as directly and consistently as he or she would confront a worker's underproduction. The following suggestions apply to overproduction:

- Establish limits on the number of hours workers can spend at the work site.
- Discourage workers from coming to the work site on their days off.
- Where compensatory time systems are used
    require prior approval by a supervisor for compensatory time
        (This allows for close monitoring of overproduction.)
    set limits on the amount of compensatory time that can be
        accumulated
    require that compensatory time be taken as hours off within
        a specified time from its accumulation
- Avoid a system that pays for vacation days not taken. Such systems reward overproduction and the failure of workers to use time-out periods effectively.
- Make managers' rewards contingent on effective delegation.
- Confront signs of overproduction (excessive hours on job, failure to take breaks, chronic pattern of working through lunches, coming to work sick, or volunteering for extra duties that could appropriately be done by others).

- Include self-care goals in annual performance reviews (participating in health and exercise programs).
- Reward behaviors that indicate increased limit setting.

14.9 Strategies to Address Role Underload
and Role Deprivation

Role underload and role deprivation are stressors that lie at the other end of the continuum from role overload. These stressors produce excessive demands for adaptation from too little rather than too much stimulation in the work environment. Strategies to address these stressors generally fall into two broad categories: job revitalization and the creation of positive alternatives outside the organization.

Job Revitalization. One of the most rewarding activities of a supervisor can be the resurrection of an employee deemed professionally dead, and the revitalization of a role that had lost its value to an organization. Management interventions designed to achieve these ends include the following:

- Role revitalization activities seek to recapture skills and resources that are being ineffectively used by an organization. Where such loss is occurring, one option is to increase the complexity and range of role activities by redefining a job position. Flexibility is built into the role expansion such that the unique talents of the person occupying the position can be fully tapped by the organization.
- Exploring creative career-path alternatives in an organization is a second option for people who have been retired on the job. If an individual's knowledge and skill levels preclude further upward advancement, both lateral and downward placement in the organization should be considered. Although demotion is rarely considered, placing a worker lower in the hierarchy in a role of significant responsibility and stimulation may meet more of his or her needs than occupying a higher position that offers no meaningful responsibilities or rewards.
- Some workers in the preretirement category may have been shuffled into meaningless roles due to the short time they have left with an organization. By enriching such roles (through special projects, for example), an organization not only mobilizes

the knowledge and experience of these individuals, but also allows them to bring their professional careers to closure with highly meaningful work.

- Career counseling and a reinvestment in worker training are often combined with the above options to support the return of a worker to greater productivity.

Managing Disappointment/Rekindling Involvement. The above suggestions reflect systems interventions but do not address how a supervisor manages the human being who has occupied an empty role for an extended period of time. The following observations and suggestions apply to such situations:

- Assess the forces that blocked the career advancement and productivity of the employee. Was it a function of knowledge and skill deficiency? Were there problems of role-person mismatch? Were there personality conflicts with the individual's earlier supervisors? Were there personal or health problems that contributed to the loss of functioning or advancement?

- Assess how the worker has responded to the loss of previous or hoped for status and responsibilities. Most advancement-discouraged employees go through initial stages of anger, bitterness, and resentment toward an organization and its leaders, and eventually move to a stage of emotional resignation and detachment from the organization. What feelings along this continuum must be managed to reactivate the employee's passion and involvement in the organization?

- Recognize the forces in the individual that will resist change. You are asking an advancement-discouraged employee to reinvest emotional energy in the organization, to rekindle visions of professional accomplishment, and to reassert his or her ego into the life of the organization. While the encapsulation of a worker into a responsibility- and status-empty role may undermine his or her self-esteem, the invisibility that comes with such a role, while painful, does afford a level of safety. The worker may have been enticed from this shelter before to experience punishment rather than rewards from the organization. Expect resistance.

- Over time, explore systems interventions with the worker that will allow him or her to build trust and test the supervisory

relationship. Escalate affirming and stroking behaviors in interactions with the employee.

- Phase in the systems intervention slowly. The worker has been
existing under conditions of stimulus deprivation for some
time. Allow an opportunity for the worker's personal defense
structure to adapt to the increased stimulation and demands.
Increase rewards commensurate with increased role activity.
- Expect periodic regression. The employee will periodically lose
confidence in himself or herself and the process, and regress
back to the defenses used during role deprivation. Such behavior does not indicate that the intervention has failed, only that
the worker needs increased supports to continue the process.

Creating Positive Alternatives Outside the Organization. There are some
situations in which it is in the best interest of both a worker and an organization to terminate their relationship. A worker may candidly report to a supervisor that he or she has learned all he or she can at the
agency and needs to find a new, more stimulating job. He or she may further report feeling unable to achieve change because of a dependence on
current salary level or an inability to relocate. Some larger organizations
provide a formal service called outplacement counseling that addresses
both these situations and the ones created by employee reductions in
the organizations. Outplacement counseling helps employees find positive job alternatives outside an organization. In smaller organizations,
this outplacement counseling function may be taken on by an employee's supervisor. The strategies designed to help employees get out of
an organization guilt-free—enumerated in chapter 11—are applicable
here.

14.10 Strategies to Address Role Safety Hazards

Role safety hazards are those things workers regard as having the potential to cause them physical or psychological harm in the performance
of their roles. Interventions to address role safety hazards include the
following:

Analyzing Employee Health Care Data. Analyzing employee health care
data is a good way to identify role safety hazards in the workplace, particularly when the data can be analyzed by work sites, job title, sex,
and length of employment. Such data analysis is important in industrial

settings where it can reveal key areas of risk for industrial accidents or illness. The data can dictate a need for improved equipment or performance procedures and reveal risks for industrial disease from exposure to toxic substances that may not as yet be defined as toxic. Health care data analysis is equally important in nonindustrial settings, where threats to safety may be more psychological than physical.

Implementing Risk-Management Programs. Many organizations have effectively used a formal risk-management program to reduce safety hazards for employees and to service recipients and visitors who enter a work site. Through orientation and training programs and improved procedures, for example, many hospital risk-management committees have reduced puncture wounds from hypodermic needles, injuries from lifting and transferring patients, and injuries to patients from falls. A risk-management committee can be an extremely effective tool in identifying and reducing role safety hazards. I encourage readers to explore the growing body of literature on risk-management in numerous occupational settings.

Responding to Worker Issues of Role Safety. While effective, risk-management programs tend to focus on issues related to regulatory and licensing bodies and liability risks. Though important, those issues may differ significantly from role safety concerns identified by employees. Employee feedback should be used to identify and address role safety hazards experienced by workers. The major hazard for an eleven-to-seven shift hospital nurse, for example, may not be tied to the nursing unit, but to an isolated and poorly lit parking lot through which he or she must enter the facility at night.

Addressing Threats to Psychological Safety. It is helpful if the manager or committee reviewing role safety hazards includes threats to psychological safety in overall assessments and intervention processes. In human services organizations, for example, workers use a very inexact science to make judgments with potentially life-and-death consequences. Consider the following possibilities:

- An alcoholism counselor writes in a report that a client has successfully completed an educational and counseling program following the client's arrest for driving under the influence of alcohol. The report, which further states that the client cooperated fully with the program and is unlikely to repeat the offense, assists the client in retaining or reobtaining his or her driver's license. A month later, a mother and child are killed in a head-on collision with the intoxicated client.

- A counselor intervenes, as the on-call crisis worker, at a mental health center where a woman is making vague threats of suicide. After two hours of talking with the counselor, the woman seems composed, more hopeful about the future, and has agreed to come in and see the counselor at the center the following morning. In the judgment of the counselor, the woman is not at high risk of suicide and not in need of immediate hospitalization. The woman is found dead the next morning from an overdose of aspirin and sleeping pills.
- A probation officer conducts a presentence investigation of a man convicted of assault and battery against his wife. The presentencing report recommends probation rather than jail, based on the following facts: It was the man's first criminal offense; he and his wife had reconciled and agreed to get marriage counseling; he demonstrated remorse over the incident; jail would burden the wife and children with financial hardship and jeopardize the man's job of twelve years. The recommendations are accepted and the man is given probation. Two months later the wife is shot and killed by the husband in a violent argument amid accusations of the wife's infidelity.

While such incidents, fortunately, are rare in the professional lives of most human services workers, the level of psychological vulnerability for these workers is great in any situation in which they alone must make decisions that can have such profound repercussions. A key to reducing such vulnerability is to implement a policy (usually a component of the code of professional practice) that requires all clinical situations involving potential physical harm to a client, potential harm to others, and any other general threat to public safety to be immediately brought into the process of supervision. Such policies ensure that the full expertise and clinical judgment of the agency has been used to address the situation, and thereby prevent the awesome responsibility of such decisions from resting on the shoulders of one worker.

A broad spectrum of threats to psychological safety that vary greatly by occupational setting can be identified and addressed through interventions that parallel the one described above.

14.11 Strategies to Address Role Insecurity

Role insecurity is the degree of uncertainty a worker experiences regarding his or her future role in an organization. Role insecurity may be an individual concern that can be alleviated through the feedback strategies that were identified earlier in this chapter, or it may be a collective concern of workers that permeates an entire organization. Given the macrosystem issues that have currently sparked layoffs and company closings in industries as diverse as steel and health care, this section will focus on the collective aspect of role insecurity.

Worker Access to Information. Workers should have access to a consistent flow of accurate information about the financial status of their organization and the implications of that status on their future roles in the organization. This information serves multiple purposes, including preventing the sense of personal violation workers feel when they learn of financial information outside their organization and have been told nothing by organizational leaders, providing a reality base from which workers can form responses and avoid the excessive emotional wear and tear that can result from unfounded fear, apprehension, and rumor, involving workers as equal partners in a financial crisis, and using workers as resources to generate cost-containment activities and develop broad strategies of crisis resolution.

Providing Rumor Control. The fear and apprehension generated in organizations that go through rapid change or periods of financial crisis generate a constant flow of unvalidated information and conjecture. Such gossip can be a powerful destabilizing force in an organization. All complex organizations inevitably generate elaborate and sometimes very sophisticated informal networks of intelligence gathering and dissemination. Many people who hold no formal power in an organization, such as a housekeeper or an elevator operator, wield considerable influence and status based on their reputations for extracting reliable information from such networks. Providing clear, straightforward information through formal communication channels in a timely fashion maintains the credibility and power of the formal channels and decreases the power of the informal rumor network. During times of uncertainty, every meeting with employees, no matter what its agenda, should function as a mechanism of rumor control.

The Management of Employee Reductions. There are a number of principles and guidelines that can make needed layoffs less painful for the employees involved and less disruptive to an organization overall. While some of the following suggestions may seem obvious and simplistic to a reader from a large, complex organization, the material may be helpful to those from small health and human services agencies who have never had to address the issue of employee layoffs.

- Develop a layoff policy before it is needed. The key component of such a policy, as it relates to role insecurity, is the clarity with which the layoff decision-making process is defined. Will layoff decisions be made by seniority or some other criterion? Are there any policy differences between salaried and hourly employees? If seniority is the primary criterion, how is it defined? By work site? Department? Total employee pool? Having such policies allows each worker to make a realistic determination as to the level of vulnerability he or she faces in the event of an employee reduction.
- Involve employees at early and successive stages of a financial crisis. Workers can be either active partners with managers in crisis resolution or passive, impotent bystanders and victims of managerial decisions. Provide workers with the cost-cutting goals to see whether they can identify alternatives to employee reductions. In many organizations, workers have come up with concrete, practical alternatives that prevented the loss of employees.
- If a layoff decision is made, avoid false or unfounded promises about the length of the layoff. If the layoff appears to be permanent, communicate this to the workers so they can plan for their futures accordingly.
- When a layoff occurs, examine what supports can be extended to the effected employees. Can a representative of the unemployment office be deployed at the work site to facilitate worker access to unemployment benefits? Can access to services from an employee assistance program, such as budget counseling, be extended to workers on layoff status? Can

workers still be acknowledged by organizational leaders for their contributions? Can outplacement counseling services be used to help connect some effected employees with jobs in other organizations? Can opportunities be provided for workers not effected to talk about the layoff in order to minimize survivor guilt?

14.12 Strategies to Address Worker Isolation

Worker isolation is usually a consequence of a role that entails high levels of boundary transactions and minimal dependence on other members for effective role performance. The sales representative, the outreach worker, or the staff working in a remote satellite office may experience high levels of stress, but without access to the supervisory supports available to other organizational members. While such isolation often increases the vulnerability of staff members, there are exceptions in which isolation may be a buffer to excessive stress. There may be such a high level of stress and turmoil in a primary work site that the detached worker actually has greater immunity to the effects of the conflict by virtue of his or her isolation. Excluding such exceptions, a supervisor should build in special mechanisms of support for the most isolated roles in an organization. The following mechanisms may prove helpful:

- Build in a higher frequency of supervisory contacts for the isolated worker under the assumption that the worker lacks many of the peer supports available to other workers in the organization. A supervisor may not be one of many sources of support and acknowledgment for isolated workers, but the sole source of support.
- Create opportunities for the isolated worker to participate in the group activities of the organization. Worker inclusion and reinforcement of peer-relationship development can be facilitated by such interventions as scheduling the worker to be at the primary work site for staff meetings, in-service training, and other group activities. The worker's travel and assignment schedules should be manipulated to ensure that he or she is included in major events in the organizational family.
- Visit the worker in the field. Help the worker identify and manage the stressors of his or her role that may differ radically from those experienced by other workers in the organization.

- Build in time-out periods from field assignments that allow the worker to spend some concentrated time reestablishing his or her senses of identity in and belonging to the organizational family.

14.13 The Supervisor and Microsystem Health

There is probably no more abused, yet no more important species in the American work force than the mid-level manager/supervisor. The importance of this role must be fully articulated before closing the discussion on microsystem strategies for reducing role stressors and increasing role supports. All of the strategies outlined in the last two chapters hinge on the health, knowledge, and skills of the frontline supervisor. The best thing a company can do for its employees is to provide them fair, competent, and nurturing supervisors. If a supervisor, however, is to provide support, he or she must in turn be supported.

There is a rapidly growing technology that enables a company to humanize the work environment and promote worker health while enhancing its production goals. It is perhaps the ultimate sin of our economic system that such technology lies dormant on bookshelves while organizations and individual workers alike self-destruct. It is not enough that new management technologies fire the vision of organizational leaders. Such technology must be transfused, through support and training, into the most basic unit of an organization—the relationship between a supervisor and a worker.

14.14 Strengthening the Personal Defense Structure through Health Promotion

The third component of the microsystem model for addressing stress is, in addition to reducing role stressors and increasing role supports, the implementation of company-wide and work-unit programs to support the physical and emotional health of workers. These programs, often classed under the rubric wellness and health promotion, encourage lifestyles that enhance the overall well-being of workers and, in so doing, reduce their vulnerability to disease, illness, and injury.

Many companies have made substantial commitments to employee health promotion activities. In the area where I live, one company purchased a vacated public high school to create a company recreational facility at which its health promotion activities are coordinated. Made available to the company's 1,500 local employees and their families, the facility hosts an extensive variety of recreational activities, including company basketball and volleyball leagues, weight lifting, aerobics classes, and jogging and walking clubs, with a wide variety of additional activities on the drawing board for future implementation. The company's formal health promotion program includes health screenings, monitoring, and follow-up in addition to a regular contingent of health promotion classes on lifestyle issues ranging from smoking cessation and weight loss to stress management. Companies like this are part of a growing movement in American business and industry committed to integrating health promotion into the corporate culture. These companies have found that enhancing worker productivity through improved health can also help halt the drain on company resources caused by escalating health-care benefit costs. Most of the companies I know of that have implemented health promotion programs have quickly concluded that they are both a good idea and good business. A somewhat ironic twist to this trend is that health and human services agencies, while marketing health promotion programs to business and industry, have lagged behind in implementing such programs for their own employees.

Given the systems perspective on worker distress outlined in this book, it should be clear that health promotion programs can and should be an essential component in the overall strategy to address professional distress in the workplace.

14.15 Responding to Casualties

Even in the healthiest organizations, situations may occur in which an employee experiences a deterioration in performance related to his or her experience of distress in the work environment. Companies with comprehensive programs to address stress-related problems build in mechanisms to identify such worker problems and intervene to enhance the worker's return to health and productivity. The most important of these mechanisms is the establishment of formal employee assistance programs in the companies.

Employee assistance programs (EAPs) are confidential assessment, short-term counseling, and referral services available to employees on a voluntary or supervisory referral basis. EAPs often serve as a resource for the resolution of problems experienced by employees long before the problems affect job performance. When problems do affect performance, an EAP is then an important resource for supervisors. With an EAP to rely on, a supervisor can focus on job performance and avoid the usually unsuccessful attempt to combine the roles of authority figure and amateur psychiatrist.

EAPs have historically focused on problems experienced in a worker's personal life that progressively affect role performance on the job. EAP counselors have focused most of their energy on such employee problems as alcoholism and other forms of chemical dependency, behavioral and emotional disturbances, marital and family problems, and financial troubles. While such efforts provide a highly needed and valued service to employees and organizations alike, EAPs have only recently reached the sophistication to address directly those distress-related problems caused by experiences inside an organization. This development places the EAP counselor in a position to respond to the distress-related impairment of a worker, and also creates the sometimes unenviable role of communicating to organizational leaders the existence of debilitating working conditions in the organization. The only alternative to this employee-advocate role is to provide emotional support to workers and then send them back to the same unchanged conditions that contributed to their impairment in the first place.

EAPs are an essential component to responding to victims of excessive personal and professional stress. The fact remains, however, that a large number of organizations have not yet implemented such a program. In these organizations, the responsibility of assessing and rectifying performance problems remains with supervisors, regardless of the origin of such problems. The following suggestions apply to the supervisor who lacks an EAP and is confronted with a stress-related deterioration in employee performance.

Responding to Early-Warning Signs. Professional distress is a progressive loss of functioning characterized by a continuum of symptoms ranging from moderate to severe in their consequences. The disintegration of a staff person's emotional and physical health usually occurs over time, with identifiable early signs that indicate the deterioration of stress-management abilities. The most crucial intervention is to acknowledge, express concern for, and confront early signs of stress-related problems. By bringing such concerns into the supervisory process, a supervisor has an opportunity to halt the deterioration in both performance and health.

Assessing the Problem. Lacking the resources of an EAP, a supervisor must communicate with the employee to assess the nature of performance problems. When such problems spring from personal issues unrelated to the work environment, a supervisor can recommend that the employee seek outside professional assistance and sustain the focus of supervision on work performance. It is *not* a supervisor's role to offer advice or to counsel an employee about such problems. When performance problems originate from distress in the work environment, a supervisor can take appropriate steps to reduce role stressors and increase supports for the worker. If these latter interventions fail, the problem was probably not related to the work environment (the employee may be chemically dependent, for example), and the recommendation to seek outside help is again warranted.

An Assessment Model for the Health and Human Services Setting. Staff members who work in health and human services agencies have three areas of distinct needs that must be met for optimum performance and emotional health: (1) each staff member has personal needs that must be met outside the program; (2) each staff member has needs that must be met in his or her professional peer relationships; (3) each staff member has needs that must be met in his or her relationships with clients. Problems related to professional distress often occur when none of these need areas is met. A decrease in both personal and professional functioning often occurs when an employee's needs are met in one of these areas at the exclusion of the other two. By reviewing an employee's status in the three need areas, problems of imbalance can be identified and corrected. This assessment and problem-identification process should be done by looking not at the personality of a staff person, but at the breakdown of supports between him or her and the work system. The problem is defined as interactional, not intrapsychic. The assessment is to identify ways the system can be manipulated to reduce stressors and produce nourishment for staff members. It is not a diagnostic interview to enlist them into "treatment" with a supervisor.

Helping the Employee Identify and Label Professional Distress. A supervisor can be an important resource to a staff person who experiences professional distress. A supervisor can be particularly helpful in giving employees words they can use to describe what is happening to them. Many people who suffer in high-stress work environments have

296 THE INCESTUOUS WORKPLACE

not identified this as the source of their distress and simply believe they are losing their minds. Identifying and labeling work-related distress can, in and of itself, free up energy for employees to begin to remobilize their personal resources.

Communication about Professional Distress to Employees. When communicating to staff members regarding professional distress use pronouns of inclusion (*"we* often find *our*selves . . ."; "It is a common experience for those of *us* in the field to . . ."). Pronouns of inclusion emphasize a process endemic to the work environment and tend to decrease self-labeling by staff members ("I'm crazy; everyone else is okay").

Use self-disclosure and provide normative information about the experience of professional distress to reinforce effectively the following messages:

- Professional distress, in varying degrees, is something that nearly everyone who works in a high-stress occupation experiences. (You are not alone!)
- One can recognize and abort the escalation of professional distress before it produces serious consequences. (You can take control!)
- One can make clear decisions and take actions that produce the nourishment necessary to reenergize and reestablish the balance between one's work and personal lives. (You can regain personal potency!)

Providing Structure and Mobilizing Resources. The primary role of a supervisor in addressing professional distress is to identify and label the source of a problem, to assist employees in mobilizing resources to speed their replenishment, and to manipulate the level and intensity of role stressors and supports to enhance workers' returns to health and productivity.

14.16 A Personal Note in Closing

It is only proper that I should conclude by examining how to respond effectively to the victims of professional distress, for it was precisely the concern over such casualties that compelled the studies and consultation work that served as the foundation for this book. In the process of conducting those early studies, I had the very disquieting experience of listening for many hours to workers who were caught up in the incestuous dynamics and role conditions I've described here. I interviewed workers whose health self-destructed from sheer physical exhaustion, workers whose marriages were only memories, workers who fell victim to the self-medicating effects of alcohol and other drugs, and workers who fell apart emotionally. Nearly all of these individuals either left or were extruded from their work settings under conditions of extreme emotional pain. Many continued to struggle years later for emotional closure on their work experiences. They continued to seek some rational understanding of what happened to them and others in their organizations. Many of those leaving health and human services agencies received less respect, concern, and support than would have been extended to any client seeking services in the agencies in which they had worked. Such exiting workers often became the pariahs and untouchables of our field, and those of us who remained continued in our blindness or arrogance to see ourselves as immune, believing that what happened to them could not happen to us. If there is any message that collectively emerges from the stories of distressed workers, it is that we are all potential victims of these processes. Today's respected worker may be tomorrow's untouchable.

To those who may have experienced the group processes and role conditions described in this book, I hope at least some part of your review of this material has been healing. To those readers who haven't experienced much of what I've written about here, I hope the material will set off warning bells that will prevent you from becoming a casualty of organizational processes you might now be able to recognize.

It has been more than two decades since the studies that would culminate in this book began. I conclude with my ongoing belief that we will address the issue of professional distress when we begin to define it as a breakdown in the relationships between organizations and workers and stop defining it solely by the personalities of our casualties.

Glossary

Boundary. The invisible skin that encloses a system, separates it from its environment, and distinguishes insiders from outsiders.

Boundary Management. The conscious manipulation of the frequency and intensity of boundary transactions as a management tool to control the pace of change and the level of adaptational demands placed on workers.

Boundary Permeability. The intensity of resistance encountered in moving people and ideas into or out of an organization. Closed systems are characterized by significant resistance (low boundary permeability), and more open organizations have little resistance (high boundary permeability).

Boundary Transactions. The reciprocal flow of people and ideas across the boundary separating an organization from its outside professional and social environments.

Career Ladders. Planned sequences of vertical promotions in an organizational hierarchy or professional field of endeavor.

Career Paths. Planned sequences of role changes that, while enhancing professional development, may involve upward, downward, or lateral movements in an organization or in one's professional field.

Closed (Enmeshed) Organizational Family. A rigidly closed organizational family characterized by low boundary permeability. The inability of staff members to make transactions outside an enmeshed organizational family for support and replenishment produces a high level of professional distress.

Closure. A sudden or progressive reduction in organizational boundary transactions that results in a loss of outside replenishment for—and increased intimacy among—organizational members.

Code of Professional Practice. The explicit definition of the ethical standards, aspirational values, folk wisdom, procedural directives, and organizational etiquette that guide decision making in an organization.

Decompression Rituals. Regularly performed actions that signal to us and others that one part of life (work) is ending and another part of life (personal) is beginning.

Distress (Authoritarian–Moral Approach). The managerial denial of the existence of professional distress via the definition of stress-related behaviors as problems of a worker's character, values, and motivation to work.

Distress (Clinical Approach). The definition of professional distress as a personal emotional problem of a worker.

Distress (Cognitive Approach). The definition of professional distress as emerging from an individual's irrational and unrealistic beliefs and expectations regarding a workplace.

Distress (Environmental Approach). The definition of professional distress as a problem of unhealthy physical and social conditions in a work environment.

Distress (Organizational). A stage of deteriorating organizational health that occurs when tasks essential to the survival of an organization fail to be adequately completed due to the stress-related decline in performance of key organizational members.

Distress (Professional). A deterioration of one's personal and interpersonal functioning directly related to continued contact with a high-stress work environment.

Distress (Systems Approach). The definition of professional distress as a breakdown in the relationship between a worker and an organization.

Distress (Training Approach). The definition of professional distress as a problem of skills deficiency—both technical skills and stress-management skills.

Double-Bind Communications. Contradictory verbal messages communicated over time to workers by organizational leaders and supervisors with an accompanying prohibition against seeking any clarification of the incompatible messages.

Ecology (Organizational). The study of the relationships and interrelationships among workers and their organizational environments.

Ecosystem. The multilayered environment that encompasses a professional role and the organization of which it is part, including

- the basic work unit (microsystem)
- the total organization (mesosystem)
- the family, neighborhood, city, county, and state (exosystem)
- the broad political, economic, and social forces in the culture and world at large (macrosystem)

Environmental Scanning. The ability of an organization to accurately perceive changes in its operating environment.

Exosystem. The political, economic, professional, and social environment in which an organization exists.

Extrusion. The forced exit of a worker from an organizational family (often through a scapegoating process).

Feedback. The transmission of self-affirming or self-correcting information to workers on the adequacy and outcomes of their professional performance.

Gatekeepers. Those people in an organization who control who, when, where, and under what conditions people and ideas enter or leave the organization.

General Adaptation Syndrome (GAS). Hans Selye's concept of the body's automatic three-stage response to any demand for adaptation: (1) alarm reaction, (2) resistance, and (3) exhaustion.

Ghost (Organizational). A former organizational member whose emotional significance was so great, or whose exit was so painful, that remaining members continue to operate as if the person was still in the organization.

Health Promotion. Organizational strategies and programs that promote healthy lifestyles and enhance employees' overall wellness and quality of life.

High Priest/Priestess. The charismatic leader of a closed organizational family.

Implosion. The inward collapse of a professional and social network.

Incestuous Workplace. A stage in the life of an organization marked by workers increasingly meeting their personal, professional, social, and sexual needs inside the boundary of an organizational family. Incestuous workplaces (like incestuous nuclear families) are marked by abuses of power and the progressive violation of intimacy barriers in worker-worker relationships.

Job Restructuring. The reorganization and redefinition of task responsibilities in a job position.

Macrosystem. Political, economic, and social processes and structures in the nation and the world.

Mesosystem. An entire organization, including all of its organizational units and employees.

Microsystem. The smallest organizational unit surrounding a worker: a division, a department, a bureau, a section, a project, a team, a shift.

Organizational Family. The conceptualization of an organizational group as a family system; those people identified as organizational members and any other people, who by virtue of frequent interaction or influence on internal decisionmaking, constitute the organizational group.

Organizational Family (Extended). The professional, social, and intimate relationships of organizational members that serve the organizational family collectively by both buffering it from and linking it to the outside world.

Outplacement Counseling. A formal program provided by an organization to facilitate the hiring of its workers by other organizations. Outplacement counseling provides healthly pathways of exit for employees who no longer have a viable role in an organization.

Personal Defense Structure. An individual's historical pattern of thinking, feeling, and behaving when confronted with personal or professional distress.

Porous Organizational Family. An organizational family that is characterized by high boundary permeability.

Professional Closure. The isolation of an organization from its outside professional environment—a condition that forces organizational members to meet most, if not all, of their professional needs within the organizational family.

Professional Stress. The demand for adaptational change experienced in the performance of one's professional role.

Professional Distress. A deterioration of one's personal and interpersonal functioning directly related to continued contact with a high-stress work environments.

Projection. Attributing one's own feelings, desires, fears, or motivations to others (for example, a worker blaming others for his or her mistakes).

Replenishment Network. The number and intensity of nurturing and affirming relationships and activities available to a worker.

Risk Management. A formal program designed to assess and reduce the vulnerability of workers to injury, illness, or disease in a work environment.

Role Ambiguity. An employee's inadequate knowledge of (1) role expectations, (2) task priorities, (3) methods for task completion, (4) accountability structure, and (5) rewards and punishments for task completion or incompleteness.

Role-Assignment Misplacement. The misplacement of employees with skills in interior organizational positions into boundary positions (promoting people from technical positions to supervisory positions without knowing whether they are constitutionally suited for the new role).

Role Balance. The relative balance between role stressors and role supports. Role balance allows workers to adequately perform their roles without distress-related disruptions of their physical or emotional health.

Role-Boundary Management. The ability of a worker to maintain a distinct separation between his or her personal and work lives.

Role Breakdown. A failure of an individual's distress-response system that results in decreased role performance and decreased physical and emotional health.

Role Conflict. Incongruous demands and expectations from two or more simultaneously held roles.

Role-Connectedness Problems. One's degree of isolation from, or overconnectedness to, other members of an organization.

Role Deprivation. The sudden or gradual removal of all significant responsibilities from an individual—forced retirement on the job.

Role-Feedback Problems. The lack of regular information on (1) adequacy of role performance, (2) methods of improving performance, and (3) adequacy of personal adjustment to the work milieu.

Role Insecurity. The degree of uncertainty experienced about one's future role in an organization.

Role-Integrity Conflict. A conflict between one's personal values and the values of one's work milieu.

Role Overload. Excessive and unrealistic expectations regarding the quantity and quality of work to be completed in a given time frame.

Role-Person Mismatch. The incongruity between (1) an individual's knowledge and skill level and the skills required to perform a particular role, (2) an individual's level of stress tolerance and the level of stress in a particular role, and (3) an individual's style of stress management and the methods of stress management officially and informally sanctioned by an organization.

Role Revitalization. The restructuring of a job role to increase its level of professional stimulation and its importance to an organization.

Role Safety Hazards. The degree to which one experiences apprehension about potential physical or psychological harm in the performance of one's professional role.

Role Stressor. Any condition in a work environment that decreases one's ability to perform organizational tasks and decreases one's self-esteem.

Role Supports. Any condition in a work environment that increases one's ability to perform organizational tasks and increases one's self-esteem.

Role-Termination Problems. Problems caused by a failure to provide permissions, procedures, and processes to allow members guilt-free exit from an organization.

Scapegoating. The projection of blame for systemic problems in an organization onto a single organizational unit or member.

Self-Regulated Organizational Family. An organizational family that regulates its degree of organizational closure through both internal and external feedback. Boundary permeability fluctuates depending on worker needs for outside support and replenishment during periods of health and for organizational closure during periods of transition and crisis. The lowest level of professional distress is experienced in this organizational model.

Self-Talk. The internal dialogue that enhances or inhibits acting on certain feelings or thoughts.

Sexual Closure. The meeting of most, if not, all of the sexual needs of organizational members within the boundary of an organizational family. Sexual closure arises out of isolation and a sexually stunted organizational culture that views extrasystem intimacies as a threat to organizational stability and intrasystem intimacies as a medium of increased organizational commitment and cohesion.

Sexual Culture. The ethics and values related to sexuality in an organization that are expressed through language, artifacts, attitudes, roles, and the spoken and unspoken rules governing relationships among organizational members.

Social Closure. The meeting of most, if not all, of the social needs of organizational members within the boundary of an organizational family.

Stress. The demand on the human body for adaptational change.

Stress Response. The generalized and specialized reactions (adaptations) of an individual to stress.

Stressors. Those situations, conditions, or people that trigger stress.

Triangling. A pattern of communication between two people in which significant messages to each other are communicated through a third party.

Type-A Personality. A personality style marked by the compulsive need to achieve more and more in less and less time.

References and Recommended Reading

Adams, W. and Brock, J. 1989. *Dangerous Pursuits: Mergers and Acquisitions in the Age of Wall Street*. New York, Pantheon Books.

Adizes, I. 1988. *Corporate Lifecycles*. Englewood Cliffs, N.J.: Prentice Hall.

Argenti, J. 1976. *Corporate Collapse: The Causes and Symptoms*. Maidenhead: McGraw-Hill.

Bateson, G. 1967. *Naven*. Stanford, Calif.: Stanford University Press.

Benson, H. 1975. *The Relaxation Response*. New York: Morrow.

Berman, E. 1976. "Some Thoughts on Sexuality and Supervision." *Voices* (Fall).

Blume, E. 1990. *Secret Survivors*. New York: Ballantine Books.

Brown, B. 1977. *Stress and the Art of Biofeedback*. New York: Bantam.

Carrington, P. 1977. *Freedom in Meditation*. New York: Anchor, Doubleday.

Caroll, J. F. X. 1980. "Staff Burnout as a Form of Ecological Dysfunction." *Contemporary Drug Problems* vol. 8: 207–25.

Caroll, J. F. X., and W. L. White. 1981. "Understanding Burnout: Integrating Individual and Environmental Factors within an Ecological Framework." In *Proceedings First National Conference on Burnout*. Philadelphia, Pa.

Clark, J. 1969. "A Healthy Organization." In *The Planning of Change,* edited by W. G. Bennis, K. D. Benne, and R. Chin. New York: Holt, Rinehart, and Winston, Inc.

Clutterbuck, D., and S. Kernaghan. 1990. *The Phoenix Factor*. London: Weidenfeld & Nicolson.

Cooper, K. H. 1977. *The Aerobics Way*. New York: Bantam Books.

Davis, Martha, E. Elizabeth Eshelman, and M. McKay. 1988. *The Relaxation and Stress Reduction Workbook*. Oakland, Calif.: New Harbinger Publications.

Down, A. 1995. *Corporate Executions*. New York: American Management Association.

Edelwich, J., and A. Brodsky. 1991. *Sexual Dilemmas for the Helping Professional*. New York: Brunner/Mazel, Publishers.

Elstein, A. 1972. "Organizational and Psychological Problems in Developing Community Mental Health Services: A Case Study." *Society, Science, and Medicine* vol. 6: 545–59.

Emery, F. and E. Trist. 1973. "Social-Technical Systems." *Organizational Systems: General Systems Approaches to Complex Organizations,* edited by F. Baker. Homewood, Ill.: Richard D. Irwin, Inc.

Frances, V., and A. Frances. 1976. "The Incest Taboo and Family Structure." *Family Process* vol. 15 (2): 235–44.

Galanter, M. 1989. *Cults: Faith, Healing, and Coercion*. New York: Oxford University Press.

Goffman, I. 1961. *Asylums*. Garden City, N.Y.: Anchor Books.

Gonsiorek, J., ed. 1995. *Breach of Trust: Sexual Exploitation by Health Care Professionals and Clergy*. Thousand Oaks, Calif.: SAGE Publications.

Hearn, J., D. Sheppard, P. Tancred-Sheriff, P. and G. Burrell, eds. 1992. *The Sexuality of Organization*. Newbury Park, Calif.: SAGE Publications.

Hochman, J. 1984. "Iatrogenic Symptoms Associated with a Therapy Cult: Examination of an Extinct 'New Psychotherapy' with Respect to Psychiatric Deterioration and 'Brainwashing.' " *Psychiatry* 47 (4): 366–77.

Hemingway, P. 1975. *The Transcendental Meditation Primer*. New York: Dell Publishing Co.

Hoffer, E. 1951. *The True Believer*. New York: Harper and Row.

Hoffman, L. 1976. "Enmeshment and the Too Richly Cross-Joined System." *Family Process* vol. 14 (4): 457–68.

Holmes, T. H., and R. H. Rahe. 1967. "The Social Re-Adjustment Rating Scale." *Psychosomatic Research* 11: 213–18.

Jacobsen, E. 1970. *Modern Treatment of Tense Patients*. Springfield, Ill.: Charles C. Thomas.

Kahn, L., D. Wolfe, R. Quinn, and I. Snoek. 1964. *Organizational Stress: Studies in Role Conflict and Ambiguity*. New York: John Wiley and Sons.

Kharbanda, O., and E. Stallworthy. 1989. *Corporate Failure—Prediction, Panacea, and Prevention.* Maidenhead: McGraw-Hill.

Levi, L. 1981. *Preventing Work Stress.* Reading, Mass.: Addison-Wesley.

Levinson, H. 1972. *Organizational Diagnosis.* Cambridge, Mass.: Harvard University Press.

Lidz, T., S. Fleck, and A. Cornelison. 1965. *Schizophrenia and the Family.* New York: International Universities Press.

Lusting, N., J. Dresser, S. Spellman, and T. Murray. "Incest." *Archives of General Psychiatry* vol. 4: 31–40.

Mitchell, D., C. Mitchell, and R. Ofshe. 1980. *The Light on Synanon.* USA: Wideview Books.

Mithers, C. 1994. *Therapy Gone Mad.* Reading, Mass.: Addison-Wesley.

Monane, J. 1967. *The Sociology of Human Systems.* New York: Meredith Publishing Co.

Nevis, E. 1987. *Organizational Consulting: A Gestalt Approach.* New York: Gardner Press, Inc.

Pelletier, K. 1977. *Mind as Healer, Mind as Slayer: A Holistic Approach to Preventing Stress Disorders.* New York: Dell Publishing.

Peter, L. 1969. *The Peter Principle.* New York: William Morrow.

Peters, T. 1988. *Thriving on Chaos: Handbook for a Management Revolution.* New York: Alfred A. Knopf.

Rutter, P. 1989. *Sex in the Forbidden Zone.* New York: Fawcett Crest.

Schein, E. 1987. *Process Consultation.* Reading, Mass.: Addison-Wesley Publishing Co.

Schoener, G., J. Milgrom, J. Gonsiorek, E. Leupker, and R. Conroe, eds. 1989. *Psychotherapists' Sexual Involvement with Clients: Interventions and Prevention.* Minneapolis, Minn.: Walk-In Counseling Center.

Schultz, J., and W. Luthe. 1959. *Autogenic Training: A Psycho-Physiological Approach in Psychotherapy.* New York: Grune and Stratton.

Selye, H. 1956. *The Stress of Life.* New York, Toronto, London: McGraw-Hill.

———. 1974. *Stress without Distress.* New York: Signet.

Stotland, E., and A. Kobler. 1965. *The Life and Death of a Mental Hospital.* Seattle: University of Washington Press.

Tamminen, J. 1994. *Sexual Harassment in the Workplace: Managing Corporate Policy.* New York: John Wiley and Sons.

Tareberry, S. 1973. "Evolution of Organizational Environments." In *Organizational Systems: General Systems Approaches to Complex Organizations,* edited by F. Baker. Homewood, Ill.: Richard D. Irwin, Inc.

Temerlin, M., and J. Temerlin. 1982. "Psychotherapy Cults: An Iatrogenic Perversion." *Psychotherapy: Theory, Research and Practice* 19 (2): 131–41.

Weinberg, S. 1955. *Incest Behavior.* Syracuse, N.J.: Citadel Press.

Zweben, J., and D. Deitch. 1976. "The Emergence of Prima Donnahood in Prominent Psychotherapists." *Voices* (Spring): 75–81.

Index

WILLIAM L. WHITE, M.A., is a senior research consultant at Chestnut Health Systems/Lighthouse Institute in Bloomington, Illinois. Under his leadership, the institute has specialized in developing innovative training and consultation programs aimed at promoting personal and organizational health during times of rapid change. The author has conducted formal studies on personal and organizational stress, has authored more than fifty articles and monographs, and has served as a consultant and trainer to federal, state, and local health and human service agencies and private industry. Many of the concepts in this book were refined through the author's consultant role in providing crisis intervention to organizations experiencing rapid change and upheaval.